Loveland:
a Memoir of Romance and Fiction

SUSAN OSTROV

A Blackwater Press book

First published in the United States of America by
Blackwater Press, LLC

Printed and bound in Canada by Imprimerie Gauvin

Library of Congress Control Number: 2024934285

ISBN: 978-1-963614-04-6

Cover design by Eilidh Muldoon

Blackwater Press
120 Capitol Street
Charleston, WV 25301
United States

blackwaterpress.com

Praise for *Loveland*

This memoir – organized around literature, gender, and romantic love – is one of the best I've come across. Intelligent, well-informed, and above all good-humored, it is a pleasure to read!

Vivian Gornick,
author of *Fierce Attachments: A Memoir*

Loveland is a searing and confessional memoir about the growth and maturation of one woman in a culture obsessed with romantic love. Ostrov expertly shifts between her individual and family histories and her readings of philosophical, literary, and popular texts in order to illuminate passion, monogamy, sexual violence, pleasure, and, ultimately, love. By turns poignant and witty, *Loveland* is a gripping read.

Emma Barry,
author of *Chick Magnet*

A candid account of a 20th-century woman's own sexual and romantic evolution, her personal ruminations on love, sex, and romantic ideology informed by the insight of a scholar who has published important books on these topics.

Stephanie Coontz,
author of *For Better AND Worse: The Problematic Past and Uncertain Future of Marriage*

Loveland is searching, unsparing, truthful, wry, direct, unstuffily erudite, and amusing. In this lively memoir, Ostrov chronicles her growth as a romantic woman, placing the "case study" of her own love life in colloquy with the culture of romance, which she has analyzed and critiqued in the works of canonical authors, mass-market popular novels, magazines, and films. Ostrov delivers a gripping narrative of her life as a romantic including frank accounts of her sexual history. Her story is both influenced by and illuminates the culture of romance in which we all find ourselves. Insight is plentifully on offer.

Pamela Regis,
author of *A Natural History of the Romance Novel*

If you sympathise with Catherine Earnshaw, feel Anna Karenina and Madame Bovary were treated unfairly by their authors, and think a chance at a relationship with Mr Rochester would be worth taking, this memoir of an unrepentant "Other Woman" may be the book for you!

Laura Vivenco,
author of *Faith, Love, Hope and Popular Romance Fiction*

❦

This is a special book. Part memoir, part analysis of how culture shapes patterns of romantic love for us all. Ostrov proves herself a brilliant guide through this topography of Loveland, inhabited by "beautiful monsters" of passion. I followed along happily and emerged wiser.

Catherine M. Roach,
author of *Happily Ever After: The Romance Story in Popular Culture*

She’s a woman of my time
obsessed
with Love, our subject:
we’ve trained it like ivy to our walls
baked it like bread in our ovens
worn it like lead on our ankles
watched it through binoculars as if
it were a helicopter
bringing food to our famine
or the satellite
of a hostile power.
– Adrienne Rich, “Translations”

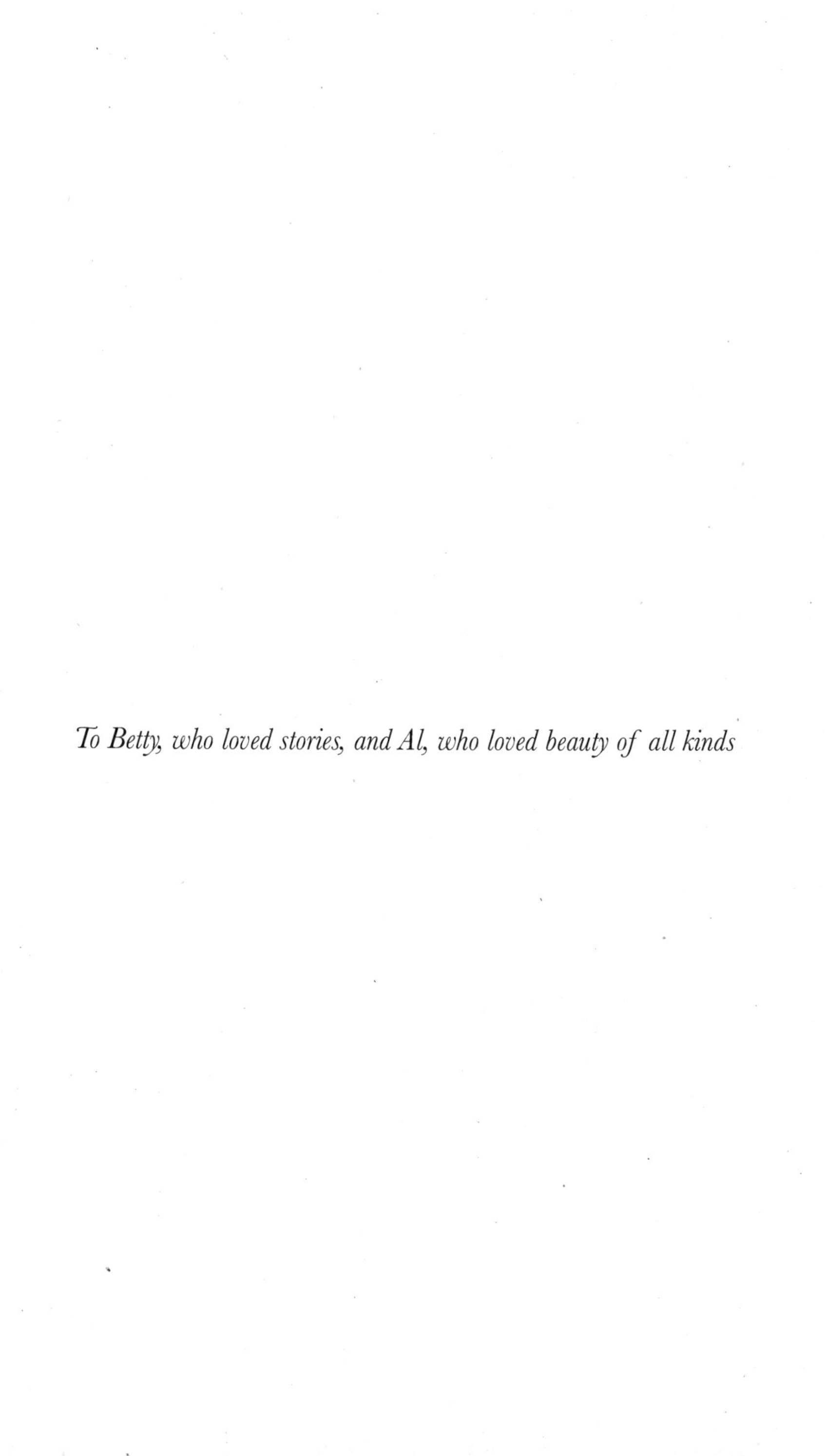

To Betty, who loved stories, and Al, who loved beauty of all kinds

Foreword

> He is in love: he creates meaning, always and everywhere, out of nothing, and it is meaning which thrills him: he is in the crucible of meaning.
>
> – Roland Barthes, *A Lover's Discourse*

Loveland is not a love story. It's a personal story *about* love, not at all the same thing.

In a college seminar I taught for years, Romantic Love in Western Literature and Culture, I always started on the first day by giving students a hypothetical to ponder:

Let's say you have to choose Door A or Door B for your future life. Behind Door A is a person you love passionately, and that person loves you the same way. But your fate is to spend a short time only with Person A, and you cannot know how long, or what will separate you. Behind Door B is a person you will be with all your life, a life of mutual affection, and you will be content with Person B… but you will never love this person passionately.

In the most recent incarnation of this course, students

suggested we add Door C, behind which there is no person at all, for those who do not wish for any sort of romantic relationship. I happily added Door C, and wished I'd thought of that myself.

Afterward, we always went around the seminar table while the students eagerly shared which door they'd chosen, and why. In some years passion won out, sometimes affection, but the vote was always close. Almost all voted for Door A or B.

The students who chose Door A explained that they want intense feeling in their lives; they thought the experience of passion was worth the grief of loss. The Door B group emphasized that their priorities were happiness and security, and passion was too risky for that. I do not share which door I'd have chosen with my students, because in the classroom I try to present all sides as objectively as I can. But if you read this book, you will know which one I'd choose. Spoiler alert: it is not Door C.

On the first day of class, I also ask students how they each define romantic love. Everyone contributes to a word cloud, where we can see their shared ideas take on a general shape. In every year, the answers were the same: romantic love is mutual trust, respect, support, kindness, commitment, companionship, fidelity, generosity, shared interests and values, and pretty much every other trait you would want in a long-term friendship, or almost any relationship. What makes it different from friendship, then? Sexuality, say a few, but then other students point out that for some, sexuality is not a priority. My students feel there must be a surplus that makes the lovers want to be more than "just friends," but what is that surplus, if not sex? Yet they reject the idea that romantic love is simply friendship combined with sexual attraction. There's got to be more to it than that! The first, confident definition begins to get blurry.

These defining traits of happy partnership clearly all belong behind Door B. And what about Door A, passion, intense longing or helpless emotion? That's always at the far margin of the word cloud, added by very few, though about half the class choose Door A as their deepest wish. Passionate desire or need is all very well as a temporary beginning to "real" love, my students say, but otherwise… they are not sure what to do with it if it doesn't evolve into the "real thing," where all your needs are fulfilled. Romantic passion, in other words, is not romantic. The definition is now slippery, if not downright muddled.

What this amounts to is that these students, thoroughly imbued with the romantic culture that surrounds them, have learned that "real" romantic love is a relationship, not a feeling. Their ideal romance is a kind of permanent super-friendship: of all the wonderful relationship traits in the students' word cloud, the idea that pops up most often is "mutual support, someone to lean on." In this version of love, you are selfless and your reward for this virtue is someone else's equal selflessness. There are no power struggles, because everyone is… well, selfless. Almost no one mentions strong feelings such as longing, desire, obsession, or just the need for attention and gratification, as part of the picture, because my students do not recognize these emotions as "true" romantic love. Needs or demands are "egotistical" or "narcissistic," and therefore unhealthy. Real love is nothing if not healthy.

I tell them that for the rest of the semester, we will be taking a wild ride beginning with Sappho and Plato, with stops along the way for medieval knightly epics, Romantic era poetry, and nineteenth century classic romances, until we arrive at our present day, with Sally Rooney and Maayan Eitan. There will be a heap of unrequited love (Sappho, the medieval Provençal poets, Dante, Goethe), and adulterous love (Lancelot and Guinevere, *The Sorrows of Young Werther, Wuthering Heights, Madame Bovary, Lady Chatterley's Lover*), none of which fits their definition of romance at all.

Students seem to enjoy the literature we read, though it doesn't live up to their standards for the right kind of love. They want to believe Sappho is writing about a happy relationship; they are puzzled as to why the troubadours seem obsessed with their "cruel" ladies; some don't quite understand why Dante rejects all romance after the early death of his beloved Beatrice, since he is young and could date again. As for Goethe's romantic lover Werther, wildly popular in the eighteenth century, the extremity of his heartbreak seems unnecessary and implausible.

Once we reach the nineteenth century, my students are on more familiar ground: true love is now linked with marriage, and in the classic novels there is a great deal of marriage-as-happy-ending love (Jane Austen, all three of the Brontës, George Eliot). But even then, the idea of romance in classic literature may be quite different from their own. Shared interests and mutual emotional support, for example, important expectations for a modern romantic couple, were not emphasized as much in an era of sharply distinct gender roles, well before our own focus on psychological wellness.

The idea of romantic love that mirrors my students', romance as a prelude to the successful couple, arose slowly over a period of change in the expectations for marriage. By the early twentieth century, marriage in the West increasingly came to be seen as the right and proper culmination of a romantic courtship, rather than an institution pragmatically favorable to both bride and groom, as it still is in many parts of the world. Not surprisingly, alongside the new view of marriage presumed to be based on "love," the values of romantic love changed too. Passion was too intense and uncontrollable to serve the interests of marriage, so the approved definition of love became those traits that foster the long-term couple's stability and comfort: all those mentioned in my students' word cloud.

"*Love is love is love*" has been a wonderful booster for the validity of same-sex marriage, but it's both ethically true (same-sex love is valid love) and also literally not-true, in that love *means* differently in history, varying according to location on the social map, as well as at successive points in people's lives.

You can see the source of my students' understanding of "real" love in a nineteenth-century magazine article, "Love, Courtship, and Marriage," which expresses the dominant idea of romance as a kind of courtship in most British and American magazines of the time:

> Courtship is to a woman the sweet consciousness that she is precious to someone; a season of favors and pleasures bestowed upon her, and a smile the only desired return; a season of ready and happy recognition by her devoted lover of her smallest opinion, of tender regard for her lightest wish…

The author then compares love in this brief pleasurable time for a woman, a period when she has the power of one who is adored, to the very different love a woman should feel in marriage. Once married, the woman must learn what love "really" is, that it's not pleasure, gratification, or attention. Instead, from the religious view below comes the students' idea that real love makes you a "better person," as the wedding toast goes:

> Perfect love is God, and the highest type of human love is Godlike. Real love is self-forgetful tenderness, that fervent wish for the highest good of its object. True love would rather see its dear one happy even with another than unhappy with self. It loves for a noble reason, and desires a noble subject… You will love the man for whose sake you will wish to be worthy, nobler, and in every way better than before.
> – *The Young Woman's Journal*, 1890

My own idea of romantic love is almost exactly the opposite: I see romantic love as a feeling, above all, ranging widely – and sometimes wildly – from short-lived and mild (which we call "a crush" or "infatuation", implying that it is not "real" love) to overpowering and compulsive. Romantic passion I take to be a stronger, more intense and uncontrolled version of love, as opposed to affectionate love, a fond attachment that is milder and more rational, which means to many that it's best suited to be long-lasting ("forever").

In my view, the emotion of love becomes a meaning-maker when it's captured by the scripts we are all subjected to in our own time and place. The philosopher Roland Barthes expresses exactly what I mean when he writes: "The love I'm talking about is not the kind you can define with rules, such as if you love me you would do X & so forth. The love I'm talking about is proved only by feeling; the proof is that it's alive in you."

But no emotions exist in a vacuum: I view love as not *only* a feeling, but also an experience, singular or shared, the meeting point of emotional need, sexual desire, and ever-changing cultural instructions for how these might or must be combined. Though Western culture has been self-consciously "romantic" since the Middle Ages, modern media have provided ever more impetus for these evolving definitions. "You complete me," for one example, from the 1996 movie *Jerry McGuire*, has been fully incorporated into what Barthes called the "lover's discourse"; we are now emotionally incomplete without a partner.

We map our own singular experience of life onto that script, and read this interpretation as a guide to future choices in our private lives. But the actual life of an individual has surprises, ambiguities, layers, unspoken agendas, deceptions and self-deceptions that don't fit well inside romantic ideology, with its received truths. These demand their own accounting.

My idea of romance is a stream of multiple and mutating feelings, a dreaming of hopes and expectations, memories and visions of the future. It is this stream that I've tried to attend to in my book. In both life and literature, romantic desire is expressed as gestures, images, scenes, landscapes and moods that no definition, theory or study can precisely explain.

My own years of courtship came just before the sexual revolution, the women's movement, the age of social media, dating apps, the ubiquitous accessibility of pornography, the LGBTQI+ struggle for rights, and the enormous changes around definitions of gender and family, just to start. Yet such shifts, including the evolving relationship between women and their own desire, make it all the more surprising how firm a grip traditional romance as a genre still has on our culture, and in a growing number of other cultures: "romance" in media and as a commercial product is now a multinational, multibillion-dollar enterprise. More than ever, most of all in Western nations, but increasingly exported around the world, marriage is expected to be based on, or at least somehow result in, romantic love. Marriage rates are declining in the Western world, but the idea of "finding your person," permanent romance locked in for life, is more ingrained than ever.

I have seen that this paradox, love as the pinnacle of extremely intimate experience and love in its commercial face as public performance and display, has produced a certain confusion in my students' generation as to the meaning of romance and the trustworthiness of romantic relations. The celebration of romantic love itself is not only pervasive but growing ever more so in romantic comedy and drama, as well as in advice columns and other self-help forms, social media, advertising, music, and so on. Reality shows like *The Bachelor* or *Bachelorette*, *Love Island*, *Married at First Sight*, *Love Is Blind*, and *Indian Matchmaker* proliferate on cable TV and Netflix, even while their success at forming permanent couplings is famously very low. Sometimes it seems that the preoccupation with romance has become a sunnier, more hopeful substitute for faith in the solidity of marriage, or even larger realms of faith. My theory is that my students cling to the idea of comfortable, "healthy" love (another favorite phrase of theirs, again from the wellness trend) rather than passion because they are shaky about the permanence of romantic relationships in general.

I find the popular contemporary model of love as either "healthy" or "unhealthy" to be suspect. The term "healthy" implies a universally accepted state of normality, comparable to the way we conceptualize illness. This suggests there is, or should be, a universal ideal of love or sex, when it's not even clear exactly what we mean by these terms, or what differences there are between them. I think it's more useful to look at a spectrum of overlapping features such as the significance of sexuality, compatibility, admiration, strength of desire, and more, all traits which have had varying weight at different times in history.

Love is a subject that has always lent itself to knee-jerk presumptions. This is why we need to interrogate these ideas rather than accept them as received wisdom. But though I resist common generalizations about love, it's true that *Loveland* is filled with generalizations of my own about romance, marriage and monogamy, based on what I have observed. This is for rhetorical convenience, because nothing anyone says about love is universally true. I recognize that some readers will not agree with what I have to say about these subjects, because they have contradictory beliefs or different experiences than mine.

I want to note that I am not claiming to represent, much less speak for, all others. I own that this book is about *my* life, *my* experience, *my* reading, *my* apprehension of (and anxieties about) romance. My point of view is that of one white, middle-class, cis-gendered, heterosexual woman, old enough to look backwards at my own experience in twentieth and twenty-first century American culture. It's reasonable to assume that romance meshes with identities, that the experience and conditions of love are not necessarily the same, especially if you, the reader, and I, the author, don't share a gender, race, age, sexuality, or culture. Nevertheless, there's a family resemblance in the international culture of romance, a kind of lingua franca that underlies and connects many of these aspects of identity. I'm not saying that love itself is colorblind, but that its representation often is.

For this reason, I strongly believe that my experience of love, both emotional and social, mirrors that of many others, especially women. If we live in a culture (and we all do), we swim in that culture, whether we like it or resist the tide that pulls us a certain way. The conventions of love, what scholars call the dominant narratives of romance, are remarkably the same, for example, in male-male, female-female, and female-male mass-market romances, or media that feature heroes and heroines of color, as they are for other romantic movies and novels.

In this book romance is a story that is about love, whether short or "forever," requited or not, committed or at a distance, legitimated by society or forbidden, lived in reality or alive in literature. The story itself gives shape and coherence to desire and emotion. Some scholars have argued (unromantically) that romantic feelings themselves, rooted in the cultural script that gives them meaning, are socially constructed. I thought about this claim for many years, and it was the impetus for writing this book. If this is so, just how is an emotion that feels so essentially human as "love," or for that matter an attraction to romance in general, shaped in the individual? In what way does it function to make sense of our lives?

Since Rousseau's eighteenth-century *Confessions*, no memoir has specifically traced the development of romantic sensibility, from its roots to its consequences, much less from a woman's point of view on the subject. When Roland Barthes examined the concept of love in 1977, he did not dwell on matters of gender ("the lover" for him is most often sexed as male). Currently, the "romantic" is often supposed to be gender-neutral, encompassing everyone with a heart. But in reality, women in our society are generally more preoccupied with romance than men are, more engaged in finding it and keeping it, as if it were their specialty.

Whether or not women are "naturally" more romantic is an old debate and belied by historical literature, but cultural evidence abounds for widespread female preference for romantic culture in our society, at least. For example, the male audience for popular romance fiction, top sellers in publishing for many decades, is about 15%, an unknown proportion of which are male readers of gay romance.

Romance is permission to dream, to *feel*, and feeling in our culture (though not always in history) is associated with women, less so with masculinity.[1] There is no more reason men should be excluded from its pleasures than there is for women's exclusion from the pleasure of sex.

---

[1] See, for example: 'Are Women the "More Emotional Sex"? Evidence from Emotional Experiences in Social Context.' Lisa Feldman Barrett, et al, *Cognition and Emotion*, 1998, 12 (4), 555-578: "Men and women do not differ dramatically in their immediate reports of emotional experience, even in contexts that are differentially relevant for men and women (control vs. intimacy). This finding raises the possibility that women's 'greater emotionality' is a culturally constructed idea, based on observed differences in emotional expression differences which are socialized from a very early age." It must be said, however, that relative degree of emotionality is very difficult to measure.

Yet women are taught to engage in a subterranean emotional calculus, monitoring *who is feeling what*, a process in which men are assumed not to participate, or encouraged not to reveal to others. That women have been and still are associated with emotion is a social fact linked to their domination of the markets for romantic culture. Romance is still a privileged place for women.

What I see is that many women cherish the idea that a man's commitment to love creates a safe zone, a legitimate, even consecrated place to exert a specific kind of authority, an emotional preeminence, in a threatening world of misogyny, denigration, exploitation, and sexual violence. While more Western women are single than ever in history, perhaps *because* marriage rates are at an all-time low and sexual culture is ever more crass, romantic love still offers women the promise of a unique value and committed protection in a world of vulnerability, sexual and otherwise. This imaginary and nostalgic adoration, described in the nineteenth-century article on courtship above, is often learned through fiction and other media even before we know what "romance" means. In a rapidly changing society, vexed and uncertain, romance restores the world to certainty, the genre itself creating a safe space for fears and anxieties. To live in a culture is to live out the dreams of that culture.

For decades I lectured and wrote professionally about the representation of love in classic novels like *Jane Eyre*, as well as in popular culture, yet never examined why I was fascinated by this topic. It was difficult to miss the irony that I was critiquing romance as a feminist scholar, yet deeply attracted to romance both in fiction and my own life.

Romance develops on two tracks: first, the idea evolves as society evolves, and second, as individuals connect emotions to other ideas and to other aspects of our own lives. I set out to explore the space between romantic fictions and the experience of romance in reality, by looking at the love story in the context of a *life story*. My idea was to invite the reader to watch it grow as a concept, incubating in a particular person, time, and situation. Then it occurred to me: to examine how romantic love operates separately in an individual woman's life, I could tell the story of the life I know best: my own.

I am an ordinary woman with an ordinary life of longing, pleasure, and loss; I think of *Loveland* as a memoir of romance itself, expressed through one person's life. That person happens to be me, but only for convenience; the romantic story is one our culture tells women, and women tell other women, over and over again, in many versions that resemble each other. What do those stories we are told, and those I told myself, say – not just to me, but *to us*, and *about us*?

Courtship and marriage, the points where romantic novels usually begin and end, are only half the story and miss the frame. I begin with origins, asking the reader to experience my first encounters with sex and romance, as I navigate a path to becoming "romantic." The first chapter bores down to the roots from which the rest of my life in romance would grow, branch out, and eventually, burst forth. I mean for the reader to see the confluence of persons, circumstances, events, and emotions that led to my longing for romance from a very young age. These strands come together in the idea of romance as a space-between, that which links fact to fiction, the real to the fantastical. This space is the realm of "Loveland."

Romance as a story is a triumph over complexity. By examining a real life, I hope to restore the complications of the formula happy ending we wish for, and offer a different understanding of "romance" as passion, no matter what we do with it.

Love presents itself as coherent, smooth-surfaced, a deep space in which to dwell and build a life. In reality it's a puzzle with jig-sawed edges, and all we have are scattered, often missing, pieces of ourselves. My goal is to lay out those parts to see how they might fit together, especially for women. I begin with one of the pieces of the puzzle: Desire.

Chapter One
Childhood: The Family Romance

> The ability to fantasize is the ability to survive. The ability to fantasize is the ability to grow.
> – Ray Bradbury

> Our stories are always intertwined with other stories.
> – M. Freeman and J. Brockmeier

My strongest desire as a girl, a young woman, then a married woman, now an older woman, was always to be loved: not only as a daughter, wife, mother, friend, but much more than these, to be loved singularly and intensely by a man I equally desired. Love has been the current of my emotional life, flickering off and on, energizing, obscuring, suppressing, but at times illuminating other parts of myself. I've had an abundance of non-romantic love, yet this seemed lacking in what was truly essential for me. Only romantic love held out a promise of the focused absorption I needed, the romance-as-story adding the infinite durability I longed for.

But women's romantic desire is so often entwined with

fear, emotional need fraught with the layered meanings of being a sexual female: censure, gratification, mistreatment, power, debasement.

It was lonely while my mother worked long hours at a summer resort, my father at work in the city, and there were no children to play with. A guest, a middle-aged man, played with me once, when I was eleven years old.

I am on a sofa with him in a deserted room of the Main House, the one with the grand old fireplace. He is hugging me while we talk, and it's very nice to be held that way. Then we are lying down on the sofa together. He is kind and warm. There's a desire like when I touch myself, a desire I can't name or stop, and I stealthily put my toes between his legs.

He doesn't speak, but I can hear his breathing.

Then I'm frightened, walk quickly outside to sit on the porch alone. He comes out to sit quietly beside me. Is he angry at me? Does he just want to chat? Does he know what I'd wanted, when I didn't know myself?

Suddenly his hand jumps deep into my shorts, rough on the cotton crotch of my panties. Fear exceeds desire. I run inside. I don't want to find Mommy, so I tell a waitress instead. She says to go back to our cabin, she'll tell my mother and he'll be "thrown out." I am relieved but ashamed that he got in trouble because *I went too far*.

My mother never mentions it, I never mention it: it is not mentionable. What is not mentionable barely exists except as a shadow that follows you around. But the scene makes flashy, lurid appearances in my head, joining other scenes like it before and afterward, a bad show no one wants to see. The boy who drives his bike between your legs as you walk a block away from home.

The jogger who comes up behind you on your way to work, thrusting his hand into your crotch without breaking his stride. A creepy pressure against your butt as you stand on a rolling, crowded subway car while no one sees your distress. Their unpredictable flash-visits punish me when I least expect it, like Betty's slap on my cheek when I wanted what I shouldn't have.

This never, ever happens in romance, not in fairy tales, not in love comics, not in *Little Women*, where pure girls are loved, where women are adored, where men sit at their feet.

And stay there.

When I was eleven, sex and romance were ready to divide into two warring camps, occupying the same disputed territory. There was real life, unpleasant and deficient, sometimes frightening, and dream life, buried like a treasure box in a wreck, beautifully, perfectly wrought. Sex was in real life, and romance was in dreams. But sex could be dreamy if two were in love, and romance was a dream you could make real when you were loved by the right person.

Or maybe: Love is the big guy from the mob with a gun, the one who can hurt you but will also protect you from harm, if you pay up.

* * *

This is the origin story of my own romantic impulse, the way I grew to be a romantic woman, one immersed in romance, fictional and real, from girlhood on. It's a story peculiar to me, but also not unlike that of many other women. I am now in my seventies, an age when I'm told I should be beyond all this, yet I am apparently not done yet. The ideal relationship for me now is one whose boundaries are all questionable: commitment, labels, monogamy, all these things are up for discussion. After a long life of dreaming and dating, marriage and motherhood, monogamy, adultery, and independence, I don't want to marry or even share living space, because I have an entirely different idea than the one our culture represents as to what "romance" is and means.

Romantics are not born, but made, to misquote philosopher Simone de Beauvoir's famous definition of womanhood. For de Beauvoir, romantic love was a kind of dependency in women, a reveling in the loss of the very freedom we say we want. For romantics, on the other hand, love is simply an occasion for the deepest delight in life. But that delight is never simple. Each love is also a potential story, the one we call romance. Romance itself is not simple, but can be simply delightful.

If romantic love is about the beloved other, romance is a story about the end game of pleasure, the pleasure of reading about romantic love. In the service of that end, it consumes the innards of other stories: the endurance of myths, the fantastic in fairy tales, the fears and threats of horror films, the thrill of pride and success in narratives of ambition. Its mode is If Only; its teleology is the couple's happy ending, where narrative and time stop forever. Yet romance isn't just read for the blissful end; it's a whirlwind, a risky venture in which life itself is powered by feeling. This book is a case study of one life, my own, and the friction between the culture of romance and a woman's experience in what I will call Loveland.

My deep convictions about love were not a result of thought. The passions I felt seemed to arise on their own, beautiful monsters from a mysterious place I knew nothing about. And so I set out to explore how this passion for the romantic was formed, to illustrate with my own life how romance absorbs meanings from our origins and experience.

No one theory about love or field of study captures all of romance, but if Freud was right, the cradle of romantic love is literally found in the cradle: our earliest bonds with our parents.

Stories of the past are like countries you once visited that are no longer like themselves when you return years later. There are stories of my life that haunt me the way spirits would haunt dark, empty houses, and love stories can feel as real and deep as a great love. Why do some tiny bits of memory shadow us throughout our lives? Why do some half-remembered stories grip you, shaking your insides until they whirl, while other, maybe truer ones, are as remote as strangers passing in a hallway?

I know that as a child, I felt more alive when I was noticed. Yet I had to hide myself in order to be a good daughter. Caught between these two truths, I was sustained by fantasies and fiction, artfully designed to express the inexpressible and inexplicable. It was natural that in childhood I loved a tale in which a girl, a heroine, perhaps unloved or at least unappreciated, becomes the center of value for others. In adolescence, the genre of romance redirected this theme of recognition, fixing it to a male who adores that young woman for life, as Rochester did Jane in Charlotte Brontë's *Jane Eyre.*

But my powerful attraction to literary and real-life romance has a deeper lineage. My first and most important stories came from that prolific and repetitive teller of cautionary tales, my mother. Before I was old enough to read grown-up novels, I knew about love through Betty's sagas of romantic love and its tragic consequences. And of course, what I saw and understood of the only romantic couple I knew well, my parents, was the most powerful shaping force of all.

Why did these two, Betty and Al, come together to make a family at all? Understanding your mother and father is comparable to imagining what it's like to be your family dog. You're never going to get it just right; you can't break through the stubborn membrane of your human bias. Those adult beings who conduct their lives in front of your nose are the most unknowable of all, because we can't help valuing and describing them in relation to ourselves. Yet they are the ground zero of romance, both the intimate relations you witness as a child and the story you are told about those relations.

Mister And Missus

> I take them up like the male and female
> paper dolls and bang them together
> at the hips like chips of flint as if to
> strike sparks from them, I say
> Do what you are going to do, and I will tell about it
> – Sharon Olds, "I Go Back to May 1937"

Long ago, in the gloomy and chaotic years of the Great Depression, Betty and Al saw one another in Brighton Beach, Brooklyn, and fell in love. Once upon a time they leaned on each other for their dreams. I have this straight from that enemy of romantic love, Betty herself.

The genome of my body is from Betty and Al, and so is the genome of my romantic sensibility. Al was sensitive and romantic; Betty was cynical and anti-romantic. As the product of these two, I am both at once: a cynical romantic, which is something like having one brown eye and one blue.

I don't remember when Betty's stories began, but her stock scenes revolved in a loop, like the previews you're condemned to watch every time you go to a movie theater before the new show. For Betty, the new show never started; there was no need for one.

"So after my sister ran away with Harold Millington – he was handsome but no good – your granddad said she was dead to us, and my mother cried. She sent me to find my sister. And my sister was bleeding, she was pregnant again, and I ran all the way home, I was scared. Daddy said we could bring her back home, she'd be his daughter again, he'd raise this child Jewish. So she had the baby, your cousin, and then what did she do?" I'd heard the story a hundred times, but I always waited patiently for what I knew was coming: "She went back to Harold Millington after she had that baby, that's what she did. Took the baby and went back to that man! It broke Daddy's heart!" A vigorous shake of the head. "That Harold Millington, he was very handsome," Betty mused, as if that explained everything, which it probably did. I knew he was a villain because he was never called by less than his full name. I thought it was a wonderful name, something out of the novels I was just beginning to read.

This story, which I could recite in great detail word for word if I'd ever been required to, was one of my introductions to the perils of romantic love. I was as familiar with this tale as I was with 'Beauty and the Beast.' And it had the same moral: It's not looks, girls, it's character that counts.

The tale of how my parents met and married was not quite Tristan and Isolde, but it was the grand narrative that framed my childhood: "When I met your father, I thought he was a genius," Betty told me – repeatedly – over tea and a bit of carbohydrate to fortify us, at our chipped formica kitchen table. "I was *in love*," she would add with a snort: "*Love!*" I may not have known what romance consisted of, exactly, but I registered the contempt in her voice. "Young and stupid," she would sigh, fixing me with her dark eyes, "and look what it got me." I had no idea what *that* meant, but there was no space to ask questions. When Betty talked, it wasn't a conversation, certainly not a discussion. It was a monologue, repeated like a sacred chant. You listened to the rhythms, the waves of emotion and the rise and fall of drama, not explored its content. Wordsworth accused modern culture of murdering Nature to dissect it; to dissect Betty's stories was to murder their point.

The grand narrative of her own love story was always the same, a melancholy opera in three acts, which could have been entitled *Betty's Downfall*:

Act I: BETTY: A Dark Beauty (idealistic, strong-willed enough as a young woman of 18 to emigrate to New York against her father's wishes, but easily duped, due to her youth and purity) could have had any man… but foolishly fell into the booby-trap of romance with AL: Tall (even I could see this was fictional), Good-looking (I frankly found that dubious too), Great Talker, Dreamer, and most of all, Overlooked Towering Talent, destined to *become something*.

SHE was so innocent she had never seen a naked man, had no idea what people did in bed. HE not only turned out to be an unrepentant skirt-chaser, but – possibly worse – had no drive, as she always put it, meaning a kind of essential Nietzschean will to power that would lead to success, a profession, if not riches. What was the use of a good intellect if you didn't *become something*? Betty had dreamed of playing the supportive wife to a hero out of Ayn Rand (not that she knew that name), a strong and ambitious man on his way up from the bottom through sheer force of character and a display of undiscovered aptitude. Instead, she was to be yoked to a husband who put more energy into finding whatever pleasure he could at the bottom than sacrificing for his family to rise to the top.

Act II: But what could Little Betty (as she called herself, referring to her height) do? Romance was a bust, or worse, a dupe, a snare into which even a clever and very attractive rabbit could unwittingly fall. She fell.

Act III: And so Little Betty found herself a Missus to his Mister. Eventually three baby rabbits emerged, and the rest was unfortunate.

Betty was in fact quite short, but she tended to refer to herself as Little Betty only at those plot points where she was threatened by circumstances and, with Herculean effort, came out ahead. She also called herself Betty the Horse when she felt overworked and underappreciated by her family, which was often.

In this Scheherazade-like tale, the undeserved trials of Little Betty the Horse were perfectly matched by her triumphant competence at running the family. Somehow she made enough money, in spite of her sixth grade education, so we didn't starve to death, as we surely would if left to the devices of our genius-level but infuriatingly unambitious father. What Al could have become hung over the marriage like a dead lightbulb that could never be changed.

The first day of Al's last and only good job, as an electrical inspector for the city of New York after many hateful years working in subway tunnels, he came home and wonderingly told a story of his own, for once: an administrator at the hospital he'd inspected had offered him money for a good report, just as they'd always done with previous inspectors. "How much?" asked Betty immediately. Al's pale blue eyes opened wide. He admitted he hadn't taken the bribe, he couldn't think of taking it, he was not only dismayed but amazed those people would expect him to. She was furious: "Don't tell me you turned it down. What about us? Did you think about us?"

My own origin was a story too: the account of why she'd deliberately had a third baby when she no longer believed in Al or her marriage. They certainly could not afford another child in the one-bedroom, vermin-ridden Brighton Beach walk-up apartment, where we lived until I was six. She purposely conceived me, she said, because she had two boys and wanted a girl, who would always be close to her, unlike boys when they married. ("I always got pregnant when he put his shoes under the bed, so I just stopped using my diaphragm and didn't tell him." She always said this as though I would admire her cleverness.) It worked: she managed to bear a girl, a relentlessly screaming infant, but it was a girl. She'd triumphed once again. As wives want to give their husbands a son in some cultures, Betty wanted to give herself a daughter. "When you were born your father took one look and said 'Missus, your daughter looks like a monkey!' So I told him, 'You don't like her face, Mister? Fine, turn her around and look at her ass instead.' That's what I said to him." I think I heard that sentimental story about my father's first view of me fifty times. Photos confirm that I was an unattractive newborn: with my long, straight dark hair and scrunched face, as if I were about to scream, I looked something like... a monkey.

Families often designate roles for children: Mel, my oldest brother, was the Handsome and Outgoing One, once he outgrew being the Sickly One; Eric, the middle child, was the family Genius, with an outsider temperament very different from our older brother's; my own role was to be Cute.

Like Betty, Al never embraced or kissed me, and there were no verbal declarations of affection I can recall. Instead: I am sitting proudly on his knee at age six or seven as he admires my long brown hair loosed from its braids, caresses my head, and murmurs "Beautiful, beautiful!" This is what it is to be adored. The pleasure of walking by his side, holding his big, calloused hand, the prototype of the deep joy I had ever after when I was in love. These memories are how I later recognized what I was feeling, the blissful familiarity of a purely imaginary long-lost and beloved home.

I remember watching my father lifting weights and admiring his strength. Sometimes he would give in to my begging – "Lift me up, Daddy!" – and hoist me up above his head as I lay horizontally in his arms, like a barbell.

This was the height of thrill when I was six or seven, the sense of being in that strong man's arms and lifted as though it were no challenge at all. I generally did not feel safe at home, which was an emotional tinderbox; in his arms, swooped up, I was protected.

Reading was the only occupation, aside from talking, that I could see my mother enjoyed. On one corner of the hard, repellent sofa, a fat novel in hand, she would settle in when she had a bit of time between long hours of work and doing everything at home that a housewife had to do. There was no talking to me or anyone then. But I would sometimes put my head in her lap, catching the occasional absent-minded touch of her hand on my head like drops of new rain in a drought. For the sake of that randomly bestowed caress, I would endure the odors of her apron, an unholy blend of potato peel and cigarette smoke. Betty (like her mother before her, she often said), did not kiss or cuddle: she called it "lecking and shmecking" ("I've never been one for lecking and shmecking, that's just the way I am. Y'see, I'm like my mother"), the very thing that I most craved withheld, though she didn't see this as withholding. Perhaps it was a conserving of resources: an emotional hoarding that felt as necessary as economic hoarding for survival.

Stories

I am sitting opposite Betty at the cheap white formica kitchen table in the afternoon after school, just the two of us drinking milky tea. She is talking… and talking and *talking*, rapidly, pushing the stories forward with her energy. I do not interrupt, except to make appreciative noises. "When we were going out together, your father found a twenty-dollar bill on the sidewalk one day. That was a lot of money in those days and he wasn't working because of the Depression, but I took the twenty from him and bought myself a nice coat with a fur collar. Twenty dollars! He hadn't seen twenty dollars in a long time, and he didn't say a thing!" That was what romantic love could do; he was powerless before her then. Romantic feeling, when someone needed you, weighted the scales of power in your direction, but made you weak when you were the needy one.

Like all fables, Betty's memories imparted their universal wisdom through specifics: usually her troubles and struggles against the almost insurmountable obstacles thrust in her way at every turn. There was my oldest brother Mel's terrible asthma and the midnight trips to the hospital emergency room, the danger of crossing Brooklyn's Belt Parkway in the dark while frantically pushing the boy in his sister's baby carriage; Eric's tantrums as a young child, so bad she had to lock him out of the apartment, howling and kicking the apartment door (the marks at the bottom of the door were still there when he took his daughter to see where we'd lived). I knew about my own incessant crying as an infant, with a temperament already inconsolably sorrowful as I demanded what I should not be asking for. The only way she could sew the factory piecework she did at home was to shake my crib back and forth with one hand, while manipulating the cloth with the other and working the treadle with her foot. She was victim or heroine, or both at once: Betty of the many limbs like some Indian goddess, including the hand that rocked the cradle and the hand that shut my angry brother out of our home, the near-magical feet that could work a treadle and fly over the dark streets to Coney Island Hospital to save the life of her wheezing child.

I barely knew the sound of my own voice. My role was listener, not teller – after all, at nine or twelve or sixteen, what did I have to say that would be interesting anyway? And I was glad to fill that position, even when it made me unhappy in some way I couldn't explain. ("On my wedding night I was so innocent that when I saw your father naked, I screamed. I didn't let him near me for three days. No one had told me, not my mother, not any of my five sisters, that a man looked that way. I never did like sex after that.") This was because I knew I was a crucial part of the ritual of recitation. The humblest vessel in a sacred rite is transformed by its necessity to the whole.

Stories, both romance or anti-romance, are part of my romantic DNA. Betty was a great storyteller and liar ("Not a *liar*," my brother Eric objects, "Say a fabulist. A fantasist"). Embellishment carried no implication at all for her of moral turpitude; she expected everyone to do it. Betty collected stories for appropriate occasions the way others might collect outfits, and could easily retro-fit the story to the purpose. My mother's ability to dip in and out of factuality was a matter of pride. Certainly her lost past in England came in handy quite often. For a short time she was hired as a nurse's aide at a hospital when she'd had no training because she told them her certificate had been lost when she immigrated from England. This was a cherished job because she was sometimes near the doctors and could see who she might have been in a different world. Another time she was hired as a bookkeeper in the garment industry. They wanted to know her education level; she went to college in England, she told them. She would be glad to give them the papers that would show she did, but they got burned up during the war. She had no idea how to keep accounts, but she claimed they did it differently in England: could they just show her how it's done in America? That's how she learned to do the job.

"See what you can do with a big mouth?" she'd say afterward, pointing out that in childhood and youth, she'd been quiet and shy like me, but life had beaten that out of her, and finally she was afraid of no one. It's even possible this was true. Or perhaps these stories about her clever lies were, in fact, themselves lies about the act of lying.

As those who pray commit themselves to an invisible world, the shifting boundary of reality in Betty's tales allowed her to shape truth as an artist does, reforming the unacceptable dullness or complexity of merely *what happened* to the far superior *what might have happened* or *should happen.* This is the seed of romance: The could-be-true is better than true.

Home

Something is missing; there is an absence, the silent ghost of what I could not name. There was no lack of strong emotions, but not those you'd want to live with.

Al was mild and cheerful, looking forward to what he

liked to do, but when he felt victimized by fate, he would cry out against his "stinkin', lousy, rotten bad luck," or for particularly bad occasions, his "*goddamn* stinkin', lousy, rotten bad luck." He had a strong sense of justice in the universe that was continually and outrageously violated. No wonder my motto is "Nothing ventured, nothing lost," given that Al felt his full glass was always being emptied, and Betty that she had to squeeze every drop into that slippery, easily-shattered glass by herself.

Betty, on the other hand, was bitter by default, not so much enraged by the universe as furious at Al. Then Al defended himself by shouting just as loudly as she did, his tone deepening while hers grew more shrill, till the high-feminine and low-masculine voices took turns flying over each other like bombers, and no one was listening, except us kids, who didn't want to. The family was a kind of hydraulic system in which steam was let off periodically so it could go on.

My oldest brother wrote to me: "I remember often lying in bed, listening to the loud screaming of our mother, our father answering back, and finally our father marching out, slamming the door behind him. One of the common disputes was that Daddy wanted the window open in the winter and Mommy wanted it closed."

Why didn't he leave, or she leave? My brother Eric remembers lying on the pull-out sofa next to our brother, trying to go to sleep, hearing our parents talk in the bedroom and thinking it was a recording they'd left there to fool us into believing they hadn't abandoned us. It seemed imminent every day.

Why did they stay? Was it love?

As a child I struggled to understand love. Once, about age ten, I had a little burst of courage and outright asked my mother if she loved me. She looked up sharply from her book and said this was a silly question.

I persisted, out of my ordinary character, determined to hear the words this one time, to get a definitive answer: "Okay, but *do you*?"

"Why would you ask me that?" she demanded. She looked annoyed.

"I don't know," I said. "But do you?"

"I never heard such a question in my life," said Betty impatiently, which was probably true: I doubt she'd have thought of asking anything so pointless of her own parents. Yet I was ready to stay with it for once; it was clear that if I were going to triumph, the words would be squeezed out hard, like the last bit of something in a tube. So I asked still one more time, which gave me this: "You're my daughter, why wouldn't I love you?"

I wanted to cry, but knew how *that* would go. Instead I asked urgently: "But Mommy, would you love me if I weren't your daughter?"

"That's ridiculous," Betty growled, and went back to reading her novel, which never asked a stupid question of her when she was tired, exhausted from doing everything, being "the man as well as the woman, the father and the mother both," as she often said.

I knew I was vanquished. It's odd now, as a mother myself, to remember my horror of unconditional love, which is supposed to be the most beautiful version. If I were someone else's daughter, she wouldn't love me, or maybe even like me. And if some other girl were her daughter, she'd love her instead. This cracked open an entirely new view of love. The one who was supposed to love you best for your whole life did not really love you for yourself. It was a matter of casual fate that you happened to be born in this or that family, out of this or that body. This was nearly unbearable.

My faith was in words, a whole genre of speaking and reading entwined with emotion that seemed my natural home. As I grew, this susceptibility evolved like a plant asymmetrically adding cells to its stem as it leans toward the light. And that growing bent towards love through language was also the pathway to my innermost life, with its secret, half-ashamed store of hope for the future.

Play

My first desires were for a love that was safe and warm. Frankie was a dark-eyed three-year-old boy down the block, whose parents fussed over their only child at a wondrous event called a *birthday party*. I went to that party. After that I *became* Frankie, cannibalizing his little sweet persona to recreate myself as a small, much-loved, indulged, happy Italian-American boy in my nightly bedtime fantasy.

Yet my childhood pretend play was not about happy families, fathers who earned princely salaries that made their wives smile, mothers whose laps were warm and welcoming, children covered with kisses. Instead I imagined daring adventures in strange lands. After we studied the American pioneers in school, these play stories had only one plot: hardy, resolute pioneers with few resources travel over perilous landscapes in search of a new life. Rather than dream of being safe where I was, I longed to be brave… somewhere else.

In the summers, most often still alone and forced outside much of the day while Betty worked long hours at a resort in the country, what sustained me was a small pink Spaldeen ball. I never actually played ball games with this ball, any more than I played chess with the chess pieces, or marbles with the marbles, or soldiers with the toy soldiers at home. All of them stood in for humans. The Spaldeen ball was my double, and the roots of imposing trees, curving above the ground and covered by the undulating green and brown moss I adored, were the scene for the adventures of this humanized rubber ball. Odd as it is to be represented by a rubber Spaldeen, I was happy as I could ever be in this territory of the imagination, where the living moss became rolling meadows and hills, and the rough roots of the trees were barely scalable mountains. Whatever these adventures were, the joy of it came from the freedom to be and imagine without fear.

Childhood play is total immersion. There's no irony, no criticism of yourself, not even humor, which is a kind of looking down at oneself and the world. Instead you swim to some subterranean cave of absorbing peace, where you can breathe for a time.

When I was almost six, my parents borrowed money from relatives to buy a tiny wretched house in a working-class Irish and Italian neighborhood in an outlying area of Brooklyn. There was a dark corner of the house, a small enclosed area behind an armchair no one sat on, next to a three-tiered end table adorned with assorted cheap plaster figurines. It was my preferred space because it was both private yet open at one end, a cavern. I could play there all day, gloriously alone while surrounded by family, an island with a drawbridge. That sort of being alone was not lonesome. In this shaded corner, the realm of dream and fantasy was weighed against reality, and reality was found wanting. This kind of play too is a romance, one that transforms the stubbornly ordinary into a better story, where joys and griefs have a point that becomes clear at the end.

Books

Before I was an adolescent, I knew that what made me unlovable had to be hidden; a greedy need to be attended to, listened to, cared for, too much. But I also discovered that solace could be found at will in slanted, oblique, even labyrinthine ways, through reading. A book may be a frigate, as the poet Emily Dickinson famously claimed, but that doesn't mean it sails only to what's far away. A book can also bring you home, including to that home you call yourself, with all its contradictions and complicating truths. Reading is the longest continuous habit I can remember, uniting my first self to my latest, and, I hope, to my last.

I recall the specific day when Betty stopped reading to me. I can see her sitting on her customary place at the end of the hard-pillowed, synthetic-blue sofa as she handed back a book I'd begged her to read. Her words seemed momentous, an edict from on high: "No, you can read this by yourself now." I didn't take this refusal as rejection; it was a signal that I was old enough at age six to have this comfort and pleasure available to me on command, my own in every way.

The book she gave back to me was the first one I was delighted to find had sequels: *B is for Betsy* by Carolyn Haywood. Betsy was six, like me, and had long pigtails, as I did – but she had the happiest, most stable, middle-class family life imaginable. Certainly Betsy had problems, but they were the smallest of troubles, overcome easily with an apology and a better understanding of the rules, smiles all around.

I was lonely at home, friendless, and afraid of my teacher, Mrs. Waddell, her white hair in a severe bun, a character more in the style of a novel by Roald Dahl than *B is for Betsy*. On our first day of school, she scolded me because I had a cough drop in my mouth that my mother had given me, and made me spit it out in the trash ("NO GUM IN THE CLASSROOM!"). I cried but didn't tell Mrs. Waddell it wasn't gum, and didn't tell my mother that I'd been scolded.

Betsy, by Chapter Two, had made fast friends with a nice girl and a jolly boy she met in her new school, and thereafter was surrounded by happy playmates who liked her best. Then too, Betsy bonded easily with her young, cheerful, earnest teacher, who recognized a good girl when she saw one. This very pretty young woman (there were illustrations) married a perfectly bland and faceless fellow in one of the sequels – surely the first time I'd encountered such an event in a book, as opposed to the unfortunate weddings in Betty's cautionary tales of life (including her own). I'd never seen a wedding, but Betsy was thrilled, especially because the teacher who doted on Betsy asked her to be a flower girl. What was a flower girl? I had no idea, but it sounded pretty.

I don't recall a single pleasant or interesting moment in the classroom, yet elementary school was a refuge for me from home, a place where the rules could be followed and keep you safe. School may not have been stimulating, but it was predictable and orderly. No one broke into angry tirades or seemed stressed by a lack of money. I barely spoke, except when forced to. Keep your head down and do your work and the day would pass quietly, if tediously.

A few years later, I began to find stories about good little girls like Betsy insipid; I wanted daring and adventure, like Albert Payson Terhune's novels about Lad the dog, the most loyal and courageous animal friend a family could have. I also wept over *Lassie Come Home* and *Black Beauty*, riveting for their drama and suspense, but also more disturbing in their depictions of animal suffering. And I whipped right through *The Swiss Family Robinson*, *Gulliver's Travels*, *Tom Sawyer* (Junior Classic editions, all from the public library), *Hans Brinker*, *King Arthur*, *White Fang*, *Bambi*, and *Dr. Doolittle*. One of my well-worn books was the D'Aulaires' *Greek Myths*, with its delicious illustrations. None of these were "girls' books" the way they would have been seen then; their heroes were all males, and that included Lad the dog (Lassie was the exceptional female, and you couldn't say she was very feminine). They offered bold experiences in unfamiliar times, and landscapes that nourished my own deepest dreams of excitement and change. When I read Twain's *Tom Sawyer*, I could not imagine being interested in pallid, whiny Becky, there only to be rescued by daring and inventive Tom.

By the time I was eight or nine, I had also discovered fairy tales, and was quickly immersed in their fantastic worlds. The library had thick volumes of them organized by color: *The Blue Fairy Book*, *The Yellow Fairy Book*, and so on. Just as for many girls, this was my primary source of information on romance, along with Disney's filmed versions.

Though real estate was the sure index of the heroines' class status, I was far more interested in the dresses they wore in the colored illustrations. I've never been much attracted to shopping in real life, and certainly not in childhood, when my tastes were not consulted and my clothes were all hand-me-downs anyway. Yet before I understood what romance meant, I feverishly wished to live in a world in which women wore long, full skirts and bodices ending in long points. I could easily see myself courted in that sort of dress. In fact the gown seemed far more desirable than the prince himself, who was never described with the slightest attempt at character. He was on a horse, and he was in charge of the place where you'd end up; that was all. It wasn't the particulars of the romantic story that enthralled me. It was a certain aura of magic, the sense that you put on that dress and anything could happen, that you *never know*.

Then came *Emily of New Moon*, a series from the 1920s by Lucy Maude Montgomery, Canadian author of the more popular *Anne of Green Gables*. I picked up the Emily books as randomly as usual in my visits to the library, and somehow missed the famous Green Gables series entirely. Emily was more than enough, in any case, because, to my wonder and delight, she was sensitive – my mother's reproachful word for me when I cried – and also a poet, which seemed appealing as a hobby because it was all about a freedom of expression I longed for.

Emily is a motherless little girl who lives in an isolated but beautiful landscape in Canada – not that I knew where Canada was – and has no friends, just books and cats and her favorite trees. She isn't lonely, we learn, because she is loved by her completely terrific father.

I could easily relate to being friendless, and also to being orphaned as a metaphor. But unlike Emily, I *was* lonely, in spite of my books (no trees or cats), though I didn't possess the emotional vocabulary to put that label on it. Before his death, Emily's father tells her that she has a special gift: "Life has something for you – I feel it," he says to his young daughter. And then he slips gently to the other side. You could only be encouraged by that message, even if no one on this side of the curtain had said any such thing to me. I was not fearless, nor did I have what Emily has inherited "from her fine old ancestors," specifically "the power to fight – to suffer – to pity – to love very deeply – to rejoice – to endure." Or rather, I had some of these traits, the suffering and loving parts, possibly inherited from my fine old peasant ancestors, but notably lacked the will or ability to fight. And I certainly didn't have Emily's "purplish-grey eyes," my own being an ordinary brown, like my hair. Why must girl heroines always possess extraordinary blue or green or gray eyes? It's enough to make a child aware she did not descend from "fine old [Anglo] ancestors," but from impoverished, illiterate Jews who'd somehow gotten stuck in the ghettos of Eastern Europe in the Middle Ages.

The sensitive, misunderstood, oppressed but strong and defiant orphan girl who finds her self-worth through trials is a common figure in classic literature, needless to say. Emily of New Moon has some clear connections to nineteenth-century Jane Eyre as a heroine. Before long, the magnitude of Emily's innate attractiveness gathers the sort of community of quirky, bonded outsiders beloved in children's books and movies such as *Harry*

Potter, as well as in TV sitcoms about funny groups of friends or co-workers. There's Teddy, called a handsome boy (clearly a future lover), who is also artistic, like Emily herself, and Perry, a kind of unsung worker-genius like my own father. When Emily smiles at him, Perry is "reduced to hopeless bondage" for life. At its core, *Emily of New Moon* and its sequels are stories about recognition: the affirmation by a community of others of the heroine's superiority and lovability, which is also key to much romance and other fictions of emotion. Both happy community and, it turns out, hopelessly bonded future lovers were entirely missing in my own childhood.

I was not yet interested in romantic stories, but that changed a few years later when I was forcibly seized by a more sophisticated work of fiction: the British author Rumer Godden's *The Episode of Sparrows*. This was the first book whose depiction of love moved me and was the focus of my interest.

The Episode of Sparrows was an interesting novel for learning about love, not least because at its center is an unusual child-heroine, a girl as fierce as Jane Eyre in her capacity for stubbornness and aggression. Strikingly, this girl-heroine isn't described as beautiful, unlike every other heroine I'd read about until then, including Montgomery's Emily. Nor is she pointedly labeled *not* pretty like Jane Eyre, who is decidedly "plain," a revolutionary act on Charlotte Brontë's part for her time. Before *Sparrows*, I'd never before come across a heroine whose looks were so little described, so unemphasized; we're simply told Lovejoy is "pale" with "mouse-colored" hair. There is nothing mousy about Lovejoy, however, nor does she ever turn into a respectable lady, like Emily of New Moon, or Jane Eyre herself. Instead she is "more like a boy" than a traditional docile girl, steals with no guilt, runs away, punches an enemy in the stomach, throws a kitchen knife at an adult who insults her, and negotiates with extravagant and stubborn "slyness" for what she wants. Yet we are clearly invited to like and identify with her as if she were entirely innocent and virtuous. This, the first independent "bad girl" heroine of my young reading life, was a revelation.

An Episode of Sparrows is set in a grimy lower-class neighborhood in London, not unlike the Whitechapel area where my father grew up on the aptly named Hungerford Street. Our heroine Lovejoy, a neglected child, is a flower among the ruins, but also a tenacious weed: she's capable of joy, though not yet of love or trust. Single-minded, irrational, gripping passions drive the plot, especially Lovejoy's passion for growing an unlikely garden in a dirt lot, and the growing adulation of a local young tough guy, Tip Malone, all of thirteen years old, for Lovejoy herself. "If he were older, I'd have said he was in love," remarks his bewildered mother at the end. Lovejoy is not in love with Tip – he's the one with romantic feeling, while she needs him to help make the garden. And probably because the novel was intended as adult fiction, it separates the pair at the end and leaves their future open, which shocked and dismayed me quite a bit. I was still young enough not to have encountered a single story that did not carry the hero or heroine to eternal bliss as their just reward. I read that ending again and again, as if repetition could make it come out the way it should.

This was quite different from the "boys' stories" I'd loved, with their physical struggles and quests for fame and power. It was around that time that my own single-minded drive (obsession, if you must) began to form, that channeling of desire and dream life into one surge that carries along all sensation to somewhere else and, most of all, to *someone* else. In the character of Tip Malone and his unnamed attachment to Lovejoy, Rumer Godden had rendered a kind of passion as I'd already begun to feel it. This was not just an unnamed desire for what I didn't have, as in early childhood, but a hope into which large emotions poured and pooled, without thought or even a specific goal.

Lovejoy, with her tough talk and reckless spunk (no charming smiles or large, beautiful blue eyes for her), combined the appeal of the daring boys who'd dominated my childhood reading with the dream of finding the love of a male that replaced it in adolescence. This was the first fiction to show me exactly how isolated and dominated girls could have a singular power over men who adore them, just as Betty, fresh off a boat in the mean streets of Depression-era Brooklyn, had conquered her man Al.

Then too, *The Episode of Sparrows* presented a hero in many a passionate romance I would encounter later: he is hyper-masculine and seems too tough for romantic love, but underneath has a gentleness that will turn him into the heroine's protector and tender lover. Godden points to what this is really about: the strong male *notices* the superiority of the heroine where the rest of the world does not. This was the perfect shape of a fantasy for my ten-year-old self. I had no trace of Emily of New Moon's calm self-confidence and noticeable superiority, or Lovejoy's "spunk" and ambition. But I had *something*, I was sure, that special gift that Emily's father believed she had – though not at all sure what it could be. If only someone would *notice*, though, if someone would turn his or her – *his* – attention to me, I would find out.

Is it any wonder that novels appealed to me? The push of the narrative towards a meaningful conclusion implied that all that happened, good or bad, meant something, was going to lead somewhere that felt right. And if life could turn out so swell in their pages, why not for me too? In the just universe of children's literature and later, in fictions of romance, virtue was rewarded by getting what you most want. I was hoping to be virtuous as hell.

Fantasy

Reading was not my only interest: I also watched a lot of TV, ritually switched on every day for the early evening news and switched off when the last adult went to bed. In our house, when you opened the door you fell into the living room, graced with a TV standing against the exact opposite wall, so that it was the first thing you saw, a testament to its importance.

My first love story was an old black-and-white Hollywood film, *One Touch of Venus*. Sitting on the floor as close as possible to the TV cabinet one afternoon after school, I gawked at the vivid beauty of Ava Gardner, wildly desired by the hero. I was young enough to wonder what made her so special. What did he want from her?

But my idea of romantic love was driven by novels. I know the precise moment when my desire for romance in my own life began. My mother and I were in the cheapest possible cabin at the bottom of an ocean liner on our way to see her elderly, ailing parents in England for the last time. I was ten. Drowsy, closing my eyes in the top bunk after Betty turned out the light, I conjured the scene in Louisa May Alcott's *Little Women* in which Meg's suitor, John, proposes marriage to her. Afterward I enacted the scene in my head, again and again, with dialogue of my own, a form of fan fiction. I did not identify with Jo, the heroine, or wish to be a boy. The suitor John's eagerness for Jo's sister Meg to accept his hand, his pining for her, the hope of a delightful future together – all these had fallen one after the other into place together, the way the bolts of a lock shift with a satisfying *thunk!* when you turn the key, into a story I didn't yet name as romance.

Not a single fantasy of mine ever centered on adventure after that. I felt too old at ten or eleven for pebbles, marbles, plastic soldiers, or chalkboard maps to represent me. All this faded almost overnight, there on the *Queen Mary* pitching in the dark.

Little Women was the first picture of grown-up courtship in my life to counter my mother's own bitter tale of marriage. Many girls who read *Little Women* are dismayed by Jo's rejection of Laurie, the lively, good-looking boy who seems destined for her. He is even rich! But impetuous, fun-loving Laurie stands for romance of the sort that is too flighty to be taken seriously, while Jo's older sister Meg occupies the necessary space for domestic courtship in everyday life. "Real" heterosexual love, as usual, is tied directly to building family and community, the kind that binds the March family together. *Little Women* and its sequels proved my gateway drug to a dream of women, courtship, and marriage not found in children's novels at that time, where female characters tended to be mothers and teachers, helpers or sometimes (as in *Snow White*) villains.

In a nineteenth-century American novel aimed at girls, it was impossible not to match Jo with *someone*, and so Alcott invented kindly, middle-aged Professor Bhaer, with his quaint European civility, his charming nineteenth-century German intellectuality, and his gentle, non-threatening reticence in courting. He is as unlike Laurie as possible, old to Laurie's young, shy to Laurie's exuberant, steady to Laurie's restless, because he represents a clear break between love that is disturbing, irrational, unpredictable emotion, and the domestic attachment that makes for an appropriately functional husband. This important (and very Victorian) division of love into suspect romantic feeling (impetuous, sexual, and uncontrolled) and marital affection (calm and reliable) is a watered-down and cleaned-up version of the difference between Heathcliff and Edgar in Emily Brontë's *Wuthering Heights*. What makes Jo's choices unusual, though, is that there's no indication she has the slightest attraction to either of them, certainly not physically. She simply likes both very much in different ways, but would only marry one.

This lack of enthusiasm for the romantic story of love reflects what we know about Alcott's own experience with romance. But as a child, or even as a teenager, I wasn't in the least curious about Alcott's life, or any author's life. In fact, I was only very dimly aware that authors *had* lives of their own – much as the way I view therapists.

Why did romantic novels appeal to me and not at all to my brothers? Where does that begin? It carries me back to that vivid memory of Daddy stroking my hair and murmuring with wonder, "Beautiful, so beautiful...": you are gazed upon singly, the focus, whereas in my actual experience later on, the boy himself and my unseen longing for him were my focus. If you are adored, these fictions say to young women, you will not be dismissed or abused, and they will not leave. You are important, you have an unshakable grip on them. This fantasy, like the fantasy of great beauty, deeply satisfying to many young girls who are still uncertain of their desirability, so easily creates an expectation that seems corrosive if unmet. Masculinity is not supposed to work this way for boys, who are meant to dream of other kinds of adulation, perhaps.

Fiction did not just express my hidden desires, it contained them, limited and molded them, it stimulated and simulated them. Fantasy and fiction made them real by being realer-than-real.

I had been Peter Pan, flying on the power of a wish, barely registering silly housekeeping Wendy in my reading. From then on, in my daydreams, and also in those gentle moments before sleep when the world recedes and the dream-world changes places with the real, I imagined only romance, including a secret fantasy that Peter was in love with Wendy. And I had transformed into Wendy.

Love

Not coincidentally, I fell in love with a real boy in the same year I read *Little Women*. I can't be sure which came first, romance in books that transported me to this new state, or my own longing that fed my attraction to fictional romance, in a kind of emotional feedback loop. All the adventure, heightened drama, and potent desires that drew me to stories were now located in an actual, embodied human.

Then romantic love became an alternate home with a door I could open at any time. It was a ferry rushing through the wide expanse of If Only.

From fifth grade on, the presence every school day of the one boy my heart had fixed on was comforting and stimulating at once. Just the wish to see him (not yet to touch him) filled my thoughts in a gratifying way. Here was my first indistinct hope that someday there might be a royal road leading from my deepest desires outward to a better future, radiant with pleasure. My interest in one quite ordinary, prepubescent youngster was sealed off from everyday life, though his appeal was exactly that he belonged to the real rather than to fiction, that he had a life of his own outside the limits of the imaginary.

I'm going to call this very young man Alex, A for alpha, because he was the first of a series of men who paraded through my romantic life, some briefly and some for decades. (The rest will have alphabetic pseudonyms, to preserve their precious privacy.)

Alex was a dark-haired Italian boy in my fifth-grade class, often smiling, more cute than good-looking, an older version of the small Italian-American boy whose birthday party I'd envied. The figure of male charm that was Alex evoked strong and singular feelings in me for no other reason than that he seemed sweet and happy, something like a brown-eyed puppy my own size, a version of me if I were sweet, happy, and male. Quickly, Alex's image became ringed round with a halo of unspeakable emotion, and the anticipation of seeing him propelled me to trudge to school by myself each colorless morning.

Alex barely ever interacted with me. I doubt I would have known what to do if he had, though I had a dim sense that I could wing it. I didn't dream of kisses, much less any form of sexuality, yet at age ten or eleven I was certainly in love, an abridged form of romance, the Junior Classics version. It wasn't "a crush," as we say dismissively; it was love in the mode of ecstatic looking, as if at a monumental statue in a museum or an idol in a shrine.

Since Alex happened to be in my class every year from fifth grade on, his presence was a reliable beacon of the City on the Hill; barring catastrophe, such as his occasional absence from school, his cute face, that uniquely pleasure-giving face, would be somewhere across the room or in the hall. And I could imagine that this day, *this very one,* would be the occasion he would notice me, perhaps even talk to me. I don't remember being terribly disappointed when each day proved to be a repetition of the others. In fact I didn't want much from Alex – a word, a look, a smile, just as the young Dante insists that all he wants from Beatrice is a greeting. At most I hoped for some hazily romantic scene, the details as impossible to imagine as the precise nature of God's presence in heaven for the pious. The rest, I felt, would take off itself.

The fact that Alex did not so much as glance my way is of course what kept this new hope going for an absurd time, through middle school and beyond, until he was replaced. This trail marked how romance would figure on my psychic map. Beginning with Alex, I was always passionately, fixedly in love. No matter how long the romantic feeling had endured, as soon as Alex, or any of them, was ousted from the kingdom of romance, what had been a pointed arrow of desire instantly became a flaccid rubber band on a slingshot ready for reloading.

My Love Story

I did not yet have a story of my own, because no one reciprocated my feelings. Real romance was supposed to be mutual or it was not real. I knew this from my mother's stories, and from my books. Books were imaginary but some books could be true. Betty's stories, however, were neither true nor not-true, they expressed truth as myth does, as the imagination does, in the no-man's land between the verifiable and the impossible.

While the children's books I'd read all ended similarly, the good repaid with exactly what they deserved and the bad dispatched, Betty's tales were an ongoing struggle against a mostly unjust fate that never ceased to plague mortals until you died.

And so I shuttled between the reality I couldn't help and its romantic version, a visionary place whose natural laws are in harmony with one's feelings, where the goal is outside oneself yet reflects the deepest level of self, and hope is confounded with expectation. Loveland had its own language, one I rapidly absorbed, as children immersed in a new culture will do. *I love you* means you are chosen, a princess in disguise who has gone unrecognized; a man's choice is a promise that you will share a space of no boundaries with the beloved Other, and he will share this space with no one but you. Your future is foretold.

My desires generally went unnoticed except in Loveland, where longing is not a weakness or an inappropriate need that must be suppressed at all costs, but the beginning of who-knows-what, a first step in the journey to a far country, with its beautiful vistas, that awaited me.

Great love stories are not only about love: they resemble love in their seductive pull, the reader's reluctance to break away, our longing to return, the disappointment, even emptiness, when the novel is over and the characters must be left behind. By the time I was ready to imagine the full story of my own life, love had joined hands with fiction and daydream, a coalition of imagination, reading, and desire.

Novels in general partook of romance, containing that very truth I couldn't grasp in real life: the pleasure of interpreting someone else's mind, of knowing the inner self of others, their secret thoughts, a sense that we know characters from the inside. For many women of my generation and upbringing, happy-ending romantic fiction reveals that the one you love *really* feels about you exactly as you'd like him to, appearances to the contrary. You as heroine are of the most value to the very one who is most valuable himself. That is your secret power: you are beloved, and you have been all along, or at least since the guy woke up to the truth. In effect, you are in love with one of your selves, the one that exists in the mind of the man who desires you.

In spite of Betty's dark cautions about men and romance, I believed, because I wanted to, that the next years, when I grew into womanhood, were going to be the most important chapter of my tale, the climax, if you will, in which I was about to encounter *real* love, with an actual and suitable young man, and specific, desirable consequences that I deserved. Those phantoms of imagination, myself and the man I loved, each of us naturally and simultaneously feeling the same way, to the same degree, and for all time, were ready to be called into life: man and woman stitched together into oneness, in a space without limits.

Betty and Al, children of immigrants, young émigrés in their turn, found new life, though no riches, in Brighton Beach, Brooklyn. And I too, on the verge of adolescence, was a migrant with no resources, clutching my ticket to a high-stakes, risky, sometimes hostile state: the majestic realm of Loveland.

Chapter Two
Courtship

> I am my longing.
> – Jon Fosse, *Melancholy*

In puberty there seemed no connection between the swell of fatty lumps on my chest and romantic love. I had loved before they were there, and I loved afterward when there was still no admirer, much less soulmate. Sex and love, body and romance, seemed, if anything, opposite realms of experience.

While waiting for my love story to begin, I occupied myself with reading. By age twelve or so, I was determined to understand the outside world as it really was. Maybe it registered that the happy, fun-loving families in the books I read had little resemblance to the real family I lived in. I started by trying to master how the world works; I had a dim sense that the more I knew, the closer I could come to making a reality from the invisible cloth of my dreams. Knowing what things really are, not how they appear or how we wish they were, is a kind of power. So I began with the encyclopedia.

Betty wanted us to have the education her father would not allow her, and the encyclopedia she'd obtained for us at a good price was a path to this. It sat proudly, stiff with reddish-brown fake leather, on a bookshelf in the living room, not far from the TV, which was the emotional center of the room. This encyclopedia, our idol of learning, was a cheap and obscure edition (how else could we have afforded it?), already outdated and probably filled with misinformation. It seemed wonderful to me, containing all the truths and facts of the world. I immediately swore to read it straight through, and may even have gotten past A, but finally settled on the pleasure of landing on random entries and reading those.

Next, I discovered the dictionary. By then I knew reading straight through was going to be too much for my lazy brain, so I jumped right away to looking up the dirtiest words I could think of. Adolescent urges were beginning to "rear their ugly heads," as my middle school teacher once put it, so the mildest of sexual connotations aroused me. I remember a conversation with several neighborhood children on one of the rare times I sat with them on a stoop. "I bet you don't know what *fuck* means," said a very young man. There was a heavy silence, because no one really knew. We waited for him to enlighten us. "Fuck," said this young man importantly, "means all the dirty words put together." We admired his erudition. But "fuck" wasn't in the dictionary or the encyclopedia, so there was no way to confirm this. I had to settle for "penis," "vagina," "intercourse," and the newly discovered "erection." "Clitoris" was a major find, in every possible sense.

When I reached the age of reason, my brother Eric, who regularly read fiction, as well as science, psychology, philosophy, law, and political economy, began taking me with him to Greenwich Village in Manhattan to browse used bookstores for new finds. The stoicism of Epictetus he highly recommended was beyond me, but when he wasn't home, I browsed through his shelves of books the way he browsed the bookstores. My personal favorite was *Pornography and the Law*, which detailed the history of legal censorship, illustrating each case with excerpts from the confiscated books. I skipped impatiently over the law and spent many a happy moment with the obscene passages.

These erotic delights were little buds of promise, like my new breasts, but there were no principles for rational living here to help out with my future life. I would have done better with Epictetus ("What you love is nothing of your own: it has been given to you for the present").

In my new mode of wisdom-seeking, I stumbled on a quotation in a letter by Thomas Jefferson that rang out to me like a personal declaration of independence: "We are not afraid to follow truth wherever it may lead." Brave words! It's what I vowed to do for the rest of my life. I had no idea that Jefferson was describing the radical principles of a new university, later the University of Virginia, based on the "illimitable freedom of the human mind." I felt that was my own purpose exactly, to cultivate a free mind, sharp and tough enough to know the difference between all I hoped, wished, longed for, and the often ugly, disappointing reality of life. Something wasn't true because you wanted it to be true; that was my founding principle. Romance was a suspect pleasure, and knowledge could overcome passion. This was the first shot in a lifelong battle between the reason that grounded me and the bliss of imagination that kept me aloft, the *what is* versus *what if*.

Jefferson's letter grandly concludes that a liberal education "will not tolerate any error so long as reason is left free to combat it," which seems quite relevant to our present day. The "errors" in belief he had in mind referred to the contemporary conflict between religion and superstition on one hand, and the rigorous discipline of science and reason he admired on the other. Yet Jefferson himself was poisonously irrational when he listed the supposedly inferior traits of "the Black race," such as the inability of "Blacks" to feel love or grief – based, of course, on his own self-interested perspective as a slave owner. I did not know this at the time. Now it stands out to me in my own battle between emotion and reason; they are not, maybe never are, wholly separate.

Truth is not "self-evident," as the Declaration of Independence claims: it has to be fought for. Not only that: truths are not simple, and even Jefferson, an enlightened political figure (for his time), was directed by the "truths" he preferred to invent. As for me, I still struggle incessantly to be honest with myself, to see the truth of my life as it is, the way some people battle with sin every day and strive to be perfect. And like sinners, I never quite get there.

The Occupation

Betty was still talking, more abundantly than ever now that I could understand more, but my reading was expanding even faster. The idea of a just, if stern, natural order was the principle of my mother's stories (*hard work will pay*, *talent will out*, and *virtue will eventually be rewarded*, if only through having successful children). This had always mirrored the world of childhood fiction, where the good are compensated by the universe (which is to say, the author). On the other hand, the larger world view of my parents – the lousy, rotten luck, the never-ending nearness of catastrophe – directly opposed the idea of the cosmos as a meritocracy. As I grew, the contradictions only sent me deeper into the alternative world of story, where life made sense.

In spite of my longing for truth to conquer my desires and set me free, no sooner did I enter the uncharted territory of adolescence than my mental space became colonized by romantic love. Romance as an actual relationship was far in the future, but it already felt like my new, permanent home. You could say that Loveland absorbed me into its citizenry, occupying its lowest caste.

I no longer was satisfied to catch a glimpse of my beloved every school day. The love that looked and adored began to long for more, for touches and caresses.

Whenever I determined to breach the walls around the real world, the sea of desire surged, and imagination embraced the life that spilled over into this longing. As my unnamable inner cravings began more and more to take on the shape of love, I feared the emptiness of never having what you were supposed to get. This was like my childhood fear of flood water slowly rising till it surged into my bedroom, drowning us, except the opposite: the fear that the life-giving water would never come. I should have feared the flood and the surge instead.

Something was missing from my life, but of course I could not have told you what it was. At age thirteen or so, I knew I was trapped in a particular body and burdened with self-consciousness, but I had no idea why, or what could be done about it. As soon as I asked myself that adolescent question "Who am I?", I found myself responding "But who's asking 'Who am I'?", and then "Who's asking, who's asking?" It was fiction that answered those turtles-all-the-way-down questions, or at least raised imaginary, hypothetical answers.

Stories frame experience in a way that bends us in a certain direction. While nothing of significance appeared to be happening in my day-to-day life, the novels I read recast the specific question, "How do I get away from Betty and Al and live a different life?" as a new problem: "How do I find love?".

Reading was like watching a version of my life from the outside as an audience. Literature wasn't so much a distraction from reality as it outlined a way to find a new one: a visit for a short while to a place that is both like but also delightfully unlike your ordinary self and everyday experience, a purpose that remains just out of reach. It's both similar enough to connect you to it, and dissimilar enough to wake you to a new story of a life, one that's both truth and untruth.

They say you never get over your first love, or will ever like any music better than the music you loved when young. Neither is true for me. But the novelists I still love most deeply, as opposed to merely admire, had seized me before I graduated from high school, which is to say before I really understood them. Language was my bridge to the world; I lived under that bridge, homeless.

Besides the classic love stories, I was also reading titillating love comics, where the apogee of desire was a lingering kiss on curvaceous lips. This, and Hollywood movies, led me to believe romantic kissing was a lengthy pressing together of closed lips, the longer, the more romantic. I did not learn about French kissing, as it's called, until much later, when I was rather horrified by the idea, as well as the practice.

Adolescence opened up blurry possibilities for what I could do or be, beginning with certain books that focused my yearning with unbearable clarity. For the first time, I knew I was unhappy, because I began to learn the words to voice this unhappiness. As I came to understand that my life was a problem to myself, some of my reading – the doomed intensity of Dostoevsky, beautiful language of longing in Thomas Mann's *Death in Venice*, the vividness of subterranean feeling in Faulkner's *The Sound and the Fury* – traced a path of what I now knew as loneliness and emptiness. Great authors showed these states as existential and universal, which was gratifying only intellectually. But in romance fiction, when you find the one who recognizes you at some deep and eternal level, it could be all right. You could be two against the world.

The idea of romantic love began to penetrate my life in unexpected ways. Like so many teenagers then, when I read the very unromantic *Catcher in the Rye*, I recognized myself in Holden Caulfield, who never felt at home in the social world. His focus was on the inauthenticity of others he labels "phonies," though unlike Holden, my beef was not so much with the phonies but the happy ones. But I also saw that Holden's journey was what *boys* could do. While the adventure books in my childhood were almost all by, about, and for males, fictional heroines passively found romance. And so as a young teenage reader, I found a third way: I dreamed of being Holden's girlfriend, the romantic beloved who would understand him, the way Cathy in *Wuthering Heights* is the only one who understands Heathcliff… or Betty imagined she was the one who'd discovered Al's genius.

At the same time I was reading romantic fiction, I was preparing myself to experience real romance, like a runner practicing for the Olympics.

I was born into Betty's stories, but they rarely included me. I appeared as a prop occasionally, as in the story where my father didn't recognize me in the street one day because Betty had cut off my braids, which displeased him; that anecdote was really about my father and his preference for pretty girls with long hair (meaning women, rivals to my mother). But in my reading, I could imagine myself as the focus, written into the increasingly complex books I read, as well as in the movies I saw and the music my older brothers played. Almost all films and songs were concerned with love, or were entirely about love.

This particular time of my life, from puberty to full adulthood, coincided exactly with the period of courtship in the novels I read. Young womanhood in these novels was the time when a girl grows interesting *as a romantic heroine*, and her fictional life as a heroine is marked by a series of significant events that flow in one direction: a male loves her, leading to the bestowal of the Magic Ring of commitment by her future husband. This could be clearly seen in the novels that meant a great deal to me: in *Pride and Prejudice* and *Jane Eyre*, real love led to marriage and happiness, while in *Wuthering Heights*, Catherine and Heathcliff love passionately and bring ruin on themselves. What I understood through these fictions was that love must culminate in marriage, because passion without marriage was a disaster.

Wuthering Heights was the first novel I had ever read in

which love ended badly. At least Rumer Godden, in *The Episode of Sparrows*, left the future open. I almost couldn't believe Brontë had played this trick on me, and I wasn't sure what to do with it. Yes, Heathcliff and Cathy may (or may not) have been together as ghosts after death, though that hardly felt like a satisfying conclusion. Was that all Emily Brontë could offer the reader? Even Romeo and Juliet might have been happily married if they hadn't been such idiots as to take their own lives in a preventable misunderstanding (a rookie mistake I felt I could avoid).

And so the hope for happy endings that had fostered a secret optimism in me, that had provided the expectant pleasure of happiness hereafter that carried me through the difficult years of childhood, funneled easily into a genre read, it would appear, mostly by women. My own early experience of love for Alex, yearning for the object of my desire without return or recourse, was never represented in the fiction I read, and so the fantasy of romance with a happy ending was the only hope to follow. These romances implied that when the boy I desired did not notice me, it was probably the first stage of a true romance, a temporary condition that would ripen into the revelation of love that took place in every courtship novel with a happy ending. My wish to be loved and never left was assured by a relationship in which I had emotional and sexual power over the man I wanted. You just had to hold out until the end.

The relationship between book and reader, art and audience, is much debated by those who defend mass-media romance against the charge of being immature or unrealistic: they argue that readers can easily tell the difference between reality and fantasy, so romance doesn't raise unrealistic expectations, at least in any simple sense. But works of the imagination don't affect us in a simple sense; they represent a culture, enforcing it or subverting it, often both at once in different ways. Romance fiction sorted and classified my emotions, gave me a vocabulary of words, signs, styles, and images to understand what I felt: I am sad, loveless, hopeful, and so on. But structures of feeling are also strictures… the way they're lived out may feel like a choice, but what we do with them is just as likely to be a negotiation with what's on hand in the reality of lives.

Romance roused a secret part of me that had belonged to that shadow life and placed it into the world, in ready-made roles designed to absorb and shape it.

Romantic love is an idea, felt in the mind and body. As soon as an idea is named, it molds all its messy, unruly aspects into the thing the label says it is. It becomes the real thing, which is superior to whatever can't be contained and controlled by the label. Because now we believe we know what love is, and therefore also what it is not.

The Favorites

My favorite novels were the classic love stories, and especially three: *Pride and Prejudice*, *Wuthering Heights*, and *Jane Eyre*. The odd contrast between Jane Austen's style – calm, witty, finely observed – and the Brontë sisters' – high drama, in a world of open and often forbidden desire – was not lost on me, but I could project myself into all their literary worlds.

I secretly suspected I combined the best traits of all three of their most famous heroines: the lively intelligence and wit of Elizabeth Bennet, the passionate nature of Catherine Earnshaw, and the suffering sensibilities of Jane Eyre. Or at least the latter. I might not have had Elizabeth's "fine eyes" which entranced Mr. Darcy, or Cathy's charming face, but even plain Jane Eyre had Rochester at her feet. It just took longer.

The heroes in Jane Austen's novels are for the most part shockingly unknown and unknowable; they speak occasionally, but more often they *look* what they supposedly feel, blank screens for our fantasies of the heroine's future. Austen's courting lovers, Darcy in *Pride and Prejudice*, Edward Ferrars or Colonel Brandon in *Sense and Sensibility*, Edmund in *Mansfield Park*, Mr. Knightley in *Emma*, are either aloof or priggish or barely described. Though the hero in romance may be imperfect (that pride of Darcy's! The wildness of Brontë's Rochester!), the important point in a novel with a happy ending is that he is *perfectable.* The courting hero is educable in the way of being the man the reader wants him to be, and the heroine will school him.

Darcy is one of the most popular heroes in the history of romantic novels, his descendants in series like *Twilight* or *Fifty Shades* extruded endlessly by literary machines, yet he's a complete cipher – or maybe "yet" should be replaced with "because." The worthy romantic hero is often like a marble statue coveted for a new parlor. He can be described with a limited number of adjectives that signal his superiority: *Tall. Richest man in the neighborhood. Handsomest man around. Proud, coldly aloof, unemotive, appears obnoxious*, apparently flaws that can be cured by falling in love with the heroine, while still retaining the virtues of wealth and good looks. There's no clue at all as to Darcy's inner life, though we do learn later (and second-hand, through a servant) that he is a good "son, brother and friend" and virtuous "master" to his servants too, a trait that makes him marriageable in the old non-romantic sense. Laurence Olivier captured this blankness perfectly in the 1940 film *Pride and Prejudice*, whereas more modern attempts to give Darcy some human expression, complexity of character, overt bare-chested sexiness, and the sort of vulnerability that modern audiences enjoy and expect, feel artificial and anachronistic to me. In Austen's novel, Darcy must be the smooth-surfaced shell whose inside is a hole rather than a whole, one filled up with the female reader's own longings for herself and her surrogate, Elizabeth.

Who these days would want to marry a guy who has little to say for himself, even if he's rich, even both rich and handsome? All right, there are probably plenty even now, judging by the popularity of *Fifty Shades of Grey* and *The Real Housewives* franchise. But most would agree this is hardly an ideal to look up to. Would Darcy be so attractive if he weren't a man of social and economic power, the sort who could make or break a woman then? Try to picture Fitzwilliam Darcy as a shoemaker instead of a rich landowner, but speaking and behaving the same way – same dialogue, wooden gestures, entirely humorless and without invention or spontaneity. Would Elizabeth look at him, would *you* date him? The appeal of the romantic hero's distance is tied to the fantasy that a suitor who thinks he is superior really *is* superior.

In all the romantic books I read as a teenager, the heroine never, ever looked for love, but found it anyway.

Darcy appears one day when least expected; *Pride and Prejudice* opens as Elizabeth hears he's coming to their town, and she does nothing, does not need to do anything, just be. It's her mother who takes charge of the pursuit, a source of humor, because it's vulgar for a woman, even a mother, to do that. Elizabeth Bennet, Jo March in *Little Women*, Maggie Tulliver in *The Mill on the Floss*, and the entire troop of famous and uncelebrated, memorable and forgettable other heroines, would never dream of seeking out a man for love, or making the first move, or consciously using wiles to catch him. Before I was twelve years old, I knew how the story went: someone of great personal value (and often monetary value as well) notices how special you are, usually through your good looks, but also personal charm, wit, and interesting mind. I believed I could qualify, if only the right man were there to perceive and reward this. Moral purity was a necessary ingredient – that would have to be faked – but then Cathy Earnshaw in *Wuthering Heights* did without it.

I was sure I would not have rejected Rochester for such a silly cause as a mad wife in an attic, leading to all kinds of unnecessary trouble, and I would certainly have stuck by Heathcliff to the end. On the other hand, I found Jo March's choice of kindly, older Professor Bhaer unsatisfactory, as did many other readers, for its deliberate lack of romanticism.

All of Jane Austen's novels, Charlotte Brontë's *Jane Eyre*, and Emily Brontë's *Wuthering Heights* still seem entirely present to me. This is what the best fiction does. It cuts the legs off time.

Desire

All these romances, the movies I saw, and the love comics I read, had one thing in common: the heroine was intensely desired. In *Pride and Prejudice*, Elizabeth Bennet is valued for her intelligence and wit; in *Jane Eyre*, Rochester can't resist our heroine for the depth of her soul and her ability to understand him; in *Wuthering Heights*, Heathcliff is near-pathologically (or if you like, pathologically) obsessed with Catherine Earnshaw. This passion is unquestionably singular, in that it must be *this* woman and no other, and it lasts forever, i.e., a lifetime. The romance narratives they spawned centered around this: how to provoke male desire, how to sustain it through troubles, how to guide it to the goalpost of domestic coupling. The lovers either succeed as a couple or die, as in *Wuthering Heights* or as Maggie does in George Eliot's *Mill on the Floss*. Sexuality is part of this system, covertly or not, but it's not the point; emotion is the point. This has changed little in much of modern romance, except that sexual coupling is now likely to precede the proposal of marriage. But Desire itself, physical or emotional, is problematic for women in more ways than one.

In adolescence, Desire seemed something that had no name and you couldn't help. It took you over like a pleasurable infection, made you do something about it, or for it, like it or not. Sex was real but disturbing. Romantic craving elevated you to a world where sexuality, like everything else, is good, a space you could fashion by yourself.

Betty caught me once with my pajama pants around my thighs under the covers, when she unexpectedly came to tuck her baby in. She said nothing and I said nothing but I could tell she knew. I hated masturbation after that but did it anyway, once along with the girl in the tiny attached house next door, who proposed that the first one who finished should knock on the thin wall separating our bathrooms. I forget who won the race. Neither of us knew there was a name for what we did.

The one playdate that Betty ever arranged turned out to be a sex date. The other girl, from a "nicer" family than mine, had a big house and later attended a prestigious university. She showed me how she secretly rubbed herself against the curved piano leg in the study. That day I learned three things: some people have more than one bathroom, you could have a room just for a piano, and what you could do with the leg of a piano. I refused to go back, without saying why.

I had felt my own sexual desire in childhood as pleasure and shame in equal measures. But in adolescence I felt the sexual desires of men as both an enticement and a risk of great harm.

One day early in high school, as I waited in vain for a city bus to school in pouring rain, my heavy burden of books in my arms, a car stopped in front of me and the driver asked kindly if I needed a lift. Of course I hesitated; this was a stranger, an older man alone. He looked normal to me, meaning like dozens of other dark-haired, respectably dressed, slightly overweight middle-aged men I saw in my neighborhood. What decided the matter was the little statue of Jesus on the dashboard, ivory and pure, a signal that the man was religious and therefore meant no harm. I hopped in and told him where my school was.

As soon as we set off, he casually reached across me to the glove compartment and took out a fistful of cheap lipsticks and other girlie accessories of the kind I never used. A whole lifetime later, I can still see ELVIS PRESLEY pasted on the lipsticks. "Look, I'll give you these if you go to the city with me for the day," he said, "You can skip school, it's okay. We'll have fun." My heart squeezed into itself and I stayed perfectly still, murmuring that I couldn't do that, thanks anyway. He put them back in the Elvis Presley-filled glove compartment, but I saw he was displeased. He asked again, "Are you sure, I'll show you lots of things you don't know," and I repeated "No, I can't," terror rising in me. Why had I let myself in for this? Where would he drive me now? He had all the control and I had none. I was helpless in this damn car that I'd chosen to get into, against all the advice I'd always been given, and all because it was raining.

To my enormous relief, he pulled over at a quiet street near my school. But before I could get out, he suddenly grabbed my face and mashed his mouth and tongue down on mine, his last chance to take what he could get. Terrified, without thought, I bit his lip hard. Before I could move, he pulled away angrily, screaming "Bitch!", drew his fist back and punched my head. It banged against the door. Then he reached across me, this time to open the door and shove me hard onto the sidewalk, throwing my books at me as I struggled to get up and run.

As his car screeched away, I screamed after him, "You're going to burn in Hell!" Because although I was near hysteria with fear, I somehow hoped in that instant, my last chance to retaliate, that the Jesus figure meant something to him after all.

The street, pretty with well-cared-for houses, a much nicer one than my own, was entirely empty of other people who could have witnessed this. Trembling, I gathered my books and walked these pretty streets to my high school… where I went through my day and told no one. Not friends – I had none – not a teacher – they barely seemed to know me – not the college counselor whose office I worked in for service credit – she never seemed to like me, and one day had told me to ask my mother for deodorant. I was alone.

But when I was finally safe at home, I did tell my brother Eric, because by this time we had begun to confide in each other. The first thing he said was "What's the matter with you? Why did you get in that car?" I had no rational answer. "Don't tell Mommy, or anyone," he went on. That was the motto in our house: Don't tell. "She'll be furious." In fact he seemed angry, where I thought he'd console me. "Don't you *ever* do that again," he said, and we never once mentioned it after that. I understood: if my sweet, understanding brother couldn't comfort me because it was my fault, then no one would.

Not talking about it didn't make it go away. I found myself feeling warmly toward the boys my age walking near me, just because they weren't middle-aged men. They threw snowballs at me in winter or called me names once in a while, but they didn't yet drive cars and I couldn't imagine them doing *that.* Afterwards, older men appeared in my fantasies: cold, dominating, unattractive, greasy men seducing pretty, innocent, but secretly sexual pubescent girls with their desire. That these ugly, compulsive fantasies aroused me, alongside my hatred of older men, was a shameful dissonance. There was no way to puzzle it out; I had to live with it. Tell no one, including yourself.

Beauty

Sexy women were beautiful. Daddy liked beautiful, sexy women; he had a nude Marilyn Monroe calendar above his workbench in the basement, with pale skin and red lipstick and nipples. Women who were loved romantically were beautiful too, though you saw less of their bodies and more of their clothes. The issue of female looks began to loom large as I grew into wanting real romance for myself. The sexy girls, the romantic ones, the movie stars, the song lyrics celebrating youthful female beauty, were everywhere, selling everything. It was the beautiful among women who got what I wanted.

Everything hung on that hook of good looks. Desire, both sexual and romantic, appeared to spin on beauty, mostly the beauty of the female.

When I was a little girl, Daddy said I was pretty… but it was a problem in adolescence, because no one else did.

At a party when I was sixteen, a boy I didn't know yelled that I had a fat ass (which I did), to general laughter. I was shocked as well as humiliated – I had my mother's ass, and my father seemed to like it a lot – the most affection I'd seen between them was his playful slap on her full bottom. But the same ass that was desirable on my mother was ugly on me. From then on I wanted to be pretty but had no idea at all how to go about it. My mother rarely bought new clothes for me or herself, and I didn't know how to dress or look stylish in general. It was a question that had never come up before.

In Jane Austen's novels, the weight of beauty is enormous, though one of Austen's innovations as a romance novelist is the emphasis on the heroine's cleverness and wit. But it seemed being clever (and good, of course) was valued only because Elizabeth Bennet and all other heroines were not only clever and good but *also* pretty enough to get their man.

Brontë's *Jane Eyre* is a startling exception. The novel begins in girlhood when Jane is an orphaned ten-year-old and ends with marriage and motherhood, in conformity with the Victorian view that this trajectory completes a woman's life. But Jane's unremarkable, plain exterior, as well as her sarcasm, outspokenness and strong will, set her sharply apart from the sweet and adorable girls often found in Victorian fiction. We know that Charlotte Brontë insisted over her sisters' objections that her heroine must be beautiful, as convention required for romance; according to her biographer, Elizabeth Gaskell, she told her sisters Emily and Anne, "I will prove to you that you are wrong; I will show you a heroine as plain and as small as myself, who shall be as interesting as any of yours."

The love story of Jane and Edward Rochester includes many feminist elements, including a sharp critique of the way women are valued for pleasing manners, rank, and beauty. Especially interesting is the way Jane demands that Rochester treat her as an equal, not a doll or a fairy, stereotypes of Victorian femininity. Rochester finally declares, "My bride is here… because my equal is here." This is highly charged for the mid-nineteenth century.

Jane is an unconventional romantic heroine also in her insistence on the validity of her own emotions, entirely contrary to the passivity and modesty required of respectable women: "The vehemence of emotion, stirred by grief and love within me, was claiming mastery, and struggling for full sway; and asserting a right to predominate: to overcome, to live, rise, and reign at last; yes – and to speak," she tells us when she believes she must part from him. Many critics in her time were scandalized by the immodest way in which Jane asserts her feelings, desires and her right to express them.

There was no other novel that spoke so well to my confused adolescent desires and the fear that lack of beauty, lack of money, lack of appeal to males in general, would hold me back. For me, as for many modern readers, Jane's cry to Rochester, "I care for myself" and "I will respect myself" was a feminist rebellion that overrode the religious dictum in Jane's refusal to live "in sin" with the man she loves.

From *Jane Eyre* I took the idea that beauty was a false value in romance, and a woman could speak her own wishes without waiting for the man to lead. Perhaps Jane would have replied to that teenager's bullying remark about my "fat ass" with a bluntness that would take him down.

Not-Dating

Puppy love is supposed to be cute and near-universal, but there was no puppy to be had in my teenage life. Instead, I was like a puppy in a book for children, unhappily sitting in a store window waiting to be bought by my forever master. At last I abandoned my enduringly futile childhood hopes for Alex, but only when he was replaced in mid-adolescence by Bob, who was then overtaken by Chuck at the end of high school. All of these took place in my head only, but were central to my existence. Imagination had been my shelter and asylum, yet also a thrilling place, when I was a child, and being crazy in love seemed less a state of feeling than a way of being. The depth of my childhood longing for affection and recognition was exactly the strength of my love in adolescence. While as a child I was weak and helpless, in the realm of love I was strong with romantic desire, though it had not yet met with another's equal desire.

If emotions were money, I was working class in both reality and metaphor, earning enough to get by day to day, but not enough to feel at ease. As far as actual finances went, I hadn't noticed that we were poor, since almost no one I knew had very much, but I did know that some boys and girls had girlfriends and boyfriends, and I felt impoverished emotionally. I also saw that some of the girls who dated were not all that pretty, but the boys they dated were unthinkable in my book.

The answer to that was clearly love. And love meant romance, not only desire, in which I was wealthy.

Courting and being courted was a kind of imaginative play, and I felt I had learned the rules of the game, such as these:

1. Being in love is a yes-or-no condition, like pregnancy or death.
2. Love comes in two kinds, "real" and fake.
3. When love is real, however you feel, so does the other.
4. If you find true love, you will never be lonely, neglected or abandoned.

Romance is not just the validation of the secret emotional life, of emotions in general; it begins with and is a surrogate for our needs, beliefs, and hopes. Romance lubricates other emotions, other desires, connecting loneliness and fear of abandonment to an alternate reality, a story of an abundant life in joy.

In the 'conventional' heterosexual love story, such as has been instilled in a good portion of the collective imagination, a man *needs* a woman both sexually and, more importantly, emotionally. Of course, in most romances, the adored woman is also hooked on the man in question, but that doesn't matter because love will be equal, and power therefore equally distributed. Within this closed circle is the heroine's value, her potential, even what the Victorians called her "influence." Mere sexual desire feels demeaning without emotion, or at best uncaring, but the beloved woman, a heroine, by contrast, was exalted above all others, including rivals.

My only adolescent encounter with sexuality had been about as far from romance fiction as possible, and not only because the incident took place in a car. Violence was not an issue in the world of romances that I read and saw. There is no molestation or rape in Austen's novels, though a woman here or there is seduced by a cad. The issue is simply this: you have what it takes to lock down the hero, or you do not.

In high school, love had no place in my real life except in my imagination. There was the summer I turned sixteen and had my first real kiss, unexpectedly, with Donald, which felt so unlike the kisses I'd seen on screens or read about in love comics that I was entirely astonished. It wasn't even as nice as pressing my lips to the pillow. It was simply… nothing, as all the kisses since then have been with men I am not attracted to. Donald liked me, which was something, a first – but not the *right* thing. At least Austen's characters didn't have to put up with a bad first kiss, since they never (as far as the reader can see) kiss at all.

Donald was a very nice young man who would have treated me well, and I rejected him due to the urgent pull of handsome, magnetic Chuck, who never spoke to me. I could have had Donald and been like one of the couples I saw forming at school. But I suspected these tedious relationships were about the desire to have someone labeled a boyfriend or girlfriend, a kind of social possession rather than any strong feeling. This kind of pairing off ("I have a boyfriend!") felt like an empty gesture to me. When I discouraged Donald, I wanted nothing less than passion.

Community

Something changed radically just after that summer encounter with Donald, and it had everything to do with love and nothing to do with romance. In my first two years of high school, my mood had sunk to a low point. In middle school, I'd had two good friends for the first time, enough to make me happy, and then one moved away and the other fell out of touch when I went to a different school. It didn't help that my oldest brother had left home to go to medical school in Chicago. I cried in the car when we drove him to the airport because there was one less buffer between me and my parents, and home was lonelier.

My life was walking back and forth to high school, working my way through mostly dull classes, talking to almost no one, wishing to make friends and not knowing how. Why had I lost the ability to connect? I'm still not sure, because as years have gone by I've found it absurdly easy to make and keep friends. It's true my head was in the dream of romance that sustained me, but that can't be all of it. Yet there I was, with no one to speak to all day, trudging home to the empty house, doing homework, listening to Betty talk when she came home from work on weekdays, listening to Betty and Al fight on weekends. Besides my fantasies of love, only reading and sometimes talking to my brother Eric sustained me, but reading was not life and a brother could not be the only emotional center of that life.

Many years later I was crossing the street when someone touched my arm and said she knew me from high school. We hadn't been friends, but I recognized the name and face. After we caught up, I impulsively asked her what impression she'd had of me in high school. An odd question, but she replied immediately: she didn't know what I was like, because I was always so aloof. *Aloof?* This was enlightening. Did I, in my painful isolation, appear cool, indifferent, even snobbish? Did I radiate to others, *I'm better than you, stay away*?

Was I silent with others because Betty needed to talk so much?

When this sense of disconnection was at its worst, it paradoxically drove me to isolate myself more, rather than be around a group that laughed and talked together, excluding me. Everyone else seemed happy and confident. Once, unable to stand the sadness, I found an empty classroom to escape the crowds of students, and went to the great windows to look out. It was on a high floor, and the thought came to me that I could open that window and jump out. I imagined what the others would say, how they would talk about me, a connection at last. The idea had some allure until I looked down at the concrete courtyard below, and knew with certainty I did not want to do it. Miserable as I was, I was going to live and see what happened.

What happened: in the middle of my junior year in high school, after my best class, an advanced honors class in modern literature, a nondescript girl I barely knew from class approached me as I was dreaming down the corridor. I was guarded, wondered what she could want. "Hi," I said, probably in an aloof way. She was not put off and asked me to come to a meeting of the high school literary magazine, a publication read mainly by the relatives of the staff, though I'm quite sure Betty and Al never learned of its existence. She said I really should be, must be, on the staff. This was Alice. My memory is that she not only pushed me to join the group, something I'd never have ventured on my own, she physically led me there, brought me with her. I felt awkward and stiff, but once there, I fell in with Marj and Jane, who ran the little journal along with Alice, and a boy or two on the fringes of the inner circle. In a stroke, it was all different.

Here was the little community of like minds I'd read about in my childhood books, bound together by noble pursuits (that is, literature and high culture), shared experience, gossip and laughter. It was like being in *Little Women*, but without the family. This was better than home, devoid of family tensions and worries. If there were quarrels, I don't remember them. We helped each other and loved each other, sympathized and discussed. We often hear in romances that when a lover finds the beloved, it changes his or her life forever. These close adolescent friendships lasted for longer than I could have guessed, long after we took off for other places, became middle-class professionals, married and had children. They had as much effect on my life as having some dreary boyfriend – much more, in fact. For the first time, I could talk as well as listen, laugh with others at people we thought were absurd, joke about ourselves as students of literature way too sophisticated for us. (What to make of Thomas Mann's *The Magic Mountain* or James Joyce's *Portrait of the Artist as a Young Man* at age sixteen? It didn't matter. We knew it was grand that we'd read them.)

Marj was sharp-tongued, witty and opinionated (and still is); Jane was warm, sweet-tempered and gentle (and still is); Jerry was cheerful and political (and still is). I loved all of them, but the best of them was Alice. She was generous, true, odd, funny, homely, lively, and unpretentious. I've rarely known such goodness. And for some reason she liked me. But then we were all fast friends: I remember the day we girls instructed Alice on how to find her clitoris, and she promised she would try it out that night. There was a pleasant equality about us: no one's family had much money, no one was very good-looking, no one dressed well, except for Marj, whose nickname was The Lady in Pink, but we all felt we were on the brink of exciting, sexy, culture-filled lives.

The snake in this garden was me. The truth is that there was tension after all, and it centered around Alice, my savior. I'd been adopted late into the group, and the strain I could not admit to anyone was that I never felt I was as much a part of the inner circle as the others were. This might have been true or not. I knew Alice's value, I enjoyed her company, but jealousy caused me to resent her – because the others, everyone, loved her. It seemed to me Alice had a natural gift for life that I'd had to work too hard for with very little pay. Yet she was never less than kind to me. When I drank too much at a party, she asked her mother to let me sleep over so I wouldn't have to go home drunk. I vomited on her bedroom floor before falling into a deep sleep, and when I awoke it had been cleaned up. Yet this wasn't held against me, because Mrs. Gilbert was just as kind as her daughter. I couldn't admit my sour feelings about Alice to anyone, knowing they were unfair, and least of all to Alice herself.

This came to a head one night when Alice asked me to go with her to a Bob Dylan concert in Manhattan. Alice had been born with what was called "a hole in her heart," now a matter of surgical repair at birth or even before, but not fixable at the time. Because of this condition, she had a blue tinge to her lips, like a baby newly born, and was always out of breath. We were a bit late to the concert, and I was annoyed that she couldn't walk quickly from the subway station to get there on time. The concert was starting and it disgusted me that I was supposed to wait for her. I knew it was wrong, but I deliberately walked ahead while she panted behind me. Finally, when she caught up to me standing sulkily at the door, she told me, breathing heavily, that she was glad I hadn't waited for her. Why? I asked, startled. "You're the only one who treats me like I'm normal," she said.

Right, anyone else would have waited for her. And did I say "No, Alice, I was just being a bitch"? I did not. I took her gratitude as though I deserved it.

Afterward, I did not apologize or even talk it out with her. We never quarreled; I might have told her the truth if we had. Instead I distanced her even more. But she continued to pursue me when I went away to work for the summer – unlike me, she could never leave home because her parents worried about her fragile health. Her letters were delightful and made me laugh; I saw how childish I had been, how much I liked her. We made plans to see each other in the fall. Alice wrote that miraculously, she had a boyfriend at last, and I was flirting with the young man who would be my first boyfriend too, so there was plenty to look forward to talking about.

But I never saw her face or heard her voice again. At the end of the summer came the news that Alice had died suddenly while coming home with her new boyfriend after a party. She collapsed to the ground under a street lamp waiting for a red light to turn green, and did not return to consciousness. She was seventeen, maybe eighteen. I did not go to her funeral, or speak to her bereaved parents. I couldn't bear the horror of her death, or my own guilt in treating her as I had.

When I had my first baby, I named my child after Alice. Only her middle name, because my daughter's first name was chosen with my husband. But even a middle name keeps Alice close in a way I didn't allow when she was alive.

Dating

My dream of college was living away from home in a dorm and sitting around seminar tables with serious, interesting students, as I saw in college catalog pictures. But I had no idea how to apply to these colleges, and Betty, who made these decisions with alarming finality and no information that wasn't financial (expensive versus free), could not see why I should not live at home and attend the same large public university as my brothers, at the same convenient cost of near zero. And so it was there I went.

Nothing much happened the first year of college that I remember, except that I became an English major. The moment I decided this is clear in my memory: to my amazement, my teacher, Professor Fodaski, a beautiful, leggy blonde who dangled nylon-covered crossed legs over the desk while she talked about poetry, had wept aloud while reading us Dylan Thomas's "Do Not Go Gentle Into That Good Night." That did it: I was going to be a brown-haired version of that professor, not beautiful but still sensitive and brilliant, who dwelt in the sanctuary of literary art and was allowed to express any emotion, even cry, in public as part of her job.

I liked these classes; I even enjoyed the required math class, Mathematical Concepts, where I learned that math actually made sense when the ideas behind the formulas were explained in a way I could understand. The professor was lively, and I was proud to receive an A in the course after a lifetime of mediocrity in math. When I bumped into my teacher in the bookstore after the semester was over, he asked if I was pleased to get such a good grade. "Yes, I wasn't expecting it," I said happily. "Well, it was mostly your legs, I have to admit," he said. It was the mid-sixties, and the era was such that you were supposed to smile coyly at this. Besides disappointment, I remember my first thought was, "How odd, I don't have good legs, really."

Romance was disappointingly not a feature of my first year in college, but the summer afterward, the same summer Alice died, brought Evan, my first real boyfriend.

Commuting back and forth from the little house in Brooklyn to my big public university had been almost identical to high school, except that I took two buses to school instead of one. My friends were still my high school friends, and no boyfriends appeared on the scene, though I flirted with a young man who'd sat next to me on a sofa in the student lounge. For the first time in my life, I'd begun a conversation with someone rather than waited for him to speak first, and I was thrilled that he then asked me out. I liked him but I never heard from him again after we went to a movie. The movie was sad and I cried a bit; I wondered if I drove him away with those waterworks, as my brothers called my tendency to weep.

But this brief encounter left me with the sense that like Jane Eyre, I could take charge and get a result. And I put this new sense of myself to good use that next summer, when my friends and I became counselors at a non-profit camp for "underprivileged children," as they were called. As new counselors, we were given a tour of the campgrounds. There was nothing unusual to see, except for the stunning body of the lifeguard, poised on the dock, illuminated by the sun behind his back, showing the counselors the regulations for swimming.

I was much less interested in either the regulations or swimming than in the natural beauty of this finely built young man. So I made sure to be where he was from time to time, and smile frequently with no aloofness whatsoever. It didn't work at all. Neither did striking up conversations: Evan was very quiet, reserved, didn't laugh a lot, flirt, or chat. Not that I minded this; I took his silence for strength of mind and his reserve as a sign of mysterious depth. But it came to me that if I wanted this to go somewhere interesting, I'd have to be the driver of that cart. Here I was, an eighteen-year-old virgin, and it felt time to get this journey started.

There was a bonfire one night for the counselors down at the lake, where as usual, Evan seemed unaware of me. I felt this was my time. Sidling up to him, I asked if I could talk with him for a moment in private. He looked surprised, but said yes. We walked a bit in silence, my heart fluttering. Then I said very seriously that I had a crush on him (did I say I was in love?), and would be fine with sleeping with him if he'd like that. Now he seemed quite shocked. And immediately said, "No, I have a girlfriend." "Okay," I murmured agreeably, half embarrassed and half relieved. Afterward I could not believe I'd had the courage to do this. That seemed far more important than the result.

And why not? In romance novels, women seldom made the first move, it's true, but there were plenty of heroes who don't know what they want until he and the heroine are in a dramatic situation and a bolt of emotional lightning hits him. "I'm so glad you asked," Evan might have said, "I've been watching you from the first day, but I thought perhaps you didn't like me."

We parted and I did not repeat the offer, but much later, only a week before the close of summer, I saw his eyes following me. Soon, he asked to talk privately with me… and there was another walk in silence. Finally he said he was no longer in a relationship, so would I…? He didn't say "have sex." Instead, better than sex, I had an actual, factual boyfriend for the first time, at last.

In the fall, my second year of college, my life changed

again: I was now in a relationship and exploring sex, rather than reading about it in *Lady Chatterley's Lover*. We both lost our virginity and I found my so-called womanhood, with an act that was gentle and sweet, if short on sexual pleasure. Evan had his own apartment, a fifth-floor walkup (bathtub in the living room) in a Manhattan neighborhood so far away from its center that there was no subway or bus line that went there. It took up a great deal of time to see him and take the subway and buses home to Brooklyn, but it didn't occur to me to question if it was worth it. What was novel and wonderful wasn't so much love as the experience of knowing someone wanted me, a young man who thought I was pretty, and enjoyed my company enough to spend time with me.

I wasn't in love with Evan, though I couldn't admit that to myself because he was an essential part of the story I was trying to live in. It was a pleasant companionship, but never one that involved strong feelings of any kind. As for the new experience of sex, it was also pleasant without a great deal of sexual gratification; Evan's wonderful physique surprisingly didn't compensate for the dullness of unimaginative lovemaking. As the year wore on, I became restless and impatient.

Evan's quiet reserve was less interesting now that I had broken through and found a limit to how much I could feel for him or how interesting I found him. It seemed to me I was swimming in shallow emotional waters. Instead of facing up to this, I complained about him to my girlfriends: he wasn't affectionate enough, it was all going nowhere, as if we had to be marching toward a goal.

The next summer, before my third year in college, I found another job as a counselor in a camp for "emotionally disturbed" children, as the catch-all term was then.

Again, in the first days I spotted an attractive young man, strong and masculine but with a more forceful personality than Donald or Evan, and immediately went to work. Rather than wait for him to make a move, I stared and flirted with my eyes until he approached me. Triumph: within a day or so, I'd replaced Evan with Frank, and no need to feel bad about Evan, as he wrote me in reply to my Dear Evan letter that he'd found someone new too. It delighted me that Frank was dynamic, articulate, funny, knew a lot about everything, and had strong opinions. I was impressed with his air of authority and his use of the cool word "flicks" for movies. We weren't very cool, since we were both living with our families in different outer boroughs of New York City, but at least his public college was in Manhattan. Next to him I felt like a rube. We were informally a couple, a summer romance, and again this was enjoyable.

Yet I was not in love with Frank either, not any more than I'd been with Evan; as with Evan, I just wanted him to be my boyfriend. What excited me was my discovery that I could be attractive to boys, that I could control the plot as if I were authoring it. But it seemed a shame to waste this feeling like an object of desire at last on just one subject. To push the boundaries, I spent a night with an extremely good-looking younger boy (I'd just turned nineteen and he was seventeen), which infuriated Frank when I confessed. It was treated as an unexplained emotional betrayal and eventually forgiven, a moral lapse like cheating on your taxes, without either of us asking what it said about our own relations. And then I lapsed again in the fall as a hail-and-farewell when I went to collect a few stray belongings from my former boyfriend Evan's apartment. This time I was too clever to confess, and simply forgot it myself, as insignificant. Neither of these brief sexual encounters was in the least enjoyable sexually. They seemed more about escape than sexual desire, or an exercise in my newfound sexual power over men, so I stored them on a dusty mental shelf. If life were a novel, this would be called foreshadowing.

When we returned to college at the end of August, I had a good time with Frank, who took me out of Brooklyn to jazz clubs in Manhattan, foreign movies, restaurants with cuisines of other countries and ethnicities way beyond my family's regular once a month outing to the cheapest Chinese restaurant in the neighborhood, where everyone ordered the exact same dish they always did. Like my brother Eric, Frank was well-read; his plan, like mine, was to be a professor. Betty took note.

Frank's family was upper-middle class; his father was a manager in a fair-sized company, and his mother (as she'd tell you frequently) had *two* master's degrees and worked as a guidance counselor. The first time I was invited to dinner at their home, a home far larger and well-appointed than mine, I made what seemed like a mistake worthy of a nineteenth-century novel. As a guest, I was served the roast beef first, and I tucked into it right away, possibly because I was nervous and it gave me something to do with my hands. Frank's youngest sibling then called out, "Mom! She's eating before you sit down!" It was clear immediately that I was out of their league because the child was told to hush. This commandment was not in my rule book of manners. No one at my home was ever expected to wait for my mother to sit and eat with us; in fact, Betty often had her dinner directly from the pot it was made in, standing at the stove while the rest of us dined, because you couldn't fit five chairs around a table in our tiny kitchen. Etiquette was not on the curriculum at the Betty and Al University of Life.

Nevertheless, Frank's family was not a great concern of mine, as we were casually dating. That fall season was generally a happy time – I had a boyfriend whose company I appreciated, and he seemed to feel equally for me. But what did we feel?

This question came up directly one afternoon almost five months after I met Frank, when my mother proposed marriage to me. We were sitting as usual over tea with milk at the formica kitchen table; no engagement ring was offered, but rather a bright image of my prosperous, stable future, a story of the rest of my life, with requisite happy ending. Betty first approached the topic stealthily, when we were discussing Frank's aspiration to be a professor of history after graduating in two more years. Her metaphorical paws were treading softly, and the first question was silky as a mere brush of the tail: "So," said Betty in a confiding way, "Do you love him?"

The unexpected question almost felled me. Betty never inquired into my emotional state. Now my feelings were up for examination. Instead, my brain calculated: if I say No, she'll ask "Then why is he sleeping here all the time?" so I quickly said, Yes, sure I do. At that, the cat's jaw snapped its quarry: "Well, I have a plan," said Betty firmly, and outlined her own calculations. There were numbers: how much she spent weekly on my upkeep and my allowance, how much Frank's parents might contribute, how much a young couple could earn working part-time and summers, the price of a wedding after deducting the cash presents. Her conclusion: it could be accomplished with some effort and initiative, like the launch of a business, or the climbing of a difficult mountain to a new country where you will dwell in peace, safety and happiness for the rest of your life.

"You'll be a professor. Married with children. And you'll have a maid to take care of everything," Betty murmured seductively. Two of these three attractive prophecies came true.

I didn't reject Betty's marriage proposal, because I wanted to see what Frank said about it when I saw him that evening. If he laughed at the ludicrous idea of two penniless students in college tying themselves to each other for life, then I would laugh too – how impractical! I'd be relieved and we would carry on merrily, as we had been, saying "I love you" every ten minutes, having furtive, rushed, uninspired sex after Betty and Al went to bed, dreaming how much better it would all be if we could have a place of our own. On the other hand, this question was a way to test Frank, an opportunity to gauge the seriousness of his feelings toward me. I wasn't sure I wanted this, but I sure wanted him to want it.

When he next visited, I flew to the door to tell him that Betty had proposed to me. Frank did not say yes or no; he looked uncertain and said he'd ask his parents what they thought, since they'd have to contribute to Betty's Go Fund Me idea to make it work. This implied that he was willing to marry me, which was flattering, but it was also like him: he was the opposite of Betty, with her carefully thought-out schemes; he tended to jump impulsively into whatever new idea came up. The pure energy of this spontaneity was part of the *joie de vivre* that made his personality engaging to me, but in his role as future husband, did not always serve me well.

We both waited for the final word from his parents, who would make or break the plan – Al, as usual, had no part in the decision-making, as he deferred to Betty in all areas having to do with feelings, family life, or any life besides his own. To our surprise, my future in-laws did not advise waiting until we graduated from college. Instead there was some talk of their own happy marriage, which had taken place when Frank's mother was nineteen, my age (because she was pregnant, a fact not mentioned at the time). They saw no reason to wait. Frank's adolescence had been difficult, and apparently this event was seen as stabilizing, a correction for his previous restlessness. It was therefore settled that it would be good for us to "settle down."

I had read about many marriage proposals in classic novels and modern romance fiction, and mine was like none of these, though the scheming of ambitious mothers was not unusual. In the language of the time, the suitor "makes an offer," which is then accepted (pending approval by parents or guardian) or else "denied" or "refused." Though constrained by the woman's duty to follow her parents' authority in this matter, by the nineteenth century, women had come far in their relatively new ability to choose a mate for themselves. But only think of the pressure on women, in love or not, the absolute urgency of finding a mate in order to secure their future upkeep and gain some autonomy outside their family of origin. In George Eliot's *Daniel Deronda*, Gwendolyn reassures an uncle urging her to agree to marry Grandcourt, a rich and well-born suitor she barely knows, as "a duty" to her family. "I am not foolish," she tells her uncle, "I know that I must be married some time – before it is too late."

Choosing a husband without much intimate knowledge of someone with whom you'd probably spent little time alone must have been an outsized burden for a young woman. In the absence of divorce and the husband's right to keep custody of the children if the wife fled, the decision was more than a risk of heartbreak. This choice was the high point of a woman's life, determining almost everything about her future, economically, socially, and emotionally. And so it was with me: my mother was not on bended knee, but the judgement call was made and went her way.

Now I was, overnight, on the lip of an entirely new life: leaving my home to form a new family, coming into my own as an adult – but not, to my great relief, a single and therefore lonely adult. It was invigorating and appealing at first. The wedding date was set for nine months away, to give us time to plan, and plan we did, Betty and I taking on our new mission to present me as a happy bride to the world. There were formal cards that announced my engagement; I was told that my sister-in-law was kind enough to lend me her wedding dress, saving us the cost of a new one; a very flawed diamond, given to Betty by her brother when she helped him profitably trade these items on the black market in World War II, was fished out of her dresser drawer and set in a band chosen by Betty and me. Betty also selected the shabby wedding hall and worked up a guest list. I had little to do with any of this, or much wanted to.

After a few months, this program began to lose the allure it had once had. For one thing, Betty's attempt to put on a proper show intersected with an unpleasant reality: my parents did not fit well with the upper-middle class pretensions of my much more successful future in-laws. I was embarrassed that my mother seemed too talkative and a bit odd, whereas my mother-in-law saw herself as the height of propriety (though she was raised in a poor family herself). My father-in-law, who presented himself as a genial but paternally decisive businessman (also raised in a poor family), seemed a world apart from my own father, dreamy and quiet, lover of nature and women, with his unglamorous job on the subway tracks. I could tell they looked down on us as vulgarians, which made Betty defensive and unwilling to please them. It was going to be her show; she had saved for this for a long time. The subterranean tensions erupted a week before the wedding in an explosive fight on the phone between Frank's father and my mother, when Betty refused to allow extra seating for my in-laws' friends at the last moment, or some such weighty matter. It made me wonder why I was doing all this.

The truth is I began to suspect I'd made a mistake months before that dreadful argument, when I slammed the phone down on my future father-in-law, to my mother's amazement. Doubts rose up and I'd squash them down, subdue them with familiar hopes and fantasies, or cower at the thought of telling Betty, my in-laws, my fiancé, my friends, my in-laws' friends, and everyone who'd responded to the wedding invitation and sent a gift, that the event planned for almost a year would not take place. It was not only that facing the humiliation of this would take enormous strength I did not have. Just as much, I believed what everyone said: nerves before a wedding are normal, everyone has doubts and fears, one should laugh at them and the Magic Ring will make them go away. As when I was an obedient child, I tried to be as good as the gold in the new ring, putting warm socks on my very cold feet.

The hidden fear, tucked beneath the pleasure and

pride of reaching my adolescent goal of finding love, was that I was not actually in love with the man I was about to marry. I already knew this when Betty asked me if I loved him in the kitchen. But I also knew I felt something for him, or at least felt better being with him, and love was as good a term as any. Here's where the slipperiness of that word as meaning either passion or domestic affection comes in handy. The turning point or conclusion in romantic fiction is often the declaration of love, but in real life words are too blurry or flippant or unreliable or undefined to be of much use. What I felt for Frank was not passion, certainly, not romantic love, but… need. Our needs happened to match at that moment. My need, and his: for change, excitement, forward movement of some sort.

In nineteenth-century novels, people either marry for love or money. The latter is a sign of desperation or low values, while the former is a sign of superior character. A woman who could not find either was supposed to settle for as close as she could come to a good match. It's far more complicated now that love has conquered as a motive for marriage, since those who want to marry are pressured to presume they're mutually in love, or at least love each other in some way. Even when a couple's marriage is arranged in a very traditional family, there's a lot of talk of "falling in love afterward," and on reality TV shows like *Married at First Sight*, the couple expects to fall in love in future if they choose to stay together. Like identity and marriage, romance has evolved as a concept and expectation.

Many years after we married, I asked my mother why she'd proposed marriage to me at age nineteen. "I saw you needed someone," she said. She saw the need, yes:

it wasn't only about breaking into a higher social class, and she was trying to help with a life plan. Yet it was the wrong need. I did not have words for it then, but what I longed for was connection, intense feeling, a mutual intimacy like no other I'd had. The closest I'd come to this was in friendship with other women, but every depiction of love I read or saw reminded me to expect still more intimacy, more pleasure, and therefore more fulfillment, in romance. Two-as-one: the couple.

This neediness itself felt wrong to me. I'd had intense romantic desires since an early age, never reciprocated by those I loved, I'd had exactly one boyfriend before this one, and I'd only just begun to discover that I could be attractive. Part of me secretly resisted closing off the possibility of new pleasures, new possibilities, at exactly the point when I'd found I could have them. Yet like the character of Gwendolyn in Eliot's novel, I was asked to weigh this against the bigger picture, a whole life secured and insured.

The truth is that I did not want to be trapped in a commitment, but at the same time I was desperate for a commitment. In Jane Austen's *Sense and Sensibility*, the heroine Marianne, who has more passion than sense when it comes to love, is wounded by her adored lover's faithlessness when he marries for money, and in the end is glad to commit her life to steady, true, good Colonel Brandon. He is much older and does not provoke passion, but will treat her well. "With a knowledge so intimate of his goodness – with a conviction of his fond attachment to herself... what could she do?" Austen asks us. It's a rhetorical question. Women without money in romantic fiction were always grateful that men of good character (and a higher class) wanted to marry them.

With Austen's approval, seventeen-year-old Marianne gives her hand to this older man (we're told he has a "flannel waistcoat" to protect him from the cold) "with no sentiment superior to strong esteem and lively friendship." A happy ending.

What would their sex life have been like for Marianne? That is not a rhetorical question.

At nineteen, I both expected romantic love in marriage and also didn't think of love as likely to be realized. The important thing at this point was to secure affection for life, the way Mrs. Bennet in *Pride and Prejudice* strove to settle her daughters socially and financially with a good catch. So in effect, I settled.

In my observation, more couples in our own time settle in choosing a spouse than we or they care to admit, sacrificing the uncertainty and unreliability of strong feeling for a lifestyle partner. It seemed impossible to reveal this was what I was doing, least of all to Betty or my fiancé, or even my friends. In reality I was following the emotional economics of scarcity: make do, take what you can get, a lesser portion is better than nothing at all, as befits the impoverished.

Yet years after I was married, I boasted that it was *better* not to be in love, that it was a stronger basis for marriage to marry your best friend, as the cliché goes in modern wedding toasts.

Reader, I married him because he was my best friend, replacing the role of my former best friends. One view of romance is to see love as a no-man's-land (but very much a woman's land) with blurred borders, where there are infinite possibilities separate from the rules of the everyday. Marriage was my move away from the unruly, the uncontrollable, the fearful power and excesses of romantic longing and sexual desire, into the committed, the predictable, the assured and secured.

At the wedding reception, as some guests were eager to tell me afterward, a mouse had run along the length of a wall. I hadn't noticed, myself.

Chapter Three
Marriage

What greater thing is there for two human souls, than to feel that they are joined for life.
– George Eliot, *Adam Bede*

You don't know a man till you've lived with him. That's an old saying, and a true one.
– Betty

Reader, I divorced him.

Romances are almost always about young and beautiful people. And there I was, as fresh and pretty as I would ever be, lovely and dewy for one quickly passing moment, and I wrapped myself in a security blanket and squirreled myself away for twenty-four years. I was a good girl, or at least had played one in childhood, and now that was assured: I would be a good wife, which is to say a good girl for life. Reading literature was living vicariously, and now I would live vicariously through my husband, as I had through the heroes and heroines in my adolescent reading.

Early critics of the novel argued that romance fiction had a pernicious influence on females, as well as the young in general. Overgrowth of imagination, they cried, leads to unrealistic expectations, or worse, irrational behavior. Such as getting engaged at nineteen to someone you've known for a handful of months.

The poet Emily Dickinson famously called a book a "frigate"; we might modernize that to teleportation. From early childhood, when a work of imagination asked me to believe in it, I responded to that call no matter where it took me, the converse of Thomas Jefferson following Truth (he said) wherever it led him. The ability to leave reality at will has double sides: for one thing, it can make you more vulnerable to shutting out what you don't want to see. On the other hand, this susceptibility is about following pleasure, and knowing how to swaddle yourself in that pleasure can be a useful skill. Wasn't it the imaginary that allowed me to endure my family in my own way?

You might well suspect that some of my willingness to be married at an early age, with no realistic notion of what marriage entailed, had to do less with emotion than with the practical situation: I was the last child trapped at home with Betty and Al, after my older brothers had inconsiderately left me alone with them. It was easy to dream of a future as the wife of a professor, who would be a clever man like my father, but better: a husband whose talents would be recognized by the world. My mother's grand illusion was her youthful belief in the Great Man theory, not the traditional Great Man Theory of history, but a traditional theory of womanhood: the Victorian idea that to help a man fulfill his destiny was her own fulfillment. Betty updated this to fit the times: Frank and

I would be professors together, a modern couple with equal investments in work and family. I could imagine the many book-lined shelves in our spacious Victorian house, walkable to the small-town university where we would both teach, while adorable children, whose care we equally split, skipped happily in the leafy background.

It often seems that what we really want in marriage is not primarily the person for him or herself, or even the advantages and social status of being a couple, but someone who will make possible your imagined best lifestyle, presumably for the rest of your life. Especially when marrying young, you marry your image of yourself in future. Ironically, in this way, marriage still seems to me more traditional than we like to acknowledge, based on the same idea I had at age nineteen.

I became a bride without ever living independently, with no bank account of my own, and never learning to drive, though my father had taught my brothers. Of course this is exactly how women throughout history had come to marriage before the twentieth century. Now I had that someone to (in theory) hover over me, manage the finances, and drive me everywhere I pleased. I was going to have a caretaker, like an estate, or an elderly person too feeble to care for herself. This was comforting to both Betty and me.

For Betty, if you were not born a man, the next best thing was to marry one. My mother was both contemptuous of men and saw love as a woman's gateway to strengths and resources that only men possessed, part of the glamour of the masculine. Like her, I was attracted to what I saw as the strength of Frank's masculinity. He appeared to be an alpha male, in contrast to my father, who for all his skirt-chasing and iron-pumping, was not the take-charge, take-care-of, determined and resourceful lord of the castle that Betty had always wanted, so she herself would not have to be the take-charge, take-care-of, determined and resourceful head of the household. Maybe Lady Macbeth wanted that too. Al was mild, unassertive, gentle, even shy, the sort of man who puts his hand over his mouth when he laughs because a show of teeth is too much exposure. And he was artistic, sensitive to the beauty of the natural world, of children, of art and science alike: traits that might have attracted literature-loving Betty in the first place, but then became distinct shortcomings when it came to propping up the castle, since they didn't pay.

My mother's view of my dad as weak, self-indulgent, unambitious, and a financial failure set the stage for me to marry someone who seemed opposite to Al in every way. Where my father was diffident, quiet, and modest, Frank was outgoing and forceful, a conversational dominator. Where my father vacillated and hated confronting problems, Frank was active and decisive, with a dramatic show of confidence. My fiancé seemed capable, protective and resourceful in ways that Betty had dreamed of for her own husband, but without success, she often said, thanks to (upper lip curled with contempt here) *romantic love*. Here was someone who could protect and defend me from the onslaughts of the world!

And all of this was both true and also not-true about Frank, and therefore rebounded on us badly. Because it turned out that while Betty was right that he *could* take care of me, in the end he didn't much *want* to, at least not to the extent I believed I needed; in fact, he resented it. My new husband was both conventionally masculine and also, in hidden ways, in need himself. I simply didn't have enough experience, of him or the world at large, to know that the spectacle of masculinity can be the hiding place of the vulnerable.

So much for my mother's dream.

The Harlequin romance hero often has the odd quality of always seeming to impersonate a tough guy rather than be one, just as a white middle-class teenager might appropriate the style of a Black rapper. The romantic hero's clenched-jaw exterior both challenges the heroine to conquer him, and also disguises a lovably sweet center from which his tenderness for her can emerge, giving her the power as well as proof of her unmatched desirability. This romance, from 'Beauty and the Beast' to *Jane Eyre* to *Twilight,* often ends with the taming of this beast. He is the love object, but it's really about the young woman herself. For example, while the heroine is usually single in mass-market romances, occasionally she is married to the hero himself, out of some plotted expediency: a wager, or a plan to preserve an inheritance, or whatever rationale the author can come up with. When our heroine finds herself in this delightful pickle, she's likely to fall in love with her own husband, which is certainly convenient. And in the course of the novel, he begins to return her feelings when he sees how utterly superior and indispensable she is. How could he not adore her?

To add to the muddle, modern Western culture assures us that this romantic passion will shade beautifully into the peaceful tedium of the everyday, just as love in arranged marriages is supposed to bloom from that ordinary soil. The process of growing marital love is supposed to be as natural as cultivating houseplants, but nevertheless is called "work," the stuff of magazines and self-help books. I had no idea what marriage would be like, because apart from Betty and Al, my model for a love relationship was chiefly romantic novels whose last pages were a promise (as the Romance Writers of America puts it) of "emotional satisfaction," – which sounds problematically like Jeanette Winterson's quote from *Written on the Body*, "Contentment is the positive side of resignation" – if not eternal bliss. The idea of attaining this enviable state just by acquiring a legitimate role seemed wonderful to me. The position a wife can leverage, after all, is the title itself, a title that quite literally and legally entitles you in more than one way; you know you matter. Not necessarily always in the way you'd like to, but still: you're important, by definition. "But I'm your wife!" women cry indignantly, in both movies and real life, when not treated as queen of the home empire and the husband's heart.

In the dailiness of the real-life domestic relationship, ordinary human ignominies are ruthlessly revealed. That someone else is willing to embrace these, and bare his or her own in an exchange, is a great selling point of marriage. We congratulate people who stay married for decades as though they have heroically conquered life; am I the only one who thinks they deserve a medal for putting up with each other for so long? Or wonders if they perhaps have low standards?

During the nearly year-long period of engagement, my sexual relationship with my fiancé had been pleasant, if unmemorable, though I'd had so little experience that there was no better to remember. Yet it went downhill the closer we came to the wedding date, which puzzled me. Surely this was tension from planning the great event, and since we both lived with our parents, once we had marital legitimacy, a shared bed, and the leisure of a great deal of time together, it would improve. Instead, on our honeymoon in Cape Cod (a wedding gift from my in-laws), I felt, with some anxiety, but entirely without desire, that it was *time to have sex* because it was awkward and disgraceful if we didn't on our honeymoon, and I suspected he was thinking the same. Since we both seemed to feel that way, it was forced, swift, joyless and perfunctory when we got around to it. But this too was not examined – it seemed impossible to say something so awful a week after you're married: Was that as forced, joyless and perfunctory for you as it was for me?

In a way this was the template for our marriage. In general, there was a good deal of dissatisfaction and eventually, complaining on my part, and bluster and evasion on his, but neither of us said what we were really thinking.

Once we were married, Frank frequently let me know that I was what he called "book-smart" but otherwise incompetent and dumb (Frank considered himself both book-smart and, it goes without saying, the other kind of smart too). Apparently, there's a thin line between being appealingly helpless and unattractively inept. He was annoyed with me because I fell too far behind him on my bike while on our honeymoon, he was angry because I hesitated to cross a wide street with cars flashing by; he exploded one night on a trip to Europe years later because I thought it was understood he'd book the hotel rooms, since he'd never asked me to do it. This was something I hadn't seen at all while we were dating or engaged; I irritated him often after we married, and he became more vocal about my flaws as the years went on and he felt less need to please me, now that I was permanently his. With his increasing habit of talking at me as though he had the Holy Grail of wisdom, at times it was like living with a male version of Betty, but without her passionate devotion that overrode everything else. I'd looked for and found someone unlike my father, and had chosen someone more like my mother.

I began to miss the traits in my dad that Betty did not give Al credit for: his sweetness and mild temperament, his tenderness and sensitivity, the open enjoyment he had in my company, his *romanticism*.

I'm very sure I was not a treat to be with: I secretly cried in the bathroom when we were on our honeymoon because it occurred to me that I would come down with flu at some point, and no one could truly care for me when I was ill the way my mother had. I was also overcome when Frank left for a day during our honeymoon to register for college, and for the whole next year, sulked when he left me alone for the evening to practice with his college lacrosse team. Isn't that why I married, so as not to be alone? We were two adult-sized babies, with needs and expectations that often didn't fit the other's, lacking any way to deal with trouble or conflicting desires in our hidden agendas.

Frank particularly disliked my tendency to weep when my feelings were hurt or he was trying to argue with me. Betty had disapproved of what she called my "sensitivity" because it was a feminine weakness that would hold me back from success; she rarely cried in my presence, only when her own mother died, and then she ran outside to be alone. Frank's distaste for my tears was based on his opinion that crying was "emotional blackmail," a callow bid for sympathy intended to manipulate the other by making him feel guilty. The effect of this unpleasant view of me was that I felt misunderstood, and so I'd cry all the more from frustration. My defense was that I couldn't help doing it, it wasn't intentional at all; he didn't buy this idea. In this he was aligned with my family. Yet to this day I cannot stop tears when I feel strong emotion. My eyes have annoyingly watered every one of the numerous times I've taught Blake's poems "The Black Boy" and "The Chimneysweep" over many years, and if I could have controlled the tears while teaching, I would have. I'm emotional by nature, yes, but my personal theory is that I simply have infantile tear ducts.

Nevertheless, my letters to my friends gleamed with happiness in those days: I loved living with someone besides Betty and Al. I loved having my very own home, a tiny attic apartment near my college, which was like playing in the dollhouse I'd always longed for. I bought a cookbook, made dinners in the tiny closet of a kitchen for our friends and even my in-laws. "We have a rollicking good time," I wrote to Marj, my closest friend, "talking and fighting and going places and keeping pace with the mad, gay social whirl. I have suddenly acquired a whole new batch of friends, all Frank's, of course, not to mention a troop of relatives, some great and some obnoxious, but all worth gossiping about, which is what really counts with relatives." I did not relate that sometimes when we made love in the usual perfunctory way, I wept afterward without being able to say why, which made Frank yet again… angry.

After college, my new husband and I left to attend graduate school in Chicago. Since my grades were better than his (book-smart), I was accepted to better schools, but settled for the best one that accepted him, so we could be together. The fantasy of singular and eternal intimacy was launched. I was now a full adult, but not, lord forbid, alone.

A year later, my husband and I had both completed Master's degrees, but only he had gone on to the PhD program. This was not my choice; our plan was to pursue PhDs in our separate programs at the university. But though I had (again) better grades than he did, he was given financial aid and I wasn't. We went to the dean and asked for an explanation, as I couldn't remain in the doctoral program without the financial support, even with my part-time job. The dean said the university policy was to give preference to men for financial aid, because women had a higher drop-out rate, due to having babies. "But you're making me drop out!" I cried. The dean was not impressed with this logic, and there was no recourse at the time. So I dropped out and began working full-time until my husband received the grant that allowed us to live in Spain while he did research for his dissertation.

We lived for three years in Chicago but inexplicably I made no new friends. Now that my dear high school friends were far away, I'd been lonely and leaned entirely on Frank for company. This pattern followed us on the exciting couple of years living in Spain, where Frank finished his doctoral dissertation, while I earned a pitiful salary teaching English to Spanish businessmen to help support us. We made friends in Madrid, but they were all historians, friends of Frank's, and my role was to make conversation with their wives. Since I'm not clever at languages, there was no one I could confide in besides Frank, who was engrossed in his own work, doing research every day in rural archives. I was more isolated than any time since before I'd met my literary circle in high school.

My journal tells me there were tensions with Frank,

as well. We had arguments about sex, which had never been very good. Before we left for Spain, he'd confessed some secrets in his past I hadn't known, and feeling pressure to join in the confessional spirit, I admitted for the first time that I'd never had an orgasm with him, only on my own. I hadn't lied about it; he'd never asked. It was like confessing to an affair, viewed as lying and betrayal. After that, there was an extended period of conscientious "working" on this problem that somehow made the years of faking it seem like the better option.

One night, Frank and I went to the Plaza Mayor to see flamenco dancing. The audience was tourist-heavy, but the club was so small we sat just a few feet from the dancers. I'd never seen a performance like it: the skill, the speed, the powerful cries and the glorious sound of stamping feet gripped me, expressing what I had no words for at the time.

In our second year in Spain, I developed a lustful crush on a handsome young man in one of my English language classes, that resulted in a graceless, fumbled kiss. The kiss was initiated by me, and repelled by him. It was a ridiculous thing to do: we'd become friendly with the young man's family, and this brief moment ruined that very pleasant connection. Even I could see this lapse was related to the circumstances of my life at the time. What I didn't see was the view I have now, the way this ill-advised kiss was an assertion, an outcome of suppressing my desire for heightened emotion, not unlike my strangely unfeminine pass at the lifeguard the summer before I met Frank.

After the sort-of kiss, I felt terrible and told my husband about it. He was angry, I was guilty and sorry, but there was no clear understanding of what this meant to us and about us after the first argument.

The solution: we mutually abandoned all acknowledgment that this impossible thing *could* happen, and soon after, I began a campaign to have my first child. Baby instead of lover; it seemed a good exchange, the right way to take care of whatever was wrong. We never once talked about my immoral attraction again: the marital shovels came out and entombed it for life.

In this matter, I took charge, though unknowingly: I changed the direction of my nameless longing toward one with a legitimate name: wanting a child. Betty had frequently claimed that when her marriage proved a disappointment, she decided to live for her children. My choice of Frank had been an experiment in unsentimental marriage, based on the pragmatic kind of affection, companionship, shared values and experiences that are supposed to follow romantic passion… but without the passion. To my babies, I would give the fierce tenderness that the (few) men I'd been with had not called out in me, a capacity for wild love that I doubted would ever be welcomed by any man I desired romantically.

All loves are versions of one another. Romantic love is incoherent, unstable (in its definitions) except (fleetingly) in its representations. Like masculinity and femininity, it's a shape with no real boundaries, both a thing in its social power, and yet also imaginary. Loving for me had always meant wanting to be intensely needed, something I'd never felt from men, except in sexual encounters, some abusive. Children were charming and beautiful little persons I could devote myself to, who would cling to me the way my husband did not, who wanted nothing and no one more than they wanted me.

Babies

Reader, I had three babies. Each time, the period of pregnancy was a deeply happy time, full of promise and new imaginings of the way life was going to be.

Yet I knew nothing much about caring for children and had little interest in them up to that point. In fact, my only real experiences with them had been unpleasant. My first job, at barely fourteen, was euphemistically called at the time "a mother's helper," meaning I was shipped away for the summer to live with a strange family and care for a toddler full-time. I had no say in the decision. In my family everyone worked during the summer: Mel drove an ice cream truck and operated rides at Coney Island, Eric was an insanely overworked and poorly paid busboy in a dreary Catskills resort. When I was too old to hang around while my mother worked at another resort, it was simply my turn to make money. As a mother's helper, I was hired to entertain a little boy from the early hour of his wakening until he was asleep at night, seven days a week for eight weeks, with no time off except for his hour-long nap. The family home was in a suburb, which I thought must be the most boring place in the world, neither fancy and aspirational nor colorfully impoverished. There was nothing much to do, nowhere to go; I couldn't believe people voluntarily lived there.

I was, at age fourteen, contemptuous of parental love: parents seemed to love their children because they were extensions of themselves, externalizations of their dreams. But I learned something else that shaped my own desire to have a baby a decade later: I could see that the child I was paid to care for wanted most of all to be with his mother, to be held by her, be near her. This made my babysitting job harder, but impressed on me the well of intimacy and a love of unfathomable depth that must effortlessly exist between mother and child, not like the fraught and changeable relations I saw between dating couples or married people.

When I was safely married, my desire for romantic passion was an excess, the dangling threads that spoil the smooth fabric. Sexual love, mutual and deeply gratifying, had eluded me, and wanting someone who doesn't want you was fatally tragic. But a baby needed exactly what I wanted so much to give, a perfect balance of giving and taking. The technique involved seemed both natural and easy: you love your child purely and with all your being, you express that love with constant caresses and the language of affection, and with this dedication, you shape the infant into the child you longed for. In dreaming of motherhood, I desired nothing more than exactly what I rejected as a child when my own mother said "I love you because you're my daughter": to feel and give unconditional, and therefore immutable, love.

By the time Frank completed his doctoral thesis in history and was offered a professorship in New York City, I was triumphantly six months pregnant. We returned from Europe to begin our life as a married couple with an actual income, a new way of living. Though birth was painful and difficult, my infant daughter Cybele was healthy. Yet to my dismay, I was more frightened than overjoyed when I took the newborn home. I'd supposed it was all instinctual, but found I knew much less about caring for infants than I'd imagined, even after reading every child-rearing book I could find.

My mother-in-law, who had raised five children, could see my anxiety on the first night home with the baby, and stayed over to help. I'd been eagerly looking forward to breast-feeding my tiny daughter, guided by misty images from a hundred advertisements and magazine articles of fuzzy heads snuggled closely (but discreetly) against a bare and swollen breast. This was "natural," meaning Nature took its inevitable course of supreme gratification for the infant, followed by sweetly restful sleep for both of us. But my newborn didn't find the eat-and-sleep cycle inevitable, or even satisfying; she woke during that first night screaming, and refused to sleep even after fitfully nursing. It was a relief but also a humiliation when my mother-in-law took her from me and put her back to sleep somehow in the guest bedroom. I sensed that she saw me as naive and incompetent, much as Frank did, not coincidentally.

The new grandmother went home to her own family the next day and I was left alone with a baby who cried a great deal, day and night, for months. I remember sometime in that first week looking at her newborn face, which seemed to me more unfinished than adorable: "Do I love her? Can I ever love her?" were the terrible questions that broke through my postpartum haze. The days went by, each the same. One terrible hour, I suffered from compulsive images of putting her in the washing machine, and then nausea that my brain could even conjure the idea. I tried talking to the pediatrician about her incessant crying, as I worried that I didn't have the required amount of milk. "Madam," he said, "You are a nervous woman, and that makes your infant nervous. No doubt that has affected your milk supply." It was my fault, after all.

I'd been so sure of the bliss of breast-feeding, the origin of the bond of perfect intimacy; instead there was a painfully indeterminate worry, the shame of wanting to fulfill the need I was formed naturally to do, but didn't seem to do well at all. Even when I finally learned how to feed the infant to her satisfaction, it wasn't gratifying to me: I often felt reduced to a living system for squirting milk in her mouth, my baby as the thing at the end of a breast.

Though Frank taught at a college in Manhattan, we had chosen (or rather Frank did) to rent a house in a New Jersey suburb from a colleague of Frank's on leave, on the premise that it would be wonderful to have an entire house to ourselves after a series of tiny, cheap apartments. But this was a mistake, as there were no playgrounds like the ones in New York City where parents and children meet one another. I was now one of the housewives in the same sort of suburban drive-everywhere-for-everything place where I'd been a mother's helper for two summers, even more lonely than I had been then. I spent most of my time trying to feed my baby enough to stop her crying, or walking around and around the neighborhood, as I'd aimlessly pushed the bored little boy in his stroller for hours to pass the time when I worked in the summer.

Once I drove with Frank to the library and asked him to stay with the baby, asleep in the car, while I dashed in. It was fifteen minutes or so to myself, a short, happy relief, but when I returned, our infant was loudly screaming and Frank was enraged. "Don't *ever* do that to me again," he growled, handing her to me. Even fifteen minutes to myself was too much! Predictably, I burst into tears, which of course made it worse. Later he apologized – saying something hurtful, then apologizing, was a scene repeated many times – but we both hated that I wasn't content, in spite of having what I'd especially wanted and planned for.

Yet at six months, the crying stopped and a joy unlike any before began… a delight in my child laughing, then sitting, crawling, speaking, walking, pretending. Apparently my supply of milk wasn't as poor as I'd thought, since the baby had grown into a plump and active toddler. Now that my daughter was beautifully energetic, inquisitive, talkative, I emerged from depression and moved to a state of restlessness. Frank liked nothing better than fitfully moving somewhere else, so when our year's sublet was over, we tried moving out to the country, another silly impulse that foundered. It was even harder to find companionship in the country than in the suburbs, Frank had a longer commute and so was home less often, and you had to drive even further to go anywhere or purchase anything. I began to long for challenge and mental stimulation besides amusing my toddler. It was time to rekindle my ambition to have a profession.

When Cyb was almost two years old, I was admitted to graduate school at Columbia University and we'd moved to a small apartment in New York City. On the days I had classes, Cyb was in daycare, though half-day was as much as we could afford. For two years, I frantically studied and wrote papers while she napped or ran around in the park, and forced myself to read fat, fine-printed nineteenth-century novels for my graduate seminars from the moment my daughter fell asleep until I dropped into bed myself. I no longer felt aimless, quite the opposite.

This was hard work but a good time, I thought, the

more so because I was now making friends, including my best friend Dora, a clever, interesting, and funny young woman with a daughter at daycare just Cyb's age. My classes at Columbia were thought-provoking, sometimes thrilling, and my thesis advisors, one an expert on Victorian fiction, the other a feminist who wrote about women in literature, were dazzling and intimidatingly learned. As a topic for my doctoral thesis, I chose a subject that fascinated me, reflecting my thesis advisor's interest in the nineteenth-century novel and my female advisor's focus on feminism: the subject was women, love and sexuality in the nineteenth-century novel. This was the best of graduate school: you chose what you most desired to learn from the best scholars you could find, then you wrote about ideas of your own. I did not, at the time, find it ironic or coincidental that the theme I'd chosen to write about, women and romantic love, had absorbed my fantasy life. It was now going to be an intellectual occupation, unconnected to my private preoccupation.

My two advisors supported my work on women and sexual love in the Victorian novel, but in general, the topic was seen as frivolous at the time. Once when I applied for part-time teaching at another college, the chairman of the English department laughed as I described my work and remarked with confidence that "there is no sexuality in the Victorian novel." I tried to argue that this view was perhaps too literal, but I was dismissed from the interview and didn't get the job. At Columbia, another professor who read my dissertation remarked slyly to me, "I sense the pressure of the personal here." This was not a compliment. I was deeply embarrassed, as though he'd exposed a shameful secret. Years later when I ran into him, he kindly told me he'd wanted to have an affair with me, but at the time, he was in love with one of his graduate students.

Then when Cyb was three years old, a crisis arose that I was entirely unprepared for. I'd taken my small daughter with me to visit my brother Eric in Chicago for a week, and called Frank as usual to say we'd arrived safely.

"Listen," he told me flatly, "Just don't come home."

"What did you say?" I asked.

"I *said* I don't want you to come home," replied Frank, angry for some reason I didn't know, "The marriage is over."

"I'm taking the next plane back," I said, for once so panicked that I did not cry.

When I was home and asked why he was moving out, Frank was… vague. I was too dependent on him; I was a weakling and whiner who didn't pull my weight in the marriage. Yes, but it wasn't clear why these long-established facts had led so suddenly to the demand for divorce. Then I remembered that not long before, we'd been walking together in the street making each other laugh, as we often did, when I remarked, in high spirits, "Isn't it wonderful how happy we are together?" "You always do this," he'd snarled, "You romanticize everything." I was hurt, but as usual, stayed silent. I could have asked: "Does this mean you're not happy with me?" As yet, the ability to ask this, even think this, was not an arrow in my quiver. The reality of the situation was too risky to be curious. I was in grad school, I had a young child, I had no prospects for a job, or any prospectus for living other than the one I'd set out years before: Get married. Have children. Be a professor. In that order. For the same reason, I not only didn't ask Frank if there was another woman involved, I did not so much as think of this as a possibility. This is what amazes me the most. So much for Jefferson's "Follow the truth wheresoever it may lead."

In any case, it was a short separation. But it was a difficult time; I developed a gruesome fear of sleeping alone in our apartment, nightmares of someone coming in the window to murder me, much like my childhood fear of a terrible flood coming in the window of my bedroom. Then gradually we began to spend time together in a friendly way, and after just a few months, Frank said he wanted to move home. My husband never really explained why he'd left, and I don't recall discussing it again. I was just glad to have my life restored to where it had been, like a car coming back from the repair shop, presumably good as new, though at some cost. It became a blip in time to me.

Shortly after, I finished all my classwork, passed my qualifying exams, and announced I wanted another baby. "But you just got back together. Don't you think you should wait and see how you two are getting along?" a friend suggested. "Not at all," I cried, annoyed, "The whole thing was a mistake. We've worked it out and it's fine now." I was pregnant with our second daughter when we left New York for another job for Frank. Looking back, if I'd taken the advice and waited a year to see "how we were getting along," I'm sure I would have come to the same conclusion – because I didn't want the advice.

Amanda's birth coincided with a move to the deep South, where Frank had secured a professorship in history. And so I found myself with a young daughter and a newborn, far from family, knowing no one, once more trying to adjust to a new home in an unfamiliar culture.

I had a goal that seemed nearly impossible: writing the dissertation, but without child care, which was unaffordable.

As an infant, Amanda screamed just as much as her older sister had, but this time I had the confidence of experience, carried her everywhere and didn't worry about my milk supply. If she was still hungry after breast-feeding, I gave her some formula, purity be damned. She grew into a feisty, curly-headed toddler with Betty's dark eyes, the child who could talk our elderly neighbors into giving her candy whenever she liked ("I just went to say hello," she explained sweetly when she'd been told to stop gouging the pushover old folk). As soon as Amanda was old enough, I enrolled her in the nearby Christian nursery school (the cheapest one I could find), allowing me to dash to the library and write for two or three hours. But the work was extremely slow for years, and it didn't help that I fell into the same creeping melancholy I'd endured before. Many days when I should have been researching and writing, miniature obsessions strangely took hold of me, and I spent my scarce free hours looking up one topic or other, unrelated to my work (why did John Lennon leave the Beatles?). Then I was appalled that I'd wasted the narrow slice of time I had, after years of longing for it, guilt compounding the depression because this was (again) my fault.

Yet unexpectedly, sex with Frank had gotten better: with maturity, I'd arrived at a simple solution to the orgasm problem, one that can be found in any modern self-help book that pays attention to women. I'd also made friends by this time, including a lifelong friend, whom I'd met because we were both "faculty wives" in the history department. Anne, both smart and kind, was and still is the closest I've come to finding Alice again. Best of all, my two daughters were flourishing. I loved reading to Cyb and seeing her act out the plots of novels in her imaginary play, while Amanda was self-confident and effortlessly independent, as I'd never been myself. My children were the main source of joy and deep emotion in my world, just as we kids had been for Betty.

As for my long-awaited career, it felt as though my chances of finishing my doctoral thesis and securing a decent academic position were not good. Again I had the impulse to extend my joy in children with a third baby, since we had a rather easy life in this Southern city, where Frank's salary was low but so was the cost of living. Frank was hesitant to have another child but wanted a son, and I was as ambivalent as he was for a good while. Then Frank decided we should go ahead and get pregnant, though, he told me later, only because he could tell I wanted it and would therefore resent his refusal.

Various entries in my journal the year before we had our third child make me wince:

Something is wrong, something is missing.

Frank is constantly angry at me: for tripping on the stairs in the dark, or for unthinkingly putting my purse on the seat next to me at a concert, without realizing that there was a man in that seat – instead of laughing about this, it was a sign of my 'incompetence'.

My response to these private thoughts was to berate myself in my journal for taking offense at this, due to what I wrote was my "fragile self-esteem." I hoped that having another baby would cure me, since my narcissistic neediness for love and attention was the problem.

Yet remarkably, I still thought Frank and I were overall quite happy together, and certainly would have said so if you'd asked me. Various entries in my journal that year feel pathetic to me now, an attempt to justify what I put up with because I did not know what else to do:

The last couple of days I felt that I didn't love Frank, that I didn't like the way he treats me, that I missed romance and sexual excitement and wanted to be in love and have an affair. Then after that I felt the reverse: how much our companionship means to me, sexually attracted to him, happy about our mutual love of our children, shared past, shared values. We are close again, sharing our laughs, our gossip, our small dreams for the future.

Soon I was pregnant with my son. My happiness in this pregnancy was just as I'd hoped it would be: all melancholy drifted away as my belly swelled. The new-baby cure worked for a time; my third child, Billy, was my first infant who was not colicky and difficult, and I delighted in his sweet infancy.

Yet less than a year later, we left the South and I lapsed into a blue mood again. For one thing, we were under tremendous financial pressure now with three small children in a new place that required more income than we had. The stress was palpable, and the arguments ongoing.

For years we'd both been eager to leave and return to New York, near our families and old friends, and to have the children in better schools than the public schools in the South at the time. The problem with the schools wasn't only about reading and math; Cyb came home one day and asked why it was only Black boys who were paddled in front of the class. Another time she related that at a holiday assembly, the principal had called on her "in front of everyone": "Cybele, you're a Jew, why don't you explain Hanukkah to the other students?" Then too, I hoped if I had personal access to my advisors, I would finish the thesis, instead of dreaming off in the library.

On the other hand, New York was much more expensive, and Frank had left his tenured position. There was no plan in place as to where Frank would find a new job after leaving academia, much less how to secure an affordable apartment and work the complicated school situation for our girls. This would be a huge move, and I was apprehensive about the sudden tornado of changes in our present unsatisfying but calm and secure life.

Frank, as always, did not appear apprehensive, but instead was confident, sure that all would be well; his anxiety always emerged as bluster.

When Billy, the new baby, was seven months old, my husband announced one day that he'd already put the move into motion; we were going to leave imminently. I'm a planner, so my instinct had been to put it off for a year to figure it all out, and this headlong decision made me extremely nervous. Frank was exasperated with my misgivings, as he so often was: I was always afraid of something new, wouldn't take risks, I didn't trust him yet wouldn't make decisions myself, I was a downer. Since all of this was not untrue, I was intimidated and fearful of his resentment if I didn't go along with what seemed to me an impulsive and possibly disastrous choice. Just as he'd agreed to have another baby to fend off my despondency, I felt I had to submit, unprepared as we were, because I was afraid of his anger.

Children

The next years after our sudden move to New York were much more trouble than even I had imagined, financially and in other ways. The tensions felt enormous – too little money, too many children, inadequate housing, and not least, unemployment – and the instability affected all of us. The bright spot was that I was working steadily on my thesis at last (the terror of it: sitting next to my advisor, Steven Marcus, an eminent authority on the Victorian novel, while we went over his handwritten comments on my dissertation. Many of the comments were a simple "Meaning what?", forcing me to explain exactly what I meant, oh lord). Later, while the children were still young, I scored a part-time position assisting a famous cognitive psychologist, Jerome Bruner, with an exciting project in narrative and selfhood. I would never have had this opportunity, which proved to be important to my later work, if we hadn't returned to New York.

But though Frank had anticipated quickly landing a decent job after being a well-published professor, he worked only spottily at little pay for some time, borrowing money in secret from relatives, including my own mother, to get by. He had assumed the world was waiting eagerly for him when he left his secure job; it was not. We were stuffed into a crowded and run-down graduate student apartment, one we could hardly afford. The move was hard for our daughters, who seemed unhappy for the first time in their lives at the upheaval, while my sweet-natured, contented baby son had become a difficult toddler and then problem child, easily upset and often angry.

Some of this was surely caused less by the move to a new city than by conflict in our home. The worse our finances became, the more irritated Frank was with me for not dropping the dissertation and getting a full-time job to help our family. That would have helped financially, of course. But for once, I insisted that I finish. I knew I could do it, and I knew that leaving off writing at this point would doom my ambition to be a professor, hard as it was for us to hang on. In this, I was Eve in the garden, committing the female sin of putting her desire first. His disgust with me mounted; he hadn't held my hand when we walked together for a long time, but now he regularly walked two steps ahead of me.

Frank floundered, working a bit here and there, and making quick jabs at various businesses of his own, which kept him away for long periods while I was home trying to keep the children busy and on track. As Frank kept coming up with dubious new business ventures, each requiring travel and the necessity of investing money we barely had in order to (in theory) make money from the investment, the household grew more and more chaotic. My journal entries reflect unrelenting anxiety, a sinking sense caused by a lack of steady income, being overwhelmed by the children's needs and difficulties, and increasing conflict between Frank and me:

This morning we had a fight duplicating other ones exactly. I am "negative" and "not supportive" of his new business; also my "inability to love him if he doesn't live up to the image of the great academic." There's a grain of truth in all this, as usual, but of course, as usual too, he's extremely defensive and unrealistic about his own situation. This goes to the heart of our feelings about ourselves and each other: I want increasing stability as I get older: two rising and prestigious careers, good income, decent housing and schools, a future to dwell on with satisfaction. Frank's constant dissatisfaction and impulsive moves are threatening to me. He sees me as scared, conservative, threatened by any venture into the unknown, snotty and narrow in my expectations of him and our life together, selfishly unwilling to support him if anything goes wrong, yet expecting him to constantly 'lead' and take care of the major decisions. All this is entirely fair.

I want him to say "Don't worry, honey, I'll make it all right," and he wants me to say "Don't worry, honey, I'll love you even if it isn't all right." And neither of us can say it and mean it.

Fight with Frank this morning because he had to look for me as I waited for him on the wrong level of a bookstore, having misheard him. This big issue led to twenty minutes of screaming and name-calling. He claimed I should have apologized right away for waiting in the wrong place. I claim he made such a frontal attack over so little that I was too angry to apologize.

Another big fight with Frank last night, finally resolved with compromise. He said afterward that I am a romantic dreamer, always expecting too much, forcing myself to an impossibly high standard, but never getting enough from anyone else, especially him. "As for your need for 'romance'," he said, "men and women are different," meaning men don't and can't comprehend this need. Is it true that men don't fall in love the way women do?

The truth is I had fallen in love, in a sense, right around this time, though it was with an avocation, not a person. I was ashamed to tell anyone, but I'd begun to flee from the troubles in our marriage and my sense of suffocation in our home by a retreat into romantic comedy, soap operas, and even more, Harlequin novels. This seemed harmless, if mortifying, until one day I began to write down a romance fantasy that had taken shape in my head. For an entire year or more, I suffered from an obsession, as if from an illness, with writing (after the day's work on my thesis was done) a novel that grew ever longer and longer. Yet I was never happier than when I was in this world and entirely mastered by my fierce compulsion to give it shape; the act of writing from my imaginary life was exhilarating, far more than any love or sex I'd had. And this sustained me for a couple of years, though it didn't make for superb mothering.

The worst of it was that when I was with my children, I only wanted to be alone so I could write; once little Billy asked to sit on my lap by requesting that I "move my 'tory," a pad of paper on which I'd been writing while I was hoping he'd play and let me be. As if the novel were a lover, I could think of nothing else. Just as the stereotypical housewife longs to get away for a tryst, I wanted more and more to sneak out under cover, to explode out of prison, to write.

I couldn't allow myself to admit my present life as a wife and mother wasn't what I wanted, and instead had thrown myself into writing that 500-page monstrosity of a romantic novel. In a way the romantic imagination saved me at a time when I did not yet have the ability to find a path in reality.

After this, when I finally saw the manuscript would not go anywhere, I understood that I'd neglected my children and delayed the already long-delayed dissertation even more, and felt ghastly about it. The romantic in me had come back to do its damage.

Romance offers this: the "I need you" of romantic

emotion is ideally not weakness or dependency when the need of the beloved Other is equal. But children alter that formula. There's an inherent *inequality* in loving them because they *literally* can't live without us, yet can't possibly love us back as full humans when they're young (or maybe ever): they love you but never really know you, or want to. Those small beloved Others had given me the depth and certainty of love I missed in my marriage, in their need of my love, my supremacy in their lives, my exclusive worth to them, all that was not secure in romantic relationships. Yet though my feeling for them exceeded romantic love in strength, the mother-child relationship lacked a specific pleasure I hoped for in a romance: being seen and desired for oneself, equally giving and taking attention and devotion.

This love for children was not, it turns out, a substitute for the recognition of my whole self, at the core of the romantic dream. You must love children for who *they* are, not because you hope they love you for your true selfhood. Their purpose in your life is not to fulfill your needs, but for you to adore them and try to fill theirs. That purpose was absorbing and important; I saw why my mother wanted it so much, and it gave me much. Nevertheless:

Ten years as a grad student and more children than we can afford, a way of life chosen by me, is ridiculous – because while I love children and of course love my own children, it drives me nearly insane to stay at home alone with them.

Children had temporarily fulfilled my desire to give and have love, to be needed, yet still left half of me in a state of permanent and unrecognized suppression and longing. In fact, the gratification of having children, both my absorption in their problems and delight in them, obscured that longing, while the maternal ideal of self-sacrifice made my romantic desire even more shameful.

Betty had lived for her three children, she told us, yet always seemed unhappy; could I live to serve others' needs only?

Happiness

We tend to classify marriages as either happy or not happy, and when a marriage breaks up, people often ask which spouse was the one who left. Sometimes the answers are clear, but often, it's not an either-or: marriage is too complex for these labels.

My husband was clever, spirited, interesting, and often enjoyable company. His presence could liven up a group, as if holding court (our friends in Europe called him The Pasha); his best moments as a father were when he'd spontaneously tell the kids to get in the car to go somewhere or other for fun. But again, as in my childhood, there was an absence, a silence. The truth is that marriage is no more insurance against loneliness and emptiness than a checkup ensures you won't get cancer.

These ten years, still in my thirties, after we fulfilled our wish of moving home, meaning to our city of origin, had exposed some fissures that had been well hidden before that time. It had been easy to blame geography or finances or rambunctious children for discontent. If there was a turning point when the marriage began to crumble, it was then, before the more dramatic events that followed. This was the period of our long-married life that destabilized the foundations of who we thought we were, and who we were to each other.

We'd had traditional roles in marriage, in some ways, though modern enough to be a two-career family – a significant change in our culture, due to the women's movement and the growing need to have two incomes to belong to the middle class. Betty and I had wanted a strong male figure who could protect and take care of me, but what we didn't see was the feminist insight that protection and "taking care of" often comes with control, except in romantic fiction. The expectations of masculinity are also a burden on men who are told they must lead, be the breadwinner, make the important decisions and then be blamed for them if all goes downhill afterward.

Before we had children, Frank and I struggled to live on just enough money, but this had not been a source of strife. The gulf between us was revealed in those years following our return to New York with three young children and no job, when money and managing the household became a central focus of discord. I'd always been passive about money, since girls were supposed to be cocooned from the world. Even as a teenager, when I worked or was given a bit of money for my birthday, I never saw it: Betty put it into a bank account that was mine. I had no idea how much it was, but I knew when I turned over my summer earnings that the savings must be accumulating, which felt good. And it was accumulating, but the entire sum was spent on my wedding, without my knowledge, on the principle that this was what women needed money for.

In the great era of the social novel, the nineteenth century, the relationship of marriage to money and class was explored in the challenge to find the right match. Just keeping up with the detailed calculations of landed property and commercial income that determined who was eligible for a "good" match would entail hiring a financial advisor these days. Throw in the all-important bargaining chips of beauty and social status, and the precise social or economic payoff for a suitor or lady to marry up, or at least not marry down, and you'd need an anthropologist as well. But we so rarely see the outcome of all this in literature, how the married couples fare economically, especially in English-language fiction. It isn't that money is no longer of interest after the ceremony, but that so many novels stopped at the wedding. (Virginia Woolf called George Eliot's *Middlemarch* "one of the few English novels written for grown-up people," because it's a brilliant exception to that rule.) In romances, after the important decision to marry is reached, the theme of marriage and money tends to disappear. Even in modern fiction, finances are not usually the most interesting problem the couple has. Yet in all those articles listing the most common stressors in marriage and reasons for divorce, money is always at or near the top of the list.

Frank insisted on controlling our money, not unlike a Victorian husband, because he liked to spend and didn't want me to have a say in how much he spent. After marriage, by unspoken agreement, I never saw all our bank accounts or paid any attention to where or precisely how much we had. When I later worried about money and rebelled against his secretive habits, Frank gruffly refused to allow me any financial control. His justification was that he'd never said I couldn't buy anything I wanted (I wanted very little, fortunately). I felt helpless to change this; he was immovable, and what could I do, divorce him?

I never once imagined leaving him; it didn't cross my mind, even before I had children, to be alone. Wasn't that why I married in the first place? And then when I had babies, I felt my ankles sink ever deeper into concrete. Children made more space for love in my life, but with each child, opening another room for love was also closing off the escape hatch to a different way of living.

Where do you draw the boundaries between what you want, what you need to have, and what you can't have? When do you really know what you must do to have it?

"You never drew a line in the sand," Frank liked to say accusingly after the marriage was over, as though it was my job to police his bad behavior. Instead, I accommodated more and more to the feeling, after the children came, that Frank didn't always seem to like me and didn't want to be there, without noticing (or only temporarily noticing) a gradual change. I was like the frog in slowly heating water swimming around the slippery sides, never alarmed enough to take the leap above the top until it's too late and the water boils. Because, as every self-help book and every film and magazine article on the topic will tell you, you *need to accept your spouse as he is*, love him unconditionally. But where does unconditional love end, and standing up for yourself begin? When is a compromise too compromising?

Twice when we were living in the South, I was startled by the possibility that Frank might be involved with another woman. The first time was when I waited for him in his office while he was down the hall, and picked up his ringing phone: "Hi Sweetie!" chirped a female voice, and when I asked who was calling, the phone clicked off. Frank said it was a wrong number, perfectly plausible. Then sometime later (weeks? months?) I was driving to the city and saw Frank in his car at an intersection, with a strange woman next to him. This time I didn't ask about it: it could have been a colleague – or a girlfriend; I was pregnant with our third child, and I couldn't think about what it might mean, so… I didn't.

The things we do for love is sometimes a romantic way of counting up what we will do to keep the peace.

This was something like the pattern so many women pursue – I think of it as particularly a woman's problem, but maybe it isn't entirely – you want something you're not getting; you complain, or perhaps timidly ask, repeatedly, to no avail; then you feel dismissed; you're afraid to keep asking, much less insist, for fear you will be accused of nagging, afraid the mate will be put off by the pressure and move even further away as a result… so you ignore it until it can't be overlooked any longer. Then comes trouble, which, startlingly, does not go away just because it's been ignored or postponed.

Frequently we fought over the Housewife's Dilemma, which has changed a good deal since 1963, when Betty Friedan wrote about the "unhappy housewife" in *The Feminine Mystique,* but still affects an enormous number of women – and also househusbands. The spouse who does not earn money, or earns less money, is responsible for the upkeep of the home and the constant supervision of the children. When the wage-earner comes home, they want respect, not in the sense Aretha Franklin meant it, but in the form of being left to relax from the efforts and tensions of the (paid) working day. This expectation coincides exactly with the moment the one at home with the children and domestic duties is ready for a break from a long and not necessarily quiet (and often tiresome) day. On weekends and holidays, those fun family trips with Frank to playgrounds and parks I'd fantasized about before having my children grew ever fewer, and they had never been plentiful. There were other things he wanted to do, and he did them.

Everything that had not been good between us before was now worse. Frank told me that our sexual relations, which I'd assumed had gone pretty well since I'd figured out the female orgasm problem, were not satisfactory, since he did not directly produce my orgasm, as a man should. I'd thought of it just a technical problem of the female body, but to him it was a judgment of his prowess as a male. The entrenched idea of heterosexual sex was that any pleasure for a woman must flow (literally and metaphorically) from the man. When it comes to women's desire, *only he can fix it*, to paraphrase Donald Trump. In other words, an ordinary solution to an ordinary sexual problem had turned into yet another problem.

This was when popular romances fed something I did not know how to name. Reading romance was like watching my inner desires projected in a continuous loop on the screen.

When my students say their grandparents "are still in love" and eternally happy, I wonder if that has to do with the "separate spheres" (as Victorians called it) and well-defined expectations of traditional marriage, where the limits were simply accepted without question. If your mate is dependable, of high enough status, has a good character, contributes to the family as he or she should, and treats you reasonably well… you might very well be happy (and lucky), or at least happy enough. And I understand the deep affection, the enduring marriage as a pillow that tenderly supports your head, the blanket that warms and covers your body

Attachments with someone you spend a life with can of course be deep. This is how arranged marriage worked (and still does in much of the world): the priority is the institution that organizes and directs whatever affection grows, if it grows at all, the forms it takes, the behaviors it allows. Particular emotions are cultivated in this greenhouse, others suppressed. But that's not what modern love in the Western model is supposed to be. "Happiness" is a word spread around like jam in modern Western cultures, but in romantic love, it hardly means today what it did in traditional society. In the popular musical *Fiddler on the Roof*, Tevye tells his wife Golde he's given permission for their daughter to marry for love, flouting tradition. This leads him to ask his wife (in song) if she loves him; she replies in a way similar to my mother's response when I asked her if she loved me: "I'm your wife," Golde says, as though that is enough, but he is looking for more, just as I did. She then sings:

> For twenty-five years I've lived with him
> Fought him, starved with him:
> Twenty-five years my bed is his
> If that's not love, what is?

This popular lyric always seems to elicit satisfied sighs, but in fact the love that Golde expresses is not quite the same as the romantic desire their daughter and future son-in-law are claiming as justification for their marriage. In fact, the pleasant, humorous song manipulates the divide between the two, merging them in exactly the way our culture blurs the distinction between passion and domestic affection to sell them both at the same time.

Long ago I had a friend who was in an arranged marriage. In India her traditional parents had tried to match her when she was in her early twenties. She kept vetoing their choices, and when she reached her middle twenties, her father ran out of patience and said this was the one, like it or not. Her successful suitor's qualifications were a) good family (including religious and ethnic sameness), b) good character, and c) prestigious profession and earning power. This couple seemed content to me, but they didn't interact the way American couples are expected to do. That is, my friend explained that though they got along well, she felt emotionally closer to, and vastly preferred, the company of her close girlfriends to that of her husband. The wife was not the husband's best friend either; he had his own important circle of friends. Their priorities were their son and economic success; my friend didn't feel the need for or expect what sociologists call "mutual emotional disclosure." I suspect he felt the same; that's just not what it was about.

After some years in America, they divorced.

Jumpa Lahiri has a wonderful story, "Interpreter of Maladies," in which an American couple visit relatives in India. The wife married early, under pressure from her traditional parents, and now longs for the excitement and attention of romance in the American way, and, eventually, forbidden sexuality. But that doesn't work for her either, and both she and an Indian driver, who has a traditional marriage and fantasizes about an extramarital romance with the American wife, are thwarted by enormous and contradictory cultural pressures and expectations from both cultures, traditional Native American and modern American.

Paradoxically, it's both difficult to make passion compatible with marriage and also difficult for most modern Westerners to imagine reverting to traditional family arrangements, with their restrictions of the past. Despite my cynicism about the connection between romance and marriage, I would not enter into an arranged marriage myself, or marry someone I didn't deeply love. There's no easy solution to these internal contradictions, though magazines and internet articles would have us believe otherwise. *Work harder!* only adds anxiety and pressure to great expectations, as romantic love in our culture grows ever more ubiquitous as personal gratification and corporate selling tool.

I am not advocating for marrying with or without romance. Some are probably more suited to romance than others, some more suited by character to the long durée of affectionate companionship with a partner, as the mate is called after the business model. My marriage didn't founder because I no longer loved my husband or even because I no longer liked our relationship. In fact, I should have disliked it much more than I did. Essentially it was because I grew to dislike the person who was married to Frank, and I could see he felt the same way.

By "the person you are with someone," I mean something other than what's called your "best self," not the good things you can do, the strength you have, the great values that people admire, but rather the shape of your inner and outer lives, both at the level of the ordinary as well as in the depths of your psyche. We all hide ourselves, but some friends and lovers bring us closer to who we are when we're alone.

Marriage for me was like realizing you're not in the movie you bought a ticket for. For a good while you still stay in your seat, just because that's where you are. The longer you sit there, the more you missed of that other, better movie anyway, which makes you still more passive and resigned. It's as if you're living the famous thought experiment where the boards of the ship are slowly replaced: it both is and isn't another ship. For me, the ship was a sense of the world and its makeup, my values (what I value, what should be valued), the fibers of my heart. Thanks to marriage, I both was and wasn't the same person I'd been when I married.

In my journal I quoted the accusation Frank threw at me: "You always think you're controlled by me and everyone and you use that as an excuse, but you never were controlled and can do whatever you want." Can anyone really do whatever they want? Yes, I should have been different, but it would have been like asking a ten-year-old to run for mayor if she wants to. I wanted to be taken care of (like a ten-year-old) by someone in charge, and it turned out that the flip side of "taking charge" was "being dominated."

Was my marriage unhappy? At times, yes, in some ways, at other times, no; the course of it was messy, with scars that healed and other wounds opening in their place. Which of us left the marriage? He did, yet I had left it in another way before that. And he had left in still another way before that. These questions have little meaning in themselves.

Deep within its structure, the very cells of the marriage had been growing malignant, silently and invisibly, a thickening that continued to swell, irreversible except by being rooted out. Just as with cancer, there were causes that were too microscopic to see. Both the physical body and the world of marriage with its emotional intertwinings are too hot with life and too cold with rational explanation to thoroughly know. Instead we feel the effects of these root changes at the cellular level: the effect on the physical body is a cancerous tumor, and on the marriage, an affair. Both can kill the host.

Chapter Four
Love

> I jumped down from the wall to see
> what would happen if fate saw me picking
> purple flowers from its hanging gardens respectfully…
> It might greet me and say:
> Get back safe…
> And I jumped down from this wall to see
> what can't be seen
> and to measure the depth of the abyss.
> – Darwish, "In My Mother's House"

1990s: You are no longer young. You married at age twenty, though you didn't much want to. And years later you meet someone, because you crossed paths in a certain place and time when you are in a certain metaphorical time or place in your life. Alarmed, you see that this is the love of your life. If you don't sleep with him, he will get away. You will never have another chance with him, or another chance at real love at all. So you sleep with him, and you very, very much want to. Though it's not at all a good idea. And people will be hurt if you do.

It began when I was safely, securely, affectionately, and loyally married forever, the questions of loneliness and romantic love long settled. I had just entered my forties. My husband Frank and I had three children, two at home, one at college. We had a middle-class income at last. This was what I'd wanted, and couldn't imagine a life, mine or anyone's, unmarried, because love was like thin air to me – I needed to inhale it deeply to survive. Marriage was a bunker, a closed space with scarce supplies in a post-apocalyptic outer world, shelter from its predations.

It turned out that love, in one of its incarnations, was one of those predations. It was romantic love that bombed the safe haven wide open, exposing the desolate spaces underneath. In modern life, romance is meant to justify marriage and also be its guarantor. Instead, I experienced the terrifying power of love and sex decades after I married.

I'd never had extra-marital sex, but I already had an enduring extra-marital relationship with romance itself. As soon as I acted on that desire, nothing at all seemed the same. One moment I was safely hunkered down in the bunker, watching life go by, as when I played in the shadowed corner of my childhood home. But now the life I was watching go by was my own.

In popular romance, in romantic comedy, passion properly and conveniently comes before marriage, which somehow both expresses and tames it at the same time. The problems of romance may be complicated, but love in popular media is not complicated; you have it or you don't. In some versions, the heroine renounces a false romance with the vain, shallow, possibly two-timing love, instead wisely choosing the Good Guy. That's the one who is always there, who will reliably take care of her, as in Jennifer Weiner's story "The Guy Not Taken," in which a woman chooses between an alluring old flame and the husband who bores her. Guess which one she (conveniently) realizes is her real love? Even Laurie Colwin, whose story "Evensong" focuses on a passionate extramarital affair with comic irony but no moral judgement, has her heroine return to the husband and her familiar family routine as a kind of relief.

This theme has been repeated over and over in Western literature, popular and classic, since love was increasingly tied to marriage in the eighteenth century. Victorian novels burst with examples of conflict between romantic passion and Good Husband Material (as my mother used to say). In *Wuthering Heights*, for example, the choice between wicked-passionate Heathcliff and the heroine's upright (and uptight) husband, Edgar Linton, is the foundation of the novel, while Maggie Tulliver in Eliot's *The Mill on the Floss* must make a choice between an alluring lover who will destroy her reputation by running off with her, or Philip, an intellectual "hunchback" who loves her tenderly. In the twentieth century, Mrs. Dalloway, in Virginia Woolf's novel of the same name, compares her unacceptable emotions for another woman in her past to her pleasant but uninteresting husband. The story of love follows the old pattern as night is said to follow day, though in reality it's just as true that day follows night. But that's what plots do, after all: they simplify the confusions of events and emotions, straighten them into coherent meaning.

Adultery, on the other hand, is treated as subversive of the story we tell ourselves, that true love is somehow a fount of morality, both private and public, unselfish and pro-social, and inevitably rewarded by coupling for life.

This wasn't necessarily the view of adulterous love in medieval Western literature, where many scholars claim our modern ideas of romance were born. Not only did the Provençal poets write unashamedly of their well-born and well-married ladies, but the prose tales of Tristan and Isolde or Lancelot and Guinevere surely encourage their readers to sympathize and align with the passion of the adulterous couples. Their sexual love is celebrated, as in the knightly epic *Lancelot, Knight of the Cart*, when Lancelot breaks into Guinivere's room (she's been kidnapped and imprisoned!) and we're told that

> the queen reached out
> Her arms and drew him down,
> Holding him tight against her breast, making the knight
> As welcome in her bed, and as happy,
> As she possibly could, impelled
> By the power of Love.

This view of adulterous love is closer to *Lady Chatterley's Lover* than to the Victorians. Isolde and Tristan unknowingly drink a magical potion that causes these two virtuous characters to fall helplessly in love, thereby absolving them of accountability, while the story of Lancelot and Guinevere doesn't bother with such a cover. Their passion just *is*, because each is simply the best of the best, she the most beautiful and high-born, he the most valiant and noble-hearted warrior, and so it follows that each would be drawn to equal superiority. Readers of these medieval tales are asked to admire the lovers' superb beauty, the intensity of their sexual feeling, and the lengths they will go for their forbidden devotion. Their joy and sacrificial pain are monumental and also the point, rather than what happens afterward.

Four hundred years after sexual morality was reformed, which is to say tightened, by the Protestant Reformation in Europe, the British and European Romantics rebelled, further nurturing our own modern idea of romance. In eighteenth-century Germany, Goethe's *The Sorrows of Young Werther* traced the mad and unrepentant passion of his hero for a virtuous married woman whose unattainability destroys him. In early nineteenth-century England, Byron dared to laugh at the hypocrisy of religious restrictions on natural desire in his narrative poem *Don Juan*, where the beautiful youth Juan and his married lover Donna Julia openly lust for each other. But since Byron's *Don Juan* is sharp-edged satire of the characters' absurdities and *The Sorrows of Young Werther* ends in suicide, neither is quite a positive portrayal of adultery.

Not coincidentally, in the modern era of love-based marriage in the West, outright sympathy for adulterous affairs that threaten the institution of marriage is hard to find before the twentieth century. In Jane Austen's novels, extramarital hankering is never love, just egoism, as in *Mansfield Park*, and the famous heroines of Flaubert's *Madame Bovary*, Tolstoy's *Anna Karenina*, and Kate Chopin's *The Awakening*, suffer from adulterous desire as if it were a disease. In popular media, affairs have been and still are often represented with cynicism and ridicule, at best well-meaning but inherently scabrous and doomed. And interesting exception from the 1990s, Robert Waller's novel *Bridges of Madison County*, idealizes a married housewife's love affair with a sensitive but masculine photographer, only to end virtuously with the wife's sacrifice of true love (and great sex) for the sake of her dull husband and barely sketched children. That sacrifice is idealized too, in the way that a dutiful soldier killed in action might be. The woman who stifles her desire is a kind of warrior of marriage, with a stiff upper lip as the weapon.

It's odd that in contemporary society, in spite of widespread sexual titillation in the many forms of popular culture, adultery is more or less excluded from the pop culture romance genre because even a shared and enduring extramarital love is not seen as a "happy ending." This is particularly striking because in life there are in fact romances with so-called "happy endings" that began in affairs all the time. Just recently I came across one of those internet articles about rare long-married Hollywood couples that included Tom Hanks and his longtime wife, Rita Wilson, whose love affair predated his divorce from his first wife. I would bet there are many more domesticated couples whose contented life together began with an extramarital affair, and they're not all celebrities. The line between the faithful and the unfaithful can be blurry, messy, rather than simply categories people belong to or not.

Love Stories

Was my own love story a farce, a tragedy. or romance? Looking back now, my memory obliterates those differences. There are no genres or categories or lines in life; we add them from a stock of concepts residing entirely in the human head.

In novels and films, a man's extramarital affair is a sign of bad character, in addition to, of course, utter selfishness: he may be a wild rake in the eighteenth century, a heartless cad in the nineteenth, an egoistic jackass in our own time. A woman's infidelity more often appears as rooted in unhappiness accompanied by boredom, especially in modern suburbs, where women in novels and movies are continually sinking from ennui. These treacherous women will always be discovered and roundly punished by not ever getting what they want (not only the lover but just about anything); the husband will leave them, their suburban homes will be lonelier than ever, their children will despise them for their cruel self-indulgence, and the world will expose their hedonistic, possibly crazy ways.

For both sexes, even where their depravity is understandable, it's never forgivable, as in the movie *Unfaithful* (2002), where Diane Lane is made to suffer for her pleasure. But women are more often punished in fiction and film than men for infidelity, likely because women are rarely allowed to put themselves first in relation to their family.

When my affair began, I was not isolated in the countryside, like Lady Chatterley, or restless and deprived of mental stimulation like Madame Bovary, or even a housewife in a suburb, like the heroine of Tom Perrotta's novel and film *Little Children*. In fact, I was happier than I'd been in many years. For one thing, I was finally living where I'd most wanted to live, in New York, the wonderful, invigorating city of my birth and upbringing. I was surrounded by friends old and new. And not least, I'd been fortunate to find a modest entry to the career

I'd dreamed of and worked hard to achieve, proud of contributing my small income to my family, and more animated intellectually than ever before by my profession and those around me.

In romantic fiction, the origin point of a woman's life (her *new* life, which is to say after she is loved) is often the meeting with the beloved – the magnetized moment of first desire. This signature feature of popular romance novels, equivalent to the bumpy, snarky, comic Hollywood movie meet-cute, can also be found in a serious and beautiful rendering of romantic passion like the movie *Carol* (2015). But the turning point in my own life story was not the discovery of love, or its massive hostile takeover; rather, it was my belated entrance into the world of grown-ups as a woman with my first full-time, money-earning job in early middle age. Until then I'd been a baby-wife, not much older emotionally than I'd been as an overprotected nineteen-year-old living at home with Betty and Al.

I'd just finished the struggle to complete a doctorate while raising three children and following my husband's jobs around the country. At last, fourteen years after beginning a doctoral program, I submitted a thesis, earned the title of professor (at the bottom-most rung, needless to say), and eventually published articles and books. Yet when I began a full-time career, I was no more a real adult than I had been when Betty's idea for me to marry while in college had been the most exciting proposal I'd ever heard. It was when I stepped into my own classroom for the first time, newly accountable to people other than my husband, in charge of young adult students rather than little children – most of all, surrounded by colleagues who listened to my timidly expressed thoughts with a respect that surprised (almost alarmed) me, who had conversations about ideas new to me, and took for granted views not necessarily shared by my husband, such as feminism – that my world changed, and I changed with it.

This was my own story now: analyzing women's relationship to romance in classic novels gave me the rational, intellectual mastery of love I'd longed for. This was not just a professional move; it was a battle in the long struggle between reason, truth, and reality on one side, and helpless feeling on the other that I'd waged throughout my life. Score one for being "book-smart", which had paid off… eventually.

I began to feel happier, more like my early idea of myself than I had been at home, some part of me rising up and firmly crossing her arms, as if to say, Yes, *here's* what I've wanted for myself. I could fail here, and badly – the clock immediately ticking on that unnervingly all-important, one-chance-only, professional lifeline, tenure – but it would be a failure out in the world, not buried in the busy, noisy silence of the walled-in home, at least not a reproach for lack of trying.

My home was no longer the shelter I'd felt it was for decades. It began to seem that its walls were keeping out what I hoped for, more than protecting me from what I feared. Some unformed, unnamed inner yearning had been silently expanding for years. I'd tried to hide it, but it was like trying to disguise a pregnancy. Now my profession, late to it as I came, lay invitingly before me, an opening to be what I'd imagined I could. The young rookie who'd been so long on the bench was finally up at bat in middle age.

This was a foreign landscape full of possibilities, the

way reading books had been for me as a child. Life as a new professor was yeasty, a rising challenge, dread-inducing and heady all at once. As it happened, earning a real paycheck, however small, for the first time went a long way to countering anxiety. I recall the moment I put my new briefcase tentatively in my office, my first curious glance around at the two desks, the shelves full with previous occupants' books, the ancient and filthy brown rug, the hideous old orange couch in Swedish Modern style outmoded even then. It was *mine*, even though I shared it for a year or two, due to lack of office space, with a grumpy colleague. My office mate was clearly not thrilled to be paired with this new person (the first woman hired in my department in years), and reluctantly showed me to the smaller of the two desks, the one far away from the window, facing a blank wall.

This is still my office and has been for decades, but now those are all my books on the shelves, its walls covered with the photos and children's drawings I've chosen. My grumpy office husband retired not long after I arrived, and I inherited the big desk close by the window with a view of lawn and trees. But the terrible orange Swedish Modern couch is still in place, losing more of its foam stuffing every year. This bothers me not at all, since I am losing my own stuffing too.

Gerald

Some years after I began work, a new man stepped into my story, not at all as if from the pages of a book or the cover of a romance. I'd heard about him first from friends, then met him; bugles did not sound and I did not tingle all over with premonition. He was nothing much like the heroes of the romances I'd read, not an alpha male, not strikingly muscled with a diamond-cut jaw. He was neither coldly aloof and proud nor passionate and violent, neither Darcy nor Heathcliff. On the other hand, he *was* tall and slim, with particularly nice hair. This was Gerald.

My memory of the first time we were alone plays out in my head as a scene from a New Wave film, Antonioni directing, with background European music. We might as well have been standing on red cliffs, wind blowing our hair, the Mediterranean at our feet:

Gerald: I like your skirt.
Me: Oh really? It's Putumayo. Fake Peruvian.
Gerald: [laughs a bit]

That's it, that's all that remains of that first private conversation long ago. You would not predict this would be a life-changing dialogue. But there are good reasons for my recall of this two-liner (and reaction shot), why it's engraved like etched ivory in some sad part of my brain. First, no one had noticed this or any other item of my clothing in about twenty years. And second, I was not used to getting a chuckle at something I'd said in just about as long. *He appreciates me.* Very *Brief Encounter.*

I still have the skirt. Not because of Gerald, but because it really is a very nice skirt, longish, full, a folky red with blue cornflowers here and there.

It's hard to imagine this as a meet-cute scene in any romance fiction worthy of its name. I not only had no indication that we would be lovers, much less long-time lovers, in fact very long-time lovers, I certainly did not desire it in this moment, or even mused over this decorous and unremarkable conversation afterward. Yet there was a shift, the point when I rounded a corner: I simply began to think of Gerald in a certain way that I had not in our few mildly pleasant meetings before that day with others present.

Both fiction and life are made up of plot points, such as the first meeting of lovers. In a romance that meeting is fraught with significance, whereas in life, it may be one fine thread in a cloth woven of invisible filaments. Or to switch metaphors, Fiction sets the table for the meal to come, while our real selves are preoccupied with trying to get the waiter's attention.

In romantic stories, you eagerly follow the pattern: the heroine is often threatened with a problem in some way at first, and the entrance of the hero may be the problem or a resolution, or more likely both, in that order. I'm creatively rearranging my own origin story as I write now, by looking backwards at the first time I encountered Gerald.

Knowing there will be a happy ending in romance not only doesn't inhibit a reader's pleasure by ruining suspense, it sustains a pleasurable anticipation. Plots seduce and control us, especially when the reward at the end makes us feel good. In reality, the moments of our lives that seem a beginning of something significant later on are often more like a fleck of dust in the dust pile accumulating in the corner. We may think we're competent readers of our own momentous experiences (and even more so the dramas of those we gossip about), but life can and does prove us wrong forever.

What we do remember, what commands our attention in life, can be a reversal of habit, of expectation, just as in literature. I was surprised and just a bit thrilled that someone found me funny, damn it, after years of laughing at my husband's jokes, of being the object of them all too often, of being the admiring sidekick at best. (Once on a trip to the Far West with Frank, I'd been unsure if a life-size wooden Native American sitting at the bar was real, thanks to my near-sighted vision. Frank told that story of my dumb mistake many times: You won't believe this, my wife thought the wooden Native American was real! Hilarious.). If I'd made a joke expecting Gerald to laugh (a mere low and brief sound in the throat, but thrilling nonetheless), I wouldn't have noticed the conversation as I did, would not recall it now.

Gerald's casual passing remark registered with me (correctly) as a sort of code, a signal blinking as red as that folky, fake-Peruvian, Putumayo skirt. Since then I've seen the look that accompanied this moment on Gerald's face many times, and not only with me – a sort of leaning in, a softening of the voice, with laughing eyes, brighter than a moment before. Call it focused interest. (Your therapist has a focused interest in you too, until time is up and it's the next patient's turn.) This sense of attention paid was different enough from what I'd known before to embed a memory groove in my brain. And that little scene found a template, buried in my mind from reading those books and viewing those movies and hearing those songs: This is love, this is how it starts.

At an age when many women worry about losing their allure, I was suddenly finding out I had some.

But I still did not dwell on him in any persistent way after that first unimpressive conversation. Or maybe just casually, with a self-satisfied amusement at his flirtatiousness, because I was married, settled and happy, sort of, or at least I supposed so, or at least I wasn't considering the question much, and he'd made it clear he was living with someone. Nevertheless, the next time I saw him, I recalled that small momentary jog of pleasurable sensation, and I knew, in an enjoyably unexpected way, that I could have this again: the same interested look, the attentive eyes, his pleased smile, the bit of superfluous brightness in his "hello" when he saw me, but above all the new sense of myself as someone who could hold a lively and amusing conversation, a woman who could make a man of looks, wit, charm, and depth of mind think I was, as he later told me, "cute," my childhood role in the family.

How strange it is, watching another person in the act of keenly observing you, the you who's a kind of double of yourself in the eyes of the other.

It's not too much to say that I never felt the same way about my life afterward and there was no going back on that path. Instead I slid, skidded down that slippery slope as fast as my heart, taking on an unaccustomed weight, would go. Some months later, Gerald was my lover; not long after that, I learned that I was far from his only mistress, some of them casual but always one of them seriously poised to be the next live-in girlfriend, an open position to be aspired to. In less than a year, I was living alone and about to be divorced, still deeply in love with Gerald, and still his mistress. And yet he had not said he loved me, and would not for a very long time; not only did I not appear to be a contender for the title of serious girlfriend, I was never even sure if we'd continue to be lovers, and in fact, during his occasional bouts of monogamy, I was sometimes told we would not.

But that isn't my point, what would or would not happen, how it would end, as in a novel. The point was a radical change in perception, not even acknowledged as such at first, but nevertheless a reorganization, an act of interpretation that was to recast and recalibrate everything, a new frame that altered the picture inside that frame. From then on, the way he saw me – or rather how I thought he might, and intensely hoped he would – was no less than who I was.

Could life feel like this always? Could I be who Gerald thought I was?

Romantic love is often much more about itself than about the loved one, yet by some magic trick of the heart, it feels exactly like it's directly caused by the other, someone or something deliberately sending a rocket into your life. The Cupid figure with his little arrow of desire symbolizes this idea. However it starts, you focus on the beloved the way a prisoner might obsess about his secret tunnel while he digs (*how far did I get today?*), though the escape is what's longed for, and the tunnel itself is barely remembered if the prisoner reaches the other side.

Let the record show that I did not fall into bed at the crook of Gerald's finger, much less because of a remark about a well-worn item of clothing produced by a company that no longer manufactures them; I had no such idea at the beginning. Instead, a very delightful flirtation was in the air. For those lovers, single or not, who find themselves in bed soon after meeting, you might be missing the many casual encounters where both parties delightedly wriggle with unexpressed mutual attraction. I thoroughly enjoyed this, but I also sincerely believed I was safe, because it was a foregone conclusion that such a morally wrong, and practically wrong-headed, project as an adulterous affair could not be undertaken, especially after decades of marriage.

It seemed to me that marriage wrote clear instructions on my body: Do Not Touch, along with the warning to myself that I carried in my heart: Don't tamper with the instructions! Yet not very long after, Gerald had pulled me aside at a party to which I'd pointedly invited both him and his girlfriend, to say in a low voice, "I've dreamed of holding you in my arms for months." This was flattering, more than a bit exciting, but it didn't make me want to toss myself headlong into adultery. Looking backwards, in the novelistic way we do when telling stories of our lives, it now stands out to me that I not only didn't angrily reprimand Gerald for his confession (I smiled nervously and said nothing, not having a handy riposte), but tellingly, I did not divulge this incident to my husband. Instead I kept it to myself as a small and private pleasure, whereas a few years before, when my husband's friend shocked me with an unwelcome kiss on the mouth, I'd been eager to inform on him. The difference between my actions after these two events (both unexpected, but only one kept secret, though an ear-piercing alarm bell) did not register in the least at the time. I was puzzled by it all, but in full control.

The dots of color in a Pointillist painting are each insignificant in themselves, but form a larger pattern when you pull away. I had no reason to pull away from Gerald, in fact had reasons not to. I was, as the French writer Colette described a female character in one of her novels, "Too bad to be good and too cowardly to be bad."

Gerald kissed me two or three months after that whispered confession, a full-bodied, all-out French kiss that terrified me. It had been more than twenty years since I'd kissed anyone but my husband that way, or been kissed romantically by my husband himself, for that matter. My unthinking response was to push Gerald away and blurt out: "I don't like the way you kiss!" This response surprised even me: what kind of kiss had I expected, a peck on the cheek, a brush of lips on the hand? Maybe the firmly pressed lips of Old Hollywood, squeezed and held for the shot? He looked amazed at my response, possibly more than if I'd cried "Stop that, you cad!" – he'd had women falling for and all over him his entire adult life, and perhaps no one had said that about his kisses before. "Show me how you like to kiss, then," he said, rather awkwardly, an invitation I found impossible to resist. "Okay," I said unromantically. I shyly showed him. This was like being in the audience at that moment in history when color first appeared in movies.

The first kiss in any relationship, even a wonderful relationship, can be very bad, whereas in romance fiction, it's almost always executed with terrific skill for maximum arousal. The reader is pulled in close, the scene is extended for at least a paragraph or two, the language is as swollen as the woman's lips. There's a whole cabinet of familiar language for kissing: how many alpha heroes cut off a heroine when she is ranting by slamming his lips against hers? Male lovers in popular romances are especially prone to feathering kisses along her jawline, something I've never experienced myself or hope to. These masculine objects of desire tend to be so obsessed with the heroine's luscious lips that they often spend the first half of the novel staring "hungrily" at them (the heroine can't think why), or repeatedly brushing thumbs over their "pillowy" or "cushiony" surfaces, as if lips are direct surrogates for breasts. In reality, if a man I'm talking to stared at my own lips, pillowy or not, I'd be likely to imagine I have a cold sore. But apparently readers eat up these descriptions of lip worship, the breakfast of love champions.

I see now that this moment, when I reached up to kiss Gerald "the way I liked it," was the next dot in the romantic picture rapidly forming in my head, after the first conversation about the skirt, and the unexplained impulse not to tell my husband what a good-looking man had confessed to me. This was an important crux in the story, an admission that I was *in* a story. He'd invited me to kiss him, kiss him the way I liked, which is to say given me the choice, the control, and after the tiniest pause of uncertainty, I'd reached up to him of my own will. It was a seal of consent, not just to the kiss, but to walking through a doorway toward a place with no real exit. Yet I still did not believe I was having an affair as long as we were not sleeping together, in the manner of some adolescents who think what they do with any part of the body is not really sex as long as it doesn't go "all the way" to full penetration.

When I did later fully lose my marital chastity, carefully preserved for twenty-odd years, Gerald cheerfully said to me the next day, "So now you're an Adulteress!" It was meant to be all kinds of ironic, of course, but it felt like a knife-wound to the breast. This wasn't just guilt – I think I understood at that moment, my heart sinking like a leaky boat, that our new relationship, while deeply and mutually pleasurable, was not *romantic* for him. That little joke, Now you're an Adulteress!, certainly wasn't what he was supposed to say in the emotional afterglow. At the time I thought of that word "romantic" as meaning a thing we all understood together. But in spite of this, I said nothing of what I was feeling about that remark, setting a pattern that persisted for many years after; who wants to expose that she not only hoped for more, but worse, expected more?

At the same time, even I could no longer deny now that I was having an affair, that I was lying to my husband, and had been lying to myself. This launched a turbulent period in which I struggled to come to terms with the cognitive dissonance of Being an Adulteress. It had always been, and still was, an integral part of my identity that I was a good wife, the *best* wife, entirely devoted to the family on a narrow path to secular domestic heaven. Now I wondered: what does it mean to be a good wife, and does that equal either a satisfied or satisfying wife?

I was bewildered to find myself in a place I could not quietly sneak away from. Once I'd punched my way out of my familiar self, the sense of being able to grow and spread in any direction was exhilarating and frightening at once: water seeping into crevices could turn into flood.

After this first kiss, I'd fallen ever more in love or it would have gone no farther. I've frequently heard the belief, usually edged with contempt, that women tend to fall in love after sex, especially adulterous sex, whereas men are only interested in getting away as soon as possible after getting off. The implication is that women are so needy and weak of heart that they use love to justify their sexual desires (while men are just pigs). This is, at least in pop science, explained by oxytocin, which is said to cause women to bond with lovers as if they were their newborn babies. If this is true, my oxytocin must be so erratic it's a wonder I was able to nurse three infants. In fact, I've had fulfilling sexual experiences without feeling the least bit of love afterward, as well as strong romantic feelings in a relationship with little sexual satisfaction.

So I doubt this inevitable connection between women, sex, and love is necessarily true, though it may have been once, when the idea of female chastity reigned. Where it holds, it seems less like a physiological difference than a reasonable response to living in a culture (which is most cultures) where women pay a far greater penalty for being "sluts" or "whores" – a word that still appears with alarming frequency on reality TV to mean a female who does not bow to the imperative for at least serial monogamy. But I do think that one of the great advantages of romantic love is that for any gender or sexual preference, it can be life's most effective aphrodisiac. Never mind Freud: think what Darwin would make of that.

What Is Love?

Once I was a speaker on a panel at a conference in the Library of Congress whose subject was "What is Love?" Is it the meeting of two souls, or a unique combination of sexuality, best-friendship and intense emotional attachment?

Not only can romantic love make sexual desire nearly impossible to suppress, it may be that romantic love is an idealization of sexual desire to begin with. Freud thought so, for whatever that's worth. Yet we know that sexual desire exists plentifully without romance. Surely love is a concept that calls out a high number of generalizations, usually to no good use (I consider myself no exception to that rule about rules).

When I consider what love is, I think of my first grand-dog, an unlovely but well-loved creature by the name of Pugsley. Puggie was a smart and sweet-natured girl doggie with an unusually expressive face and a passionless personality. Phlegmatic as her nature was, there was one occasion when Puggie consistently showed acute excitement. Pugs, who is now in Dog Heaven herself after a long, happy life of mostly resting, was completely uninterested in other dogs, with the notable exception of one particular male she encountered sometimes on a walk. As soon as she caught a whiff of this nondescript dog, even across a field or a block away, she would freeze on the spot, stare and sniff intensely, then frantically strain at the leash to get to him, with an amazing series of whimpers, growls, and yelps of pleasure and longing. (He was not uninterested, but he was more enthusiastic about squirrels.)

I often wondered, Why this one dog? He wasn't even good-looking! Yet that specific doggie, with his unique combination of pheromones, for reasons mysterious to us but entirely explicable in nature, rang Pugsley's inner bell, loud and clear; he aroused her, made her happy beyond her normal pleasures, trumping even the sofa and the dog treat. Why else does Juliet love Romeo, whom she knows on an intimate level no better than Puggie knew her beloved? And that, folks, entirely unadorned, is, I believe, a huge part of… what love is, making it surprisingly difficult to predict who an individual will fall in love with, as we see on reality shows and dating apps.

But of course humans are much more convoluted in their psychology than dogs, or at least we like to think we are. Puggie and her would-be lover (damn that leash!)

did not bark about "having a connection," or "marrying their best friend." We prefer to think that all the blather about "soulmates" or "the right person for you" indicates high-minded admiration and respect for the object of our romantic lust, pointing to an origin in the highly evolved forebrain, and only secondarily in the genitals or those hormones that get blamed for everything. For humans, passion appears to be a hot stew of excited neurons, pumping chemicals, buried memories, emotional needs, social expectations, and relational dynamics. It's enough to make you lose your appetite and settle for someone who makes a decent living.

What you think about the beloved is probably important to an extent. Certainly my intense romantic response to Gerald was more than sexual desire, the sexual pleasure he uniquely gave me, or an unconscious guilty response to that. He was also the most thought-provoking, funny, intellectually stimulating person I'd ever known, and if he hadn't been attractive to me sexually from the beginning, I would have been glad to be his lifelong friend. My sudden and awful depth of feeling for him was based on an entwining of that deep enjoyment of who he was (or who he was when he was with me) and the intense sexual bond we had. Together they made for a terribly potent brew of frustrated hopes and expectations, yes, but also some deep, and until then unknown, merger of solace and stimulation, both mental and physical.

I once asked Gerald which of his many girlfriends he'd been most in love with in his life; he named a woman from his distant past. And why that one, out of the many? I was struck by the simplicity of his answer: "She was a superior human being." I would say the same. This is not to contradict the Rule of Puggie; I'm not declaring that romantic love is *mostly* about admiration, "the one who makes you a better person," the claim of many a wedding toast. I suspect that's sheer wish-fulfillment, a Just-So story we tell ourselves. For Aristotle, true friends were those who promoted each other's virtue, his version of a "superior human being." I didn't think of Gerald as the best person I knew, if by best you mean the most virtuous or trustworthy or "good person" in the usual understanding of those words.

But neither are my friends necessarily my friends because they are "the best people," in the sense of morality or noble character, the idea touted by Aristotle; rather, they bring something to the party that makes it worth attending: the wine, the cake, an interesting point of view, a knack for empathetic cooing, the satisfaction of laughing together at the absurdities of life, and so on. No one of them brings all of it, and I wouldn't expect them to. One friend may be reliably kind and generous, if a bit dim; another is sharp-tongued and occasionally selfish, yet original; this one has wisdom and sound judgment, while that one is delightfully silly. One is a tea-party, while the next is a midnight barbecue at the beach with naked swimming; some I confide in, and others not, though I enjoy them in other ways. Why should these human variations be different for lovers who bring themselves to the festival of your life, while adding the power that mutual sexual desire has (not unlike alcohol) to make you party harder, to make the party wilder?

I knew pretty quickly that Gerald was far from the noble, perfect, or, at least, perfectable human who is the love object in a popular romance. In fact, I saw fairly soon that he had qualities that alarmed me, such as a remarkable ability to compartmentalize what he needed to put away temporarily (that is to say, me). He tended to evasion when pressed on a fraught issue, a trait he shares with many, and when pushed beyond evasion, had quite a bit of competence at deception, mostly through omission. Though we all employ these tactics when the motivation is strong enough, his proficiency was at a higher than usual level. Yet he was also paradoxically capable of more directness and honesty than I'd ever seen in anyone, in that I never knew him to say what he didn't mean, even when it could have gotten him what he wanted. Talking to Gerald, I learned to observe with a different eye what I had never questioned, including love, sex and marriage. Thanks to him, and also to the wide study I began to undertake as a new scholar, I no longer saw the world quite as I used to.

Gerald didn't discuss his relations with other women, having, for both self-serving and also unselfish reasons, a strong sense of privacy, his and theirs. But gradually, as we grew closer, I could see what was happening, and he made less effort to keep secrets from me. Maybe it was a relief to him not to deceive at least one of us. I was appalled at first, since I'd never known a man or woman who behaved like this. And of course I was also hurt and disappointed that I wasn't the One and Only… mistress, at least. But I also wanted to understand what the drive to this behavior was about, much more interesting to me than condemnation.

It was fascinating that for the tiny, privileged group of women he called "serious" girlfriends, those who'd been candidates for the next real (which is to say public) relationship, their knowledge of this hidden life of multiple involvements would have been a deal-breaker. Why in the world did Gerald always choose a woman who was fixed on monogamy? Astonishingly, they never did discover the truth until he left them, so adept was he at balancing his many spinning plates. When he was living with them, it seemed likely to me (and at times, to him) that the woman he'd plighted his troth to must know on some level and accept this as the condition of being with him. But in fact, it was revealed afterward that during their tenure as legitimate girlfriends, they had floated contentedly enough in the warm pond of denial, something I did myself when married.

In spite of his public reputation that some of them knew very well, Gerald's serious girlfriends were furious afterward that they hadn't had the relationship they imagined, namely an entirely monogamous one in which they were the sole sun in his galaxy. To my amusement, at least one of Gerald's Serious Girlfriends had *first* been one of the adulterous Mistresses herself, then later snagged the domestic crown, thoroughly convinced he'd completely repented… for love of her. Yet when the truth of his affairs emerged and she became the deserted legitimate girlfriend, replaced by a new Serious Girlfriend he liked better, how self-righteousness bloomed! Wait, the fellow who chose me for his mate, after adulterous affairs with me and others, had then gone on to have still *more* affairs? Who'd have thought?

How many fictional works are based on exactly this plot, the Rake Reformed into chastity by his purer love for the Good Woman, who rescues our hero from his wild and bad past? One suspects the audience for this pleasant fiction is mostly female.

The girlfriend of a man whose promiscuous past included her must be deeply confident in her own superiority to believe the Rake Reformed idea. What astonishes me most is the willingness of these women to put self-regard, playing the role of a reforming heroine, before any desire to know the one they claim to love above all others as he actually is. If you're imagining this person as you'd like him to be, what *do* you mean by love? We're not talking here, after all, about, say, his snoring, his lame puns, or propensity for watching horror movies at two in the morning, but a part of him fundamental to the structures of his being, your beloved's strongest desires, his most secret self.

It's interesting to think that if I'd been chosen as one of Gerald's "serious" mates, as I'd so much hoped to be, I too would not have known that important aspect of his life, the architecture of his inmost self. Or I might have looked at it only as a part of our own romance, an obstacle to be overcome before our traditional happy ending. And then if I'd found out the truth while positioned as the established love of Gerald's life, when the Rake Reformed becomes a Rat, perhaps I'd have been bitter too. Instead I was curious about how this all really worked, a trait many forfeit in order to maintain the romantic story they've woven, heroism or villainy.

As it was, I had the favorite mistress's strange privilege of seeing the hidden self of the man I loved. I may have futilely aspired to the "serious" crown for a distressingly long time, but the sense he and I had that we could be more than usually ourselves with each other went a longer way in the end, and I don't only mean a longer time. That is, what I lost in not having the formal relation and the status of the role I coveted, I gained in a more truthful and mutual understanding.

Gerald once startled me by suddenly remarking, with genuine puzzlement, "I've always wondered why women like me so much." I told him it was because he fixed on whomever he was flirting with at the time with flattering energy and focus, in the same way he concentrated his considerable mental powers on any idea or problem he cared about. (But I'm not sure how much he listened to my answer; he nodded but already looked vague, not focused. I was long past being seduced.) Discussing this was a most unusual moment, not just in our relations, but possibly for him too.

It was because I knew Gerald as he was, the dark and the light, the buried and the open, the secrets that eventually seeped to the surface, that I could see his deception wasn't something he enjoyed, like a stereotypical philanderer. Rather, he seemed to me to be coping with shameful private desires, the fulfillment of a deeply true part of who he was, that came with a discomforting, but to him necessary price. My own response surprised me: this was so starkly contrary to my own mode of thinking and living that it slapped me awake. I'd never been able to face paying any price at all for what I wanted most, and where had that gotten me?

This is where it had gotten me: to a wildly sped-up time of my life when Pandora's box exploded, sending a thousand little winged desires of my own in all directions. I'd been afraid of myself; I was right to be afraid. As soon as I stood up for my hidden life (and I would not have been able to tell you at the time what that was, I discovered it by acting it out), the rest of my known and habitual world, pleasing to others as the way one ought to live, fell around me like the set of a movie knocked down after the final day of shooting. This was something like those science fiction stories where the hero suddenly discovers, to his horror, that he is really an android, the moment the science fiction writer Philip K. Dick called "discovering that his reality consisted of punched tape passing from reel to reel in his chest."

I simply could not live in that well-known and familiar place any longer. No matter if I wanted to, I couldn't bear to. An awful fatigue suddenly enveloped me, a sense that I was so very weary of who I'd been, which was not what I was any longer. I wrote in my journal then what I hadn't acknowledged to myself or anyone for a long time: "*I'm tired of being needed and I'm tired of needing.*" I was overcome by this emerging sense of myself, as though I'd birthed a terrifying alien into my natural world: a repulsion toward the home, the routines, everything I'd loved and taken for granted, a fog of dark displeasure bearing down on my life. What I'd clung to fearfully before, perhaps *because* I'd clung to it just short of desperately, I now wanted to leave. But I also could not imagine doing that.

This wasn't only about sexuality; it was the furtive truth that I wasn't a good girl in many ways, not really. I was certainly not the ideal wife or even the wonderful mother I'd believed I was; I too had qualities that bewildered and unnerved me, just as Gerald's secret life had dismayed me. In fact, I was – no, even worse, I *wanted to be* – quite bad, in the ways that women are considered bad. Aside from the absolute and inviolable boundary of never abandoning my children, I felt that I was all at once capable of almost anything, both what society admires but also what it doesn't.

The truth is that I loved Gerald *because* he seemed to me bad, not in spite of it. This is what pushed me to question what I meant by "bad." My romantic feeling was not about finding a splendid mate, the one who courts and is true and makes you half of that darling of society, the committed domestic couple – far from it, given what I knew about him. Rather, I liked that he was true in a different way than its usual meaning of "true" as sexually monogamous. I loved him because he had the audacity and energy to act on what he knew about himself, his desire to be with many women, though never publicly, for reasons I didn't then understand. And at a time when I didn't yet know what was true about myself, he recognized what I wanted in a way no one else had.

Since it was understood that neither of us was exclusive with the other, I always confided in Gerald about my other affairs, which was great fun. Once when I was confused about how to behave with a lover who wasn't treating me well, he joked, "When you feel you really should be fair or nice to him, do the opposite."

It turned out, when I had the courage to look, that an ancient lost city, built on a volcano and entombed under layers, could be seen in the depths of the crevice that love opened. A fusion of hope and dread was my first response to this vertiginous experience of looking in; a disoriented tourist, I wanted to explore and yet felt the foreignness of this new land as a kind of menace.

Bad Boys

Pop culture, including a thousand romance novels and romantic comedies, is filled with bad boys who are wild and free, and most importantly, loved by the women who will tame them. In this genre, the tiger is put in the cage, not by a handler with whip and chains, but by a pretty woman in a becoming yet modest-enough dress, whose sexual magnetism is powerful but whose power is really her sweetness, her down-home domesticating niceness, who sees the mildness of the lamb dormant in the male tiger. This delightful cultural dream reaches back to fairy tales like 'Beauty and the Beast,' then takes on literary prestige in novels such as Samuel Richardson's *Pamela: Virtue Rewarded* in the eighteenth century, where a virtuously virgin servant girl reforms and marries her almost-rapist. The fantasy grows to fullest life in the classic romances by the Brontës in the Victorian era, and drives right on through modernity to its temporary but impressively successful stop at *Fifty Shades of Grey*.

In *Fifty Shades*, the secret and supposedly out-of-bounds sexuality of our hero is ramped up to a level meant to surpass previous bad boy lovers: badder than the wildness of the fairy tale Beast, with his silly roars, or the clumsy attempts at molestation and rape in Richardson's *Pamela*, or even the outrageous entry of Heathcliff into Catherine's room just before she gives birth to her husband's child and dies in *Wuthering Heights*. The ambition of *Fifty Shades* is to reach beyond the self-consciously "hot" sex of most category romances, so bland they make tabasco taste like vanilla. The old-fashioned social constraints of femininity that hold the heroine in her place (even as she is adored) become, in *Fifty Shades*, real whips and chains that she herself desires.

The force of this mythic tale is that it sells itself to a heterosexual female audience as personal satisfaction through power over the threatening male. The Bad Boy both expresses female passion by proxy and simultaneously satisfies society's demands on women to be conventionally "feminine." In the twentieth century, demon lovers were domesticated as Dracula never was, so you could have your cake and eat it too, at the kitchen table with your bad-boy-turned-protector husband. The popular novel *The Sheik* had an enormous readership in the 1920s, and an even larger audience in the series of silent movies. These famously starred the sexy Rudolph Valentino, an Italian-American immigrant, as the "exotic" Sheik of the novel, who kidnaps, rapes, but finally falls in love with a virtuous British girl and marries her, to their eternal happiness. The vampire lover in Stephanie Meyer's *Twilight* series (novels and films) also has frightening powers, in this case supernatural, but fortunately is an adoring protector of the young heroine.

This bad-boy-in-love idea had attracted me to *Wuthering Heights* in adolescence. But as an adult I read *Wuthering Heights* differently: Heathcliff and Catherine go down to disaster exactly because domesticity can't hold them, because they deliberately resist it, in an age when virtuous domesticity was idealized as never before. The lovers are unrepentant to the end – and beyond the end. Even the narrative can't entirely contain them. Cathy is one of the few stubbornly bad heroines in classic literary romance: she may be killed off, but she refuses to be shamed or morally redeemed, though the next generation of characters in *Wuthering Heights* conveniently does that work for her. You might say Cathy and Heathcliff re-imagine the idea, both Victorian and modern, that romance is not a love story unless it has birthed a domestic relationship, even while the novel about these two is paradoxically understood to be one of the great romances.

In any case, Gerald was no Heathcliff to my Catherine. Not only had Gerald, unlike Heathcliff, never threatened anyone with murder, brutalized his wife, tried to disinherit a rightful heir, or even ran guests out of his house with "savage looks," he was more ready than any man I'd known to be fine with my freedom to do as I pleased about him, about sex, about anything. If he had any relation to these cultural landmarks in romance, it was a contrastive one. This was part of his appeal: after many years of marriage, I was and still am allergic to the faintest sign of domineering or forcefulness in a male, even as a supposedly romantic sign of flattering emotion.

Just as many men, with the encouragement of our culture, still behave as though women can be sorted into opposing categories of Madonna (the decent kind of woman you marry) and Whore (the one you want to fuck), many women, with the encouragement of the same culture, divide men into alpha Wild Guys (to whom you are romantically attracted) and Good Guys (the decent and reliable sort of man you should marry instead). But this isn't strictly an equivalence, because there's one important difference: the fantasy of romance is often that the Alpha hero isn't really *too* bad, and in fact is ready, though he doesn't yet know it, to be housebroken. Or his wit may conceal that he is just undeveloped and secretly sad and lonely, and so in a different way needs the love of the right woman, who is a *good* woman, to put him on the proper path.

Shakespeare refused to practice this neat trick with Othello, or Antony and Cleopatra; he did not turn away from the asociality of passion. This is what I find striking about *Wuthering Heights*: Emily Brontë doesn't make Heathcliff "good at heart," or gloss over his capacity for violence and cruelty. Passion is presented with rich complexity, moving or repellent or both of these at once, affirming our deepest humanity. Films based on the novel tend to soften the character of Heathcliff, so he can conform to the romantic hero pattern, one who could have settled in nicely if the story weren't a tragedy. Yet Emily Brontë calls Heathcliff "brutal" no less than five times in the novel; she pulls no punches for the sentimental reader.

Bad Girls

Since the sixties, sexual values and expectations have changed enormously, yet cultural views of monogamy have evolved surprisingly little. The messages of contemporary mass media are striking in their lack of variety, a rerun of what was on offer decades ago. In the 1990s, for example, when I began my affair with Gerald, an episode of the popular TV show *Ally McBeal* featured a good-girl heroine, Ally, who was tempted by a mutual attraction to her married former boyfriend. This plot line seemed daring at the time, but after a forbidden kiss, the note sounded over and over was shame, even for the wish. Although the show was usually more comedy than drama, shame-and-guilt in this case weighed heavily: not only is adultery unequivocally "wrong", and the spouse "wronged," but the adulterous couple were said to be (conveniently) "wrong for each other." Now that's a whole barrel of wrong.

Fortunately, after one episode of longing and almost acting on the longing, Billy, the guy in question, decides that he only *thought* he was in love with Ally, a kind of temporary loss of mind. You see, it turns out to have been an easily rectifiable problem – his wife's distance – which, now that it's been brought to her attention, the wife will clear right up. The listing marital ship will be righted again, as is only *right*. (This is the barrel of right.) Naturally, I thought, it's never about the Other Woman. She is mostly a titillating and/or threatening accessory to what is presumed to be the Real Thing, namely the all-American domestic couple, a prop in their drama.

In *Ally McBeal*, every narrative turn after that forbidden kiss reassuringly functions to punish Ally for that slip. When her would-be lover Billy leaves to rectify his barely-forgivable error with his wife, Ally's new boyfriend walks out too, disgusted. In other words, she isn't permitted love or sex with either the boyfriend or the man she loved, or for that matter any man (at least for that season), because she has dared to want to be with someone she Wasn't Meant to Be With. Whatever that means. ("Even though we'll always love each other in a way, we were not meant to be together", the penitent Ally says afterward. Who or what means love to be, I wonder? Is it God, the Three Fates, kismet, Cupid?) All this penance and punishment, and she doesn't get to sleep with either one of them! At least Anna Karenina and Madame Bovary were granted some pleasure before dying (but they were not American).

If, like Ally, your true love chooses to be unavailable (or only available for two episodes), are you supposed to go through this inhospitable world alone, excluded from providential blessings? Decades later, there has been more cultural representation of non-monogamous love, as in the TV series *The Affair*, but the change is simply soft-focus sex scenes replacing Ally's hesitant kiss: representation isn't exploration.

The wisdom that adultery (or triangulation, as psychobabblists call it) is Not About the Lover but really a reflection of the marital issues is one of those little jewels of modern insight that seems obviously true, and yet not always true when examined closely – why can't it be both, for example? On the other hand, as a description of the way women are often viewed by married men, not to say the world in general, it seems accurate: the Other Woman must stay Other unless she somehow manages to snare the husband for herself and slips from the hot Dark Side into the warm and snug role of Wife.

Other Women are both desired and despised because they are not wives, because they are not imagined as real women doing the real thing women are meant to do – if not be a wife, then supporting the institution by trying their hardest to be one, or demonstrating the good grace to be miserable in the failure. Other Women undermine the sacrosanct nature of domesticity and therefore don't count, even as a motive.

This confusing view of adultery is not confined to popular culture. A decade after Ally McBeal, the novel and movie *Little Children* (2004 and 2006) were both admired as creative works: the novel was praised as an "intelligent and absorbing" account of "passion" by *Publisher's Weekly*, while the movie received several Academy Awards. In the filmed version of *Little Children*, Sarah, the wife played by Kate Winslet, and Richard, her husband, are "immature" (the husband obsessed with teenage ath letics and his own lost youth, the wife unable to finish her dissertation), and therefore purely selfish. In one absurdly pointed scene, the wife returns home from an adulterous overnight adventure and ignores her daughter banging on the bedroom door while she narcissistically caresses her own cheek with a smile. This scene is strikingly parallel to a dramatic moment in *Madame Bovary*, Flaubert's nineteenth-century masterpiece, in which the heroine coldly pushes her small daughter away so she can be alone with her intense emotions for her lover. Both heroines are portrayed as narcissistic. Apparently one can't be a sexual woman and also a loving mother at the same time.

"Cheating" is still a formidable plotline in popular shows, not least in reality TV. By contrast, literary fiction has begun to represent its complexity, beyond the idea that the adulterous wife is infantile. The French novelist Annie Ernaux chooses to closely observe rather than judge her character in *A Simple Passion*, based on her own memories of obsessive desire for her married lover. In the much-admired series of Neapolitan novels by Elena Ferrante, *L'Amica Geniale*, the fiercely intelligent, independent heroine Lila is trapped in marriage with a controlling and abusive husband she mistakenly chose at age sixteen. Lila, and later her friend Elena, make no apologies and have no real guilt about their passionate affairs with the men they desire intensely and for whom they leave their husbands. Neither Lila nor Elena is killed off by the author as a result, and in fact both retain our sympathy as victims of their gender, class and time. I see these heroines as descendants of Cathy Earnshaw of *Wuthering Heights*, except that both Lila and Elena live, and their lives go on. Annie Ernaux also survived her own real-life affair and wrote about it, going on to be a Noble Prize-winning author.

Infidels and Infidelity

Not only wasn't I in suburbia or bored when I fell in love, my sex life was as reasonably satisfying as it probably is for those long-married, and I loved my husband, in the same affectionate, companionable, marital-love way I had from the beginning. According to the formulas of our culture, then, there was no explanation, unless I was wicked at heart.

It's doubtful that many people enter a conventional marriage hoping to have a forbidden love affair, just as you don't get pregnant hoping for an abortion. Why, then, is adultery so common? Statistics vary as to infidelity, from a conservative twenty percent all the way to one in three American marriages, and seventy percent in unmarried committed relationships. "People in the United States almost universally think adultery is wrong even while they are doing it," as the sociologist John Gagnon amusingly said about the high rate of both adultery and the moral condemnation of adultery.

An affair may be a signal of unhappiness in a relationship, a way to ease out of it – or a way to hold onto it. It might be a fallback position when you're caught between walls that are closing in on you. Or an electric charge in the slow, thick hum of marriage. For me, it felt like this: you can sit on the bench and continue to forfeit the desire and pleasure you suppressed all your life because you don't want to break your kids' hearts, or you can take a swing at the ball, knowing you could strike out and never have another chance at bat.

I understand this seems self-serving (it is), and there are strictly moral ways to frame this: for example, You should not risk your children's happiness by taking that chance. In a simpler world, I'd completely agree. But as far as hurting your children: I think of my mother, who sacrificed any possibility of love for her family's sake, and my father's decision to stay in a loveless marriage out of guilt. Restless, stifled, unhappy parents aren't wonderful for children either. I should know.

Let's say you're certain that you'll break your children's hearts, on the one hand, or break your own on the other, and you can get enough fulfillment in the affair to keep the structure in the household and maintain the commitment (though not the promise) of the marriage: I say that might be worth a try. It may blast your life through the domestic roof, for better or worse, or deception may turn out to be the best all-round solution for everyone.

On the other hand, even if you question conventional sexual morality, the non-monogamous are still stuck with another ethical violation: what about the outright lying, the breaking of the contract, the betrayal of trust, the oath sworn aloud? So-called open marriages (sometimes called honest non-monogamy or CNM, "consensual non-monogamy", as opposed to, let's say, Unethical Non-Monogamy – why are these labels always so ugly?) are morally preferable, of course. But this idea is based on mutual consent, and jealousy is a widely shared emotion that makes honesty impossible for many, if not most. It might be better to look beyond the choice between honesty and deception to the foundation for all this: the pledge of fidelity, automatically assumed even when not discussed.

The ideology of monogamous marriage is that you make a promise of permanent single pairing and that's that: fifty years without a mistake or the promise was worth nothing. You're super-glued down for your entire life. I'm not the first to notice the wobbliness of lifelong promises, as though circumstances and relationships don't shift, as though you can predict how it will be from the standpoint of age twenty or thirty or even forty. Too bad! You swore your troth and now it's an either-or. You keep that promise or you don't, no in-betweens. On one side of the line, you're good, on the other you're a cheat, either one hundred-percent chaste or practically a criminal. And of course context counts for nothing at all, whether deep or shallow, enduring or momentary – the cheating rat can be a man who nursed a wife with dementia for twenty years and is starved for touch and companionship, or a politician who casually texts naked photos of his genitals, or me when I was married and in love… or you, whatever the conditions of your life may be. All have committed precisely the same sin and are exactly the same: rats, cads, assholes, jerks, homewreckers, sluts, "betrayers" every one. This binary you-are-or-you-aren't is unreasonable to me, something like a girl who's pure if she's a virgin and ruined if not.

Extramarital affairs are popularly called "cheating," as if human relations were a card game. But every affair is also a compromise, an adjustment in terms of trying to balance elements of inner and outer life that don't go well together.

How others construed this adulterous episode in my life at the time told me more about them than about me: according to those who knew my situation, I was either deficient in ego or had excessive ego, I didn't love myself enough or I was too entitled, I'd lost my mind along with my morals or else I was too garden-variety spoiled to say no to myself. Moralists did what moralists love to do: vigorously point out, with confidence and self-importance, how wrong others are. The sardonic mockers, like the moralists, also think of themselves as superior: Give me a break with that sixties shit, finding yourself! Put your head down and do what's good for your marriage and family, lady! And I recognize that response, having been a long-time sardonic mocker myself: how silly the American language of "selfhood" can be, how self-indulgent the grandiose note of importance it can sound. Oh, you need *me-time*, do you? What, it's all about you? On the receiving end, I saw how this mockery operates: not just to wound and dismiss, but, like morality, to control.

Some of the criticism stung as intended to: my children, for example, probably saw me as carrying on like an adolescent, a sexual adolescent. I'd like to believe this was less a problem they had with me than an issue with me in relation *to them*, reflecting what they thought I was taking away from them. It's extremely difficult for one's children to imagine themselves in their own parent's dilemma. The girls were nineteen and fourteen when I began the affair; there was snarkiness and eye-rolling, but no angry confrontations. My son was ten, and I am not sure how much he knew before Frank and I separated. I did see that he was much more upset by his father refusing to see him for months. If he'd asked me why I loved another man, I'd have tried to answer truthfully, but instead his agonizing question was "Why doesn't Dad love me anymore?"

Not nearly as important, but still dispiriting, some women, even a friend or two, told me I was a bad feminist, bad to other women by sleeping with "their" men, a charge I had to think about, because I'd rather be told

I'm morally bad than a hypocrite.

The psychoanalytic lens of interpretation is quite different from the moral or personal one, in that it's seemingly objective, even empathetic: your sexual acting out (not exactly a judgment-free phrase), specifically the (unconscious) choice to love someone with whom you don't have a public relationship, has its origin in your family dynamic, your psychic wound, your repetition compulsion, the return of the repressed, everything and anything in your past that should be explored over months but preferably years, so you can change and live a balanced, healthy, moderated life, one that, by the way, does not include what *you feel* you want… because you want it for all the wrong reasons. And just why are these wrong reasons? Because this kind of *inappropriate* love must come from those neurotic impulses that have to be worked on by further exploring your father, your mother, your wound, your repetition compulsion, the return of the repressed… and so on, till exhaustion or poverty sets in, whichever comes first. This psychological morality, so to speak, replaces the religious idea of sin and punishment for those who consider themselves culturally evolved. In lieu of moral righteousness, substitute psychic health, and for God's punishment, swap in punishingly expensive psychological correction.

In both systems, moral and psycho-moral, if my lover had left his relationship for me, so that my affair had resolved into a new, reconfigured domestic couple, my lapse might have been forgivable, an eventually forgotten blot in the history of my new husband and me, as with Tom Hanks and Rita Wilson, and countless others. Thanks to the "happy ending," our sexual history in retrospect might not be motivated by all those deeply neurotic reasons, after all. It's usually a big shrug after the initial round of hurt and scandal. The fact that this moral and psychological judgment of infidelity turns on the ability of the infidels to marry reveals how suspect that judgment is. In some cultures, rape is an outrage unless the rapist marries his victim; the outrage isn't about the moral violation but about the loss of "honor," social approval.

Since post-affair new couplehood was not going to be the case for me, just about everyone in my life hated what I was feeling and doing, and so advised me to stop immediately. But though I felt terrible, all the advice, analysis, cajolement, or shaming did nothing to diminish the desire. For the first time in my life, I did not care to be told what to feel. Only a few of my closest friends offered the sympathy I craved more than approval, and I'm still grateful to the very first therapist whose doorstep I landed on, though to my dismay, she retired not long after I found her (presumably I didn't provide the final push). Beverly's surprising view was, in quick summary: "This is your need for passion speaking out. Passion's not a bad thing even if it hurts. You'll learn to value it." She doesn't know how right she was. Remarkably, she did not immediately set to work convincing me that if, thanks to her ministrations, I would come to my senses and stop feeling this way, domestic bliss would be my reward.

More typical was a mental health professional I found after Beverly deserted me, I mean retired, who remarked with barely disguised exasperation, "You won't change because you don't *want* to fall out of love!" I thought about this very seriously, because you need to do that when insurance doesn't cover this service, before I sincerely replied, "You're right, I don't. That's not what I want from this therapy." What did I want? I hoped to comprehend better what it all meant to me, and I've pursued that ever since.

Besides the friends, family, and professionals who stuck with me (or were unfortunately stuck with me) during this trying time, I'm quite sure I was the subject of gossip, for the purpose of malice or just entertainment. In our culture, the cliché of the midlife crisis is a joke about the idiocy of going a little age-related crazy, regressing in a disgraceful manner before settling into late-years wisdom, which translates as stability and quiet. But being the subject of a joke is not necessarily a humbling corrective to your bewildered need to defy what you always thought you were. It's true that a midlife awakening isn't nearly as weighty as, for example, feeding your family, much less the hungry of the world. But I didn't think of it at the time as either a pathetic joke or a personal enterprise. I was too busy trying to keep my nose above the tsunami of my desires.

Chapter Five
Alone

Julie: "Say that you love me: otherwise – what am I?"
– August Strindberg, *Miss Julie*

Someone tells me: this kind of love is not viable. But how can you evaluate viability? Why is the viable a Good Thing? Why is it better to last than to burn?
– Roland Barthes, *A Lover's Discourse*

Journal, early 1990s:

Normal life is painful. I like to live in total control of my life, planning and analyzing and justifying. I keep talking to people to get a handle on things, but everyone has a completely different and contradictory perspective: it's about you and your depression, not your marriage; or it's about your marriage, you should work on what you have; you should leave.

Barbara scorns me: "It's all bullshit except for eating and shelter and taking care of kids; the emotional stuff is thinking with your twat." Elayne reassures me: "Anyone who isn't closed off is going to go through a crazy jolt like this." Gene laughs fondly at me: "Oh, you were a cherry ripe for the picking. Of course you just can't have fun! Remember to keep it light." Advice I am incapable of following.

As soon as the affair began, I began to write every day, instead of the spotty journal entries I'd squeezed into the tiny spaces between child-rearing and doctoral studies. Like so many journal-keepers, I was trying to figure it all out by writing it out.

I was doing all I could, trying to balance my desires with the advice of others, the increasing irritation of my husband at my moodiness, the worries about the effect on the children: a performing seal frantically juggling a sudden burst of beach balls on her nose. Trying to correct course rationally, as I always had, I was properly shamed, I was analytical, I was insightful, I made resolutions. All day and every day, I scolded-denigrated-lectured myself, looking hard at the bright side, as I was told to do, meaning I should acknowledge what I already had and be grateful for it. None of this did the slightest good. My emotions had their way with me. This inconvenient love felt less like a moral choice than an act of surgery performed on my mind and heart while strapped to a table.

I am ashamed, guilty of compromising my own moral principles and for betraying Frank and my family. How can I do this? I'm continually pretending I'm okay, and the strain of this is enormous.

That tendency of women like me, to try to pull everything together in an emotional net, to weave the world out of bonds of love – I won't give into it. Am I playing a game of seduce the seducer? Do I want to be able to say I've had this? Jane Austen plays at

Emily Brontë for a chapter or two?

I'm not just Frank's wife or Gerald's lover. What does this affair mean to me?

Only one man wanted to marry me, and I married him. Reader, I won't marry this one.

And with those questions began a long road I was ill prepared to follow. But the choice was this: follow it and find out, or stop asking those questions.

I could see this was no longer about being with Gerald, though he was the stream through which these sensations flowed, or rather the bed for the stream, in more ways than one. It was now a matter of sinking, floundering, doggie-paddling my way up to the surface for a breath, then sinking rapidly again. I had caused this crisis, not Gerald, though it wouldn't have happened without him, I think.

While I was going through this turbulent conversion experience, my husband finally noticed I was "not myself," a phrase that implies there's a solid self somewhere you don't quite inhabit. Frank did not at first suspect the truth, even when I thought it should be obvious – he was checked out, stuck on seeing me the way I was when he married me decades before. But he must have sensed a change, though not enough to talk about it, because as I found myself in a state of continual alarm and crisis, he began to be more pleasant, stopped snapping at me as he tended to do. He even spent more time with the children and me instead of leaving for the day with his usual jolly "Have to umpire a night softball game," when asked where he was headed. Once I overheard him say "Leave mom alone. She's going through something," though we had no real discussions about what that "something" might be.

But the kinder he became, the guiltier I felt, until at last, two months after the first kiss with Gerald, in a panicked moment of metaphorical and literal nausea, I confessed quite unnecessarily to the affair. This was in a moment when I was sure the sexual part of it was over, leaving only my feelings dangling aimlessly over the side of a very steep drop. And so in short order, not long after I became a mistress, I found myself on the road to becoming a divorced wife, something I had never so much as considered before it happened.

Of course it was more ragged than that; there were awkward hesitations, serious reservations, partial reconciliations, many entries in my journal about the foolishness of giving up my supposedly happy home for the great unknown of being alone and poor. My husband and I spent the next months inching a step forward toward righteous recovery, then galloping two steps backward into confusion and pain, a dreadful game of marital Snakes and Ladders. At times I clung to my affection for Frank, my loyalty to him in every sense except the sexual. I defended the way we'd been together, though it was not making me happy and he seemed no happier with me. Still, it seemed like such a slight and reparable tear in the balloon that had proudly stayed aloft for most of our adult lives. What is a laceration caused by one short extramarital relationship compared to the complex history, the strength of allegiance, dual memory and layers of feeling, good and bad, in a very long marriage?

Yet the fact was that air had leaked out of this small fissure with horrible rapidity. I found I was afraid to be *without* my husband, yet utterly depressed at the thought of being stuck *with* him. My journal from that time gives it away: "*Honestly I have to admit that if I stay married, I will have more affairs to help me through it.*" This was a statement I could never have imagined writing just a year before, even months before. Odd as it seems now, admitting this aloud, so to speak, was my way of trying to keep the family together.

I vividly remember walking on a beach with Anne, my dear old friend, telling her I was sure Frank and I would get through this, because "the bond between us will bend, but never break" (and I see that I liked this banality so much that I wrote it in my journal even before declaring it to her on the beach). She replied, with her usual sad kindness, "Oh, don't be so sure about that." A divorced mother herself, she knew better than I did. That long alliance, the close weaving together of husband and wife, seemingly so essential and resilient that I believed each of us could not conceive of ourselves without the other, was unraveling, a loose-knit scarf cut with a large pair of scissors. The worn and loved threads took on strange new colors, the familiar patterns muddled in an entanglement of disorder. I felt entirely naked without a marriage, not just my particular marriage, as in one of those dreams where you're the only one undressed and exposed while other people appear born into their clothing.

In memory it seems only a minute from that late-summer walk when I stoutly affirmed to Anne that we would, without question, recover from this breach because *we had to*, to the day I wrote in my journal, when the weather had turned cold: "*Frank will not talk to me, or work on it with me, or go to a marriage counselor with me.*" It was over, really over; the next phase of my life was about to begin, which is to say I was suddenly pushed to the edge of a cliff and told to start walking. My life as a wife had lost its boundaries among unbidden desires, my guilt for acting on them, my husband's furious resentment, my unwarranted hopes for my new love, and vertiginous cognitive dissonance. I no longer stood firmly on the concrete foundation of being a married lady. And so I said my fearful goodbyes to all that.

Yet in the end, it was my husband who made the decision, as usual.

The reality was that I'd been pushed through the wall rather than made a courageous choice: "*I feel embattled with life, but also battered by life*," I wrote the first night after my husband took me out for New Year's brunch and told me to "get out", six months after my confession. "*I'd rather keep the peace, but keeping the peace is no longer possible for me.*"

Now I was alone.

This was my chance to have the life I wanted, in theory to create myself again, a sort of female Gatsby without the money or mansion. During this time of loss, both material and psychological, I was curiously both terribly self-absorbed and also felt I had no real selfhood to speak of. Who was I besides someone who needed and was needed? How should I live now? This was partly a practical question concerning the financial problems that sprang up immediately when one of two incomes was gone, causing the eventual loss of our newly-bought home to a bank. But it also implied that I had no idea what to do by myself, meaning without a man. Once, years before, I asked Frank why men get married at all, and recorded his answer in my journal; "Men *love* to be married, taken care of, their creature comforts," he'd replied, "The problem is, they also love a lot of pussy." It didn't feel particularly good to be *either* the "creature comfort" *or* one of the pussies. Weren't there other ways to be?

But even while weeping, I was also surprised by an unaccustomed sensation of sheer freedom I'd never had, since I'd married quite young – not only the freedom to do what I liked about men and sex, but the quickening sense that my life had taken a new turn and anything could happen, that there were many unknown roads to follow. I dared to think I could choose almost anything I wanted to do, though of course that wasn't true.

My brother Eric, as always standing by me, said this was a rare opportunity for me to rethink the entire basis of my life. This was excellent, something most people never get to do, he said, as opposed to settling into what it was supposed to be.

"But it feels awful," I cried (literally) in response.

"Well, naturally, it feels awful," he wrote, "We like to compromise with our fates. We plant trees and buy houses to console ourselves, and we get to love the structures of our own compromises. It's terrible to tear these up, and most people won't take the risk. In fact they'll tolerate enormous strain in order not to change them." I thought of Al and Betty then, unable to risk changing their lives – yes, enormous strain, for them and all of us.

Though in my forties, I hadn't yet lived on my own. That first night alone, in a dismal monthly rental, was filled with panic and regret, enough to fulfill my husband's wish for revenge, if he had one. It felt hardly bearable, except for a moment I recorded, when my friend Dora, not one for dramatic expressions of emotion, made me laugh by advising on the phone while I sobbed about being forever alone, "Hey, get a hobby, get a hubby!"

As it happened, there was no time for a hobby, much

less another hubby. It was essential to show up at work to support myself and my children, for one thing. There was also the frightening necessity of getting tenure by publishing articles and books, dealing with the foreclosure on the home we'd bought just months before, and not least, children who were upset by the upheaval in their lives. The youngest one coped by trying to soothe me, which was heartbreaking; the two oldest, one in high school and one in college, thought my melancholy and tendency to tear up while listening to Simon and Garfunkel were performative and let me know how absurd I seemed to them. In the end the necessity of pulling on rubber boots and wading into the muddy fields of work probably helped more than anything else: I was reasonably good at my job and knew how to do it even in a personal crisis.

My good fortune was a mutual platonic love with Gene, my wonderfully generous colleague, who would be the stereotypical witty-gay-best-friend-sidekick if we were in a romantic comedy. In reality, though Gene was in fact my witty, gay best friend, he was not a sidekick but my mentor, coaching while I played the special game that success in academia requires. ("And now you should chair a committee," he'd say breezily, as if it were as simple as "Now take a left turn here.") And that was how I got tenure in the worst year of my life. At least I could do something right.

Love

The truth is, I did have a hobby to distract me, and that was love. Love still preoccupied me; I wish it weren't so, but the journals, hardly readable now but unforgiving in their truth-telling, reveal that this is what filled my thoughts, more than the pressing, practical questions you'd think I'd focus on. Such as where we would live with less than half the income we had before. I tackled that with a very old solution: taking in a variety of boarders (some pleasant, some not) at my new rented apartment, which meant sharing the kitchen and bathroom.

Shameful or not, the more my everyday world tilted precariously, the more I looked away and immersed myself in the suspenseful story of my romance. I was preoccupied with my longing to be its heroine, its scenes of comedy and tragedy, its jagged, uncertain trajectory, but especially what end there would be to my tale of love, happy or failed, as though these two were immutable and sacrosanct types assigned by fate. There's no telling how attractive this bundle of extreme neediness, bursting forth from long confinement, must have been to the man I most wanted to attract.

Even I could see that it wasn't looking good for the happy ending, in which Gerald would leave the current girlfriend he kept saying he no longer wished to live with, and I would take over as his next (putatively permanent) Serious Relationship, reigning Queen of his Heart. My hopes weren't pure fantasy; they were based on this simple truth acknowledged by both of us (if not universally acknowledged): not only did we have the wonderfully natural, joyful, easy relation that's called "chemistry" in bed (I think of two molecules interacting, with bubbles), one that proved enduring, we also found great enjoyment in each other's company and a satisfying emotional closeness that grew all the time. For these reasons, I thought he *should* love me romantically; it seemed ridiculous to think he wouldn't. Who would not want to be with the person who is both your most passionate lover and also your "best friend," as he described me? Isn't that what romantic love is assumed to be, finding this rare relationship, a remarkable harmony of the best, both sexually and psychologically?

This made so much sense to me that I deeply believed Gerald *had* to become aware of this evident truth sooner or later, just as romantic heroes regularly wake up and have an epiphany at last, the knowledge exploding into their addled heads – that the deserving one who has loved them from afar, or been spurned for all the wrong reasons, is really the right one after all. (As everyone knows, this is often followed by the hero's frantic chase down airport corridors to catch the beloved as she is about to fly away forever, only to grab her just as she's going through the gate, where he breathlessly delivers a sentimental and/or comic speech imparting this insight, not unlikely self-deprecating because he's been such an idiot for not seeing this sooner. And she never, ever says, Well, fuck you, buddy, too late now).

But apparently harmony of both mind and body did not necessarily involve the heart where Gerald was concerned, or whatever organ Gerald used to choose his mate. It seemed reasonable to assume that the problem was the immovable obstacle, which is to say, the present girlfriend. However unhappy in his legitimate romantic relationships, Gerald was always reluctant to leave them, tossing the idea about for years before acting, so this gratifying fantasy of the hero waking up to the sweet reality of me seemed like a solid possibility more than once. Yet when he did finally part from that current girlfriend (to everyone's surprise, very much including the current girlfriend's), there was still another Serious Girlfriend waiting in place. I happened not to be that one.

A nice trick, if you can pull it off, never to be alone. In fact Gerald always appeared to have grown a meadow of lovely flowers at his door, from which he could pick the new *one and only* of his choice. This lucky lady was now The One, to my astonishment each time. However, she was literally the only One for a limited period requiring brave and strong efforts towards monogamy on his part, undertaken almost as a task because he loved her and wanted to please her, a knight jousting for his beloved. This perfectly sincere conversion to romantic and sexual chastity, which he would promote with the unattractive smugness of the newly self-righteous, somehow never did last long, at least not in his relations with me.

Years later, when all of this seemed old, Gerald explained that he'd always loved me, had always been deeply involved with me, but "didn't want to live with me." Despite that seemingly magical combination of sexual and other kinds of enjoyment, I was never to him the romantic One who was right for forming the domestic couple. For the first time in my life, I had to face this down, squeezed between my yearning to be the sole care and center of a man's attention, which is to say (for a heterosexual woman of my upbringing) to *be normal*, and my intense desire to enjoy this particular man I loved, who challenged that One-and-Only idea, even while chasing it himself. It's odd to think that if I hadn't been rejected, there would have been no need to think about this question.

Romance, read mostly by women, positions you as an owner with an investment in your property, simply because you are the One with the unique ability to gratify the hero's desires, to fill every corner of his life so there are no pockets of desire or need that are not stuffed with… yes, you.

"Well, I would never put myself in that position," sniffed someone to me once about being a mistress, even a loved mistress, "because you'd never be *special.*" The raw pragmatism of that statement makes traditional sexual morality look noble by comparison. It suggests that monogamy is not based on some higher ideal of chastity or fidelity, however questionable; it's all about maintaining a style of living, a position that conveniently places you at the center. Wasn't that the advantage in being the wife in traditional society, the honor of being chosen for those special rights and privileges as payback for the husband's supremacy?

The very premise seems bankrupt to me: the wife is told she is *a priori* "special" by virtue of her distinguished social, legal, and sexual role, but why is anyone publicly fastened together with someone else in a couple necessarily elevated or more valued by a spouse? Of course we're trained to believe this is the way it will be, rehearsed again and again in music, in novels that bring moisture to your cheeks, in images of radiant windblown couples on beaches posted everywhere, and in all the romantic performances on screens or in wedding toasts to your relatives and friends. That was my sole template for comparison when I brooded over whether the drama of my relations with Gerald was going in the *right direction*, an arrow pointed to a domestic heaven.

Gossip about celebrities or real-life acquaintances and their cheating permits the enjoyable violation of a supposedly immutable given, the rightful romantic status of the One. Sexual and romantic gossip is the trading of stories in which the complacent romantic narrative is upended by our real-life knowledge of the shadow sexual economy. From Hollywood and the British royal family to your neighbors and friends, there are so many tales of scandal, betrayal of commitments, sudden changes of heart, indecency public and private, and (best of all) news of the infidelity of others, all of these grass-lawn common, that you'd think we'd be aware that the forever-monogamous romantic ideal isn't really a given at all.

Romance

I'd been a reader of fictional romances, and the one I wrote myself remains still washed up in some dark hole in my desk. Yet in the years after I fell in love, I could no longer enjoy reading romantic fiction. The romances that once showed me what I longed for now looked like mimed gestures, a hopeful move toward perfection. Like all perfection, romantic fiction is brittle and thin compared to life itself, missing all the complexity, ambiguity, and shades of real feeling. I suppose that's the point – not all those feelings and actions are pretty ones. We don't like to examine these unless they are rectifiable mistakes, the roadblock to the proper resolution we trust will appear in its time. These don't go with a happy ending.

While the genres of mystery, spies, or crime fiction

imply origin and explanation, romance is often represented as *just* happening. Or conversely, the technocratic version teaches you how to make it *just happen*: the pastor who supplies wisdom on the American edition of the reality show *Married at First Sight* likes to say that "love is a choice." Is desire too a choice? Aren't the two intertwined? Whichever of these contradictory ideas you espouse, finding the "right" one is treated as transformative, like coming into money.

When actual people, fundamentally unknowable to each other, operate in a real world, which is to say a world of infinite density, the ways they behave are not really foreseeable, or even explicable. A recent long-term study of tens of thousands of romantic couples concluded that marital happiness is just not predictable. The traits of a romantic hero and heroine, on the other hand, form a short list, nameable, sortable, and not least, tellable (and often all very much alike). In reality, you'd be hard pressed to find a short list of adjectives that gives you even a small sense of what one actual person is. Imagine how unlikely universal truisms are about two lovers, then, never mind a triangle, each with their convoluted histories and incoherent inner lives, always responding to their changing and changeable contexts, including the hidden agendas and secrets in their relations with each other.

Genres resolve this problem because they are labels, just as titles in relationships are labels too; the title is the sanction for what we feel entitled *to*. In fiction, we rely on the hidden code of genres to organize how to think about them, because knowing what to expect imparts a kind of comfort even in suspense, tragedy, or horror. The stories we tell ourselves about our real experiences are similarly sorted into genres: this *funny* thing happened, I was the *victim* of this natural event or that rotten individual, here's how I survived/succeeded/triumphed, at last I'm *rewarded* for my hard work, yes, that's a tragedy but it was *meant to be*.

Romance is a genre of entitlement: I was not a romantic heroine, for example, because I wasn't a single lady in love with a so-called "available" man, and he with me. Besides the proper hero, I also lacked a heroine's long, flowing hair, her firm, creamy bosoms, unwrinkled skin, and unflagging virtue. The typical American romantic heroine tends to come in two sorts: either Dark, Wild, Exotic Beauty, or Very Pretty, Well-dressed, White, Middle-Class, Sweet Girl Next Door. I was neither of these types. My husband used to call me an Upper West Side shlump, at first affectionately, later in denigrating contrast to the first girlfriend who followed me. This was a lipstick-and-heels kind of gal, his ideal of femininity. (If this were a movie, she'd be blonde, large-breasted, and talk in a silly voice. She wasn't blonde, and I don't remember the rest.) Why didn't I wear makeup and high heels too, why hadn't I tried to be sexier?, he'd lamented while packing up to leave our home for good. Frank wanted glam, but it was too late for me to become something else, especially since I had no desire to.

Frank's youngish girlfriend probably had excellent lingerie, not like my underwear, bought in plastic-wrapped packages of three, or a warm nightgown with penguins on it. (I don't mean to reduce this woman to her glam make-up and clothes. Of course there was a great deal more to her and to their year-long relationship than that. And all of that "great deal more," given that he wanted her to be my children's future stepmother, alarmed me no end.)

We know that men tend to marry sooner than women do after divorce, and at a higher rate. There are probably multiple reasons for this, but I can't help wondering if men are more afraid of being alone and therefore less discriminating about who will be taking care of them. Interestingly, the woman Frank ended up marrying, with lightning speed after shedding this first one, was more in my own style than Ms. Lipstick-and-Heels. His second wife may or may not wear flannel nighties with birds on them, but we're more like each other than we are like Ms. Lipstick-and-Heels. This too makes my point; in so much romantic fiction, if the beloved starts out as wild or exotic, he or she must repudiate this identity and assimilate into their domesticated function by the end of the story (which is to say, when the true commitment is made). Even in the 2015 comedy *Trainwreck*, much praised as a feminist movie, the heroine enacts the ritual conversion from her initial role as Wild Girl, who had meaningless sex, to prepare herself for the proper domesticated role in romance with a Nice Guy. That conversion constitutes the happy ending.

In my real life, the "pussies," as my husband had called women whose attractiveness was sexual, were trumped by the "creature comforts" provided by the wife… me. When I was no longer a creature that provided comfort, he at first briefly preferred the pussycat, then came home to comfort at a different fireside. If this all seems peculiar to me, it's because I'm a woman who's been seen as both a comfy old towel *and* a feline at the same time, as many women are.

Because heterosexual romance is, or at least has been since Jane Austen, a woman's genre, written mostly by and for women, the conventional romantic hero may or may not have those warrior traits traditionally representing the masculine – muscular, bold, confident, fearless, protective – but above all he exists specifically to be there *for her*, focused only and all the time on the heroine, adoring her, devoted to her, making her feel, as a pop song says, that she is the "only girl in the world," because she *is*, in fact, the only girl of any substance in this fictional romantic world. "Lovers are obedient men, cheerfully willing to do whatever the beloved, who holds the entire heart, desires…", says Chrétien de Troyes, writing in the twelfth century. The fantasy of the beloved woman as the perfect object of her beloved's desire is still the center of gravity of romance as we've understood it since the Middle Ages.

In the genre of romance, being elevated by another is a sign of one's power and preeminence. The heroine's superiority in a love story is the fictional reason she is adored, and conversely, the hero's adoration is a sign to the reader of the heroine's (and perhaps the reader's) superiority. Within this system, the male worship of the heroine in a heterosexual romantic story appears to raise women's value, regardless of their social and economic stature. By feeding a woman's craving for a greater sense of self-worth, this marker of her high valuation counters women's anxieties about their real power in the world. Whatever the reality of women's lives, the romantic code assures her that she can safely assume she is protected and treated well when she is loved.

In popular romance, there may be another woman who is a rival, or a clingy previous girlfriend, to provide dramatic tension (as though we don't know how *that* will turn out), or perhaps another female character is sometimes a warm or tart-tongued best friend, but no other woman can come close to the worth of the heroine herself.

The other side of that coin is the villainous male rival for the heroine's affections. The rival may be pleasant but a bore (the hero is assumed to be deep, usually with little evidence), or he may be promiscuous, which signals that he does not really love the heroine or anyone, because romantic love by nature must always have an utterly singular focus. This character is A Rat, as he's often called in pop culture, who creeps around the heroine's psychic landscape, heartlessly infecting innocent women with his emotionless sexuality. The opposition of heart and heartlessness is the coin of the romantic realm: a man is either Good Hero or a Rat, without space in between. Occasionally the hero gets to punch out the Rat, which is just as rewarding for the female audience as for the fictional hero himself (the heroine is distressed by the violence, but sees how necessary it was).

When the heroine is drawn without the artistry of great writers, we're more often shown that her character is adored than shown *why* she is. We know why Darcy loves Elizabeth because we get to hear what Elizabeth says; who wouldn't want to be always in the company of someone who delightfully demonstrates her wit and intelligence with clever observations for pages on end? I would marry her too. But in far less capable hands, we know the heroine is superior only because of the strong effect she has on her lover. In other words, she's supremely worthy solely because the hero loves her, not the other way around, and certainly not because she exhibits exceptional cleverness or a fascinating personality, much less has interesting thoughts. This shorthand – he loves her, so she must be wonderful – feeds the reader's hope that she, like the heroine, has earned romantic love by her secret superiority, which has not yet been properly noticed or appreciated (least of all by the heroine herself, because she's too modest). It certainly fed mine.

When I first cast Gerald as my romantic hero, I was primed for him to detect that well-concealed worth that distinguished me from all others he'd known. This was founded on the fact that he appeared so obviously smitten by me. In fictional romance, the moment the hero is smitten, he's caught for life, with his gaze so riveted on the heroine that he can't turn away even if he wants to (he often fights it, for reasons of his own which will be overcome, and rather quickly if the novel is short). If he'd been involved with a woman before, she now means nothing at all, just as Romeo's love for Rosaline vanishes as soon as he casts his eye on Juliet ("Did my heart love till now?"). Whether or not the hero tries to distance, dominate, or even demean our heroine, she has permanently attached him with her sexual, but more importantly, emotional power. (Of course it's not *just* sex, or it would not be a romance.) He may flounder and protest, but she wins in the end – though it's clear he's not a loser, since he's been gifted with *her*, the uniquely valuable prize that every romantic heroine is.

Though rattled that Gerald was not behaving like a romantic hero, I was amazed to realize that I didn't like him any less for it, because this unrepentant libertine was still the same person I'd loved before. It was thought-provoking, even mind-spinning, after being a secret romantic and having read romantic fiction since adolescence, to see that the True Romantic Hero could also be the Villainous Rat at the same time, something like being told that Abraham Lincoln was really a Nazi.

The discovery of my lover's multiple affairs, even after meeting extremely-worthy me, was surely the point in a fictional romance at which I'd have broken off the affair with him, the Rat, only to find the True Hero waiting to take up the baton (and bring home the bacon). And in fact some accused me of not recognizing the presence of an unknown True Hero probably waiting just off-stage, whose eminently decent and truly romantic love (i.e., for me alone) would protect me from all such villains in a reliably secured future. If I did not move quickly, they said, I was going to miss out on this super-desirable creature expressly because I didn't break it off with the Rat! Or if I was going to be so pig-headed and blind as to continue to desire the Rat, I should at least hold out for more from him, bargain for his conversion, make a good deal for myself. You can learn from fiction exactly what to do in this case, namely serve up the classic ultimatum: If you don't leave her/stop seeing others/make me your One and Only/commit to me forever – you're toast and I'm outta here! Romantic heroines in movies have been doing this forever, always to great effect. The hero, obviously not a born Rat, immediately quits his unbecoming ways and never looks back – or around – again.

But I just didn't *want* to be outta there, not when it was that good, and I doubt the ultimatum would have altered Gerald or our relations much in the end: he liked me, he loved me in some way that was not what I'd hoped for, there was no end to how much he desired me, but it came down to this: there was something about the idea of me as a domestic partner that didn't move him. He was both the irresistible force *and* the immovable object. And the deeper truth was that I didn't want to transform or redeem him; I liked him as he was, and still do.

It would be easy to fictionalize Gerald as a one-dimensional pathological maniac, whereas in real life he's an unusually interesting person with more than usual contradictory feelings and desires. Yes, when I met him and for a long time after, he had relationships with the many women who were attracted to him. In fact I was drawn to his boundless sexual energy and admired the skilled way he went about pursuing what he wanted, which at the time I couldn't bring myself to do.

But unfortunately, for both him and the few monogamous women he'd selected as the One and Only, he equally wanted to live with a long-term partner, which in our culture inevitably is assumed to define the "romantic." My guess is that he longed for the normalcy conferred by the legitimating story of "real" romance. This didn't mean he wanted a woman who wasn't his equal, or one who confined herself to the domestic space – to the contrary, his choices of partners were accomplished and high-powered, more so than I am or was. But that very modern idea of equality in domestic work and ambition between the sexes lived uneasily alongside the Victorian idea of the home whose symbol was the gently glowing Hearth: the traditional center of tranquility, warmth, and steady, low-key affection, the very opposite of intense sexuality or unruly passion.

Gerald was therefore only attracted romantically to a certain kind of woman for that domestic role, someone as highly educated and culturally sophisticated as he was, yet who somehow also possessed a June Allyson heart – an actress he once told me jokingly was his feminine ideal. (I discovered this when I happened to wear a fifties-like shirtwaist dress once, and he couldn't keep his hands off me.) In other words, romance for him was exactly the homey relationship with the One and Only, the hallmark of monogamy that his behavior perversely belied.

The result was that he never seemed to desire a "serious" relationship with anyone who did not demand exclusivity and the public imprimatur of couplehood. For whatever reason – our consuming sexual relationship? My high-maintenance emotionality? My three children, including a surly teenager at the time? or perhaps the unlikelihood that I'd be half of a power couple? – I was not marked in his psyche for the domestic partner role. It's not that I hadn't known this all along, but the idea had resided in some lint-filled pocket of my mind, overwhelmed by the desire I had for him.

I may be alone in this understanding, but what I saw was an exceptional man who at heart was a tormented sentimentalist. He was no Hugh Hefner: he never lived alone and dated many women, as you'd think he'd want to do and could have done with ease. It wasn't a matter of setting up a harem or accumulating "pussies," in the sense my husband meant that word.

But then, even Hugh Hefner married more than once. People like their domestic comforts.

Affairs may be more an indicator of the ability to compartmentalize than a barometer of happiness in a marriage. Gerald's pleasures were well compartmentalized, but anxiety about his secret life was a price he paid for them. "What does your shrink say?" I inquired once. "Oh, I don't tell him everything," Gerald smiled. And why not? "Because it's none of his business," said Gerald.

How tremendously envious I was of Gerald's seeming aptitude at making many women love him when and how he wanted them to, a skill I clearly did not have and is not teachable. As for me, I stumbled along, with no real idea what to do. I just knew that I wasn't going to give up easily, not for my own imperiled virtue, not even for the hypothetical rescuing figure of True Love (just as sexy and romantic, yet also steadfast and loyal, certainly not a Rat), allegedly hovering, undiscovered, nearby.

One day I was trying, as usual, to get Gerald to spend more time with me, and wheedled, "Let's meet up for a short time! C'mon, I don't need a lot… I'm a cheap date."

"Well, you shouldn't be," said Gerald. That stopped me in my tracks. He'd cut through to what it really was: my attempt to diminish what I wanted, in anticipation that I could never have it.

This was something else that cemented me to Gerald: I could talk to him in a particular way that I had not been able to with anyone else. Whether or not he could detect his own bull, he was my bomb sniffer; he simply had a knack for uncovering others' guile, agendas, and games. How ironic that this master deceiver (so good at it that he'd never been caught by any of the women in his life while he was with them) was the most honest person I knew in an entirely different sense. It cast a new light for me on what I meant when I thought about truthfulness – both Truth in the abstract, my first principle from adolescence on, and the neglected truth of my own life in particular.

Love is a way to begin to discover ourselves, but it's only a beginning.

Chapter Six
Wives And Mistresses

> Woman's infidelities...are natural, those of a man proceed from his duplicity and his viciousness; a healthy and intelligent woman will hence spurn no occasion to be unfaithful.
> – Marquis de Sade, *Juliette,* 1797

> "The cases are different," he replied, "It's a woman's nature to be constant, to love one and one only, blindly, tenderly, and forever – Bless them, dear creatures!"
> – Anne Brontë, *The Tenant of Wildfell Hall*, 1848

I, the mistress, am the Other to you, the married woman. You, the Wife, are the Other to me. If our roles should be reversed with time, the same holds true. We are all the Other Woman now.

While we were still married, and I was spinning in frantic circles, not to say running around, my husband was not standing still. He'd declared he wasn't going to wait for me to decide to stay with him, and with stupefying speed had acquired a younger girlfriend weeks after my unfortunate confession. I'd done it, why shouldn't he? Did I think he was going to be my safety net?

It was that girlfriend, Ms. Lipstick-and-Heels, who called me one evening after Frank and I separated, to reveal that he'd had numerous affairs all during our marriage, not just with her. She gave me this golden information, she said, because she wanted me to know she hadn't "busted up our marriage," though I'd thought no such thing. To her annoyance, I expressed some doubt about this account of Frank's many infidelities, since I knew from unhappy experience that this girlfriend was given to highly dramatic, not necessarily accurate declarations, and Frank himself had a tendency to boast. Ever considerate, she then passed on to me the name and phone number of one of his mistresses so I could confirm her story.

At first I simply stared at the unfamiliar name and the phone number I'd scribbled next to it, unsure what to do. For one thing, calling my husband's former mistress was about as vulgar and crass as you could get. On the other hand, it seemed a shame to pass up this singular opportunity to learn some part of the shadow story of my husband's life. And so, heart pulsing nervously, I called. The middle-aged woman who answered was understandably wary of talking when I identified myself as her former lover's wife. But when I told her the marriage was over and she saw I was not coming after her, no metaphorical or literal dagger in hand, she did in fact acknowledge her affair with Frank. This was one of the strangest conversations I've ever had, but to her credit, it was conducted with a surprising level of dignity and mutual respect.

After this peculiar conversation, I, as wife, had an unfamiliar sense of peace, of power, that came from possessing truth I did not have before: that satisfaction when the larger pattern of the jigsaw takes shape at last, and each piece takes on its proper significance. I was now no longer only the Mistress who knew what the Wife didn't; I now occupied, at the same time, the space of the Wife who knew what the husband had hidden. There I was, standing with one foot in each side's shoe, you might say.

In movies and fiction, when a wife is confronted with a mistress, there's either a catfight, some silly act of retribution (if it's a comedy), or a scene of outrage and revenge (if a drama). Either way, there's nearly always hatred, two women fighting for their male property, one morally and legally entitled to it, the other not. They are the legitimated and the illegitimate, the insider and the outsider, an absolute binary, like the rightful heir and the bastard. Because the husband has betrayed her, the heroic wife is presumed to own the right to do just about anything to the mistress, while the devilish mistress, who has no rights at all, is nevertheless ready to do anything to get rid of the wife.

I probably would have been furious at Frank, as wives are expected to be, if I'd known the truth a year earlier. But now that outrage would be vanity only, since I was both the betrayed *and* the betraying. Instead, I deeply wished I'd known, not necessarily about my husband's affairs, or who the women were, but why he felt impelled to have them. It seems to me that in long-term relationships, facts are less important than knowing what the other feels behind the safety of commitment. What was Frank thinking about me, about us, all those times? Was he unhappy in ways I hadn't known? What he never did reveal could have been the truth that cracked the egg, broken open the hard protective shell around our marriage. Whatever we choose to do about it, no matter that it makes us very unhappy, there's a peculiar value to knowing the deepest truths that goes beyond the value of mere happiness.

After Frank and I separated, when he thought he'd instantly found love with Lipstick-and-Heels, Frank mused to me one day about her when he came to pick up some belongings, "We kiss a lot, and when we kiss, it goes on and on. How come you and I never kissed like that?" Strange as this observation was, considering the circumstances, his uncharacteristic wistful tone was so unusual that it saddened me, especially because I had longed for those kisses. There seemed no point in reminding him that he'd been the one who didn't like to kiss, which is to say, to kiss me.

When I saw Frank after the phone conversation with his former lover, I had to ask why he'd been so morally indignant about my one affair when he seemed to have had a number of his own, a contradiction that left me equally dumbfounded and curious. His answer left me no less bewildered because I believed it was sincere: he was perfectly right to be both outraged and wounded, he said, because *his* multiple affairs were purely sexual, whereas my one affair involved *love*, the ultimate betrayal. He explained that sex-only affairs (his) don't threaten the family if concealed; sex with emotional involvement (that would be mine) destroys it. I see his reasoning, self-interested though it was: in the end the principle is to preserve the family at all costs, a view of sexuality that nicely harks back to the Old Testament, with its handmaidens. The quality of a particular marriage and family or extramarital relationship don't come into it; it's the principle itself that counts.

Frank's hierarchy of adultery, agreeably sorted into bad and unforgivable (me) and perfectly understandable (him), made me think about the general tendency to interpret what we do as the standard of what others should do. And here I'd thought of my own transgression as the more forgivable, precisely because I knew I would never have pursued an affair *unless* driven by intense romantic love. I did it for love, not casual sex! – in other words, the exact opposite of his formulation, a reversal of hierarchies. We'd each been equally confident of our own superior justification, enabling both of us to come out looking swell to our imagined audience. There's no limit to the ways the mind can come up with self-serve.

I still don't know what the former mistress I called looked like, what she had or did that attracted him, what she wished from my husband, whether she pursued or was pursued, if she loved him or was simply titillated by his attention, if the sex was terrific or just passable, whether the ending had been offhand or seemed tragic to her. Did she wave a cheerful or wry goodbye when it was over? Did she write my husband, her lover, a bitter letter, had she made fun of him afterward, or wept on a sofa for days? None of it seemed more important than that she was a woman like me, possibly just as muddled about what she wanted and what was really going on, playing out a role with a kind of script that predated and shaped her choices. We were all floundering in the same sea together, swimming hard in circles to persuade ourselves we were going somewhere, now this way, now that. For that particular specimen of husband, the Wife is one of those ways to go forward, the Mistress is *the Other.*

In the brief talk Frank and I had about his affairs while we were married, he revealed that one of these took place while I was pregnant with our second child, a pregnancy we'd planned together. What was he thinking during this time? I can't imagine it, and he wasn't about to go into it in our ten-minute conversation in the street (or ever). But it must have to do with the dissociation into types of women that men are taught: the legitimate domestic partner and the forbidden sexual one.

I was enlightened, saddened and ruefully interested in all this, to the point that I never saw the subject in the same way again. But I was not angry at my ex-husband or the mistress I spoke to, or any of the other women he may or may not have been involved with, and contrary to popular thinking, I had shockingly little desire to harm or shame them. Unlike in fiction, I didn't feel the world and the woman (the pussy, the mistress) owed some heavy debt to me, the supposed casualty of infidelity. This certainly wasn't a simple story of innocence and oppression, a moral tale of evil (a Rat) versus helpless virtue (the Good Woman). We were, all of us – husband, wife, lovers – actors in the same confused set of conflicting assumptions, unmet desires and expectations, and, I would say, rather touching hopes.

Other Women

Mistresses often envy that the Wife is the hub of the family home ("She is solid," wrote the poet Anne Sexton, "as real as a cast-iron pot"), with the prestige of a legitimated role. Yet while in theory the wife has the special rights, privileges, and dignity of a legal fixture, in reality a wife may be taken for granted and given little respect.

Whether or not the mistress is younger or prettier than the wife (many are not; I never was), a would-be mistress may first be seduced by the idea of being the sexy, desired one – glad recipient of extra attention the wife is not receiving, in spite of the *special* status of the wife mentioned by my sniffing friend who said she'd never have an affair because she wouldn't be "special." In fact, the husband may experience the mistress as *very* special, leading to her demonization as the object of hatred and envy by the wife, and by women in general.

The idea of the mistress disrupts the necessary complacency that still surrounds marriage as a system. Yet while wives, like children, are idealized in the media (Family is all that matters in the end!), popular culture is as full of wives who boss, nag and criticize as it is mistresses who are cursed as brazen slatterns. The wife is honored by her husband's (presumed) lifelong commitment, but she could just as easily be the familiar worn penny and the mistress the secret stash, a golden coin to be fondled in the husband's pocket when no one is looking. Which, then, is the better, more desirable role: to be elevated by society yet personally treated as a tiresome ball-and-chain, or to be a figure of strong desire, yet always on the shaky margin of the central relationship, of whatever quality?

We don't usually ask that question, because the answer seems so obvious: since the whole point of marriage is that it's designed to last, like a good car, I would guess most men in a triangle would say their spouse is the "important" one. After all, leaving a marriage, especially one that's long-term, is a personal revolution in a way of living, and it takes outsized motivation to risk changing one's whole life without knowing the outcome. This is not as flattering to the spouse as it may first appear, especially if children are involved in the motivation for staying.

Speaking from my own experience, it's not necessarily all about the individuals. Role and function determine significance just as much as the individual, and in this case they occupy two completely different locations on the emotional map: let's say Paris and your home town. You like both in different ways, of course, which is why you might visit Paris but live at home. Just to confuse matters, our culture insists that when you marry for love, you've made the move – Paris is your new home.

How curious, then, are those not infrequent cases when the mistress becomes the wife eventually, and leap-frogs from one area of the mental topography to the other? What a shocking change of value that must be, from sleazy-prohibited to ennobled-legitimate!

Yet women, even those mistresses who succeed in gaining proprietary rights to the man, often don't empathize with the position of other women; the Other Woman remains Other to the wife, and vice versa. Each sees the other as a despised competitor for territory, a cunning she-wolf who plays at being a human being, but isn't one. There was another strange moment in my life when a particular woman, who had imagined herself the One and Only, asked to talk with me, the Other Woman, after her public relationship with Gerald had ended, a bookend to my conversation with my husband's former mistress. I agreed because I could sympathize with a drive to know the truth. Even more, I naively believed we were going to transcend the given roles of innocent womanhood, victimized by adultery, facing off against her opposite number, Perpetrator of Illegitimate Carnality. My hope was that this odd occasion would allow us, with curiosity and even a degree of generosity for once, an unusual view into each other's separate yet intertwined experiences.

I actually thought we'd have a great deal to say to each other, to come to understand each other: what was it like for you, what was it like to be me? What has been going on here that's been unknown to each of us until now, and why? I saw myself as speaking truth, frank and sincere, she saw herself as brilliant at being justifiably devious. After an interesting beginning, here's where it went: straight to the plot of all those silly movies where the wronged wife gets revenge for stolen property, in this case publishing writing designed to humiliate me. It was the literary version of *The Real Housewives*. As half of one of Gerald's power couples, this girlfriend had the power to do it, as I did not. I'm sure it never occurred to her not to, just as a husband in some cultures has historically been allowed to assault or kill his wife's lover with impunity.

Think what you might learn about yourself, your mate, the world, by allowing truth to emerge, even painful truth, without judgment. Yet the simple joys of injured innocence, and if possible, nasty retaliation, are so much easier on your feelings. And there's little out there in culture and media, particularly popular culture, to induce that kind of opening. The romantic template is too rigid to allow for it.

As a wife, I'd encountered the mistress; as a mistress, I've faced The One and (supposed) Only. Wife and mistress are defined as existing each at the expense of the other, day and night, up and down, an eternal conceptual zero-sum game. The idea that we're natural enemies casts us as two moons who circle the same male planet in opposing directions, never in the same place at once.

After this I had a sense of double vision, that I had been, and anyone could easily be, on either side of the same street. That extended to the way I was seen by these two men, husband and lover, in these very different roles. Frank was turned off by a wife who seemed to him pathetically incompetent, whiny, needy, sexually boring; Gerald, my lover, was attracted to a mistress he viewed as exuberant, warm, playful, sexually alluring. No doubt I behaved somewhat differently with each of them, but I was the same woman. That was me in those funhouse mirrors.

Sex

It was around this time that Gerald declared one day that I was a "genius of sex," to my great amusement. I mention this, not to boast, or only partly to boast, but mainly to make a point. Because to my astonishment, shortly before this declaration, my husband had specifically accused me, post-separation and perhaps not without a motive of justification, if not retribution, of being sexually "frigid." I'm quite sure I was neither, in reality.

I had not heard that I was frigid before, but I don't think my husband said it only to wound me; however anachronistically phrased, it meant something to him that he had no other words for. And it's true that with my lover, I felt a certain way about my body and his that

I never had with anyone, an experience I'm sure is not uncommon. You might say having a lover brought out this aspect of myself. But what is an aspect of oneself, especially a *buried* aspect? Is it a thing you say yes or no to? Does it live starving underground, or bloom unnoticed by the side of a road? Is it the real you, in a coffin? Whatever it was, something in me rose up from its long sleep and began to speak like an infant learning a language. That "aspect of myself" stepped forward, the victim of an accident learning to walk again, at first hesitant and awkward, later more confident, stronger.

On one hand I'd thought of myself as a respectable professional, a devoutly committed and monogamous wife, the conscientious and loving mother of my husband's children, someone you could take out socially and be very sure she would not rip off her clothes, or throw a drink. On the other hand, there were these obscured desires and those unspoken fantasies that never emerged in marriage. What did one have to do with the other, say to each other, which was real? Of course we're all of them at once; all the complicated disguises we wear to hide from ourselves are just as much us as the outward-facing. No one sees them in their entirety. It's one terrific and sometimes terrifying bundle.

We say people change, or that they never really change, but maybe that's the wrong way to put it. We are the same person all our lives, and yet also not quite the same with different people: different with each of our children, different with each of our parents, each of our friends, and so on. Then why should it be surprising that you are different with different lovers or spouses, when they are different themselves and therefore have a different dynamic with you?

I'd been with my husband since we were little more than children, spent nearly every day with him for twenty-four years, first as students and then grown-ups, in dark moods and light moods, for richer and (usually) poorer, in good health and bad, without and then with children, and yet it seemed when *one* circumstance changed, I suddenly felt unknown by him and discovered he was not much known by me either.

Naturally I remember the "genius of sex" remark with diamond-cut clarity because it was flattering, all the more because I'd been with very few men at the time and therefore not what you'd call sexually experienced – certainly not compared to Gerald himself, who'd dallied with half the well-educated female population of these United States. But after that offhand observation, this genius had her share of bad-to-awful sex.

I don't believe the quality of my relationship with Gerald had anything at all to do with my degree of sexual competence or his plentiful experience in the field. For me intense pleasure comes from intense mutual desire, not from having sexy tricks up your sleeve; I'm sure I couldn't have competed with any professional in the tricks department. I just did what I felt like, because for the first time in my life, putting my own pleasure first was equally the pleasure of the man I was making love with, as well as the other way around. There's a four-line poem by William Blake I love:

What is it men in women do require?
The lineaments of Gratified Desire.
What is it women do in men require?
The lineaments of Gratified Desire.

When that equality of desire is there, you don't need a manual and there are no false steps. How many flannel-nightgowned women are geniuses of sex in the right circumstances, which they may never experience?

I'm sure Gerald had been with better-looking women. But this was completely unlike anything that came before: a worship of pleasure, for a few minutes or for hours, a caress not overtly sexual, or any whim we felt in the moment. Human nature, said John Stuart Mill, "is not a *machine* to be built after a model, and set to do exactly the work prescribed for it, but a tree, which requires to grow and develop itself on all sides, according to the tendency of the inward forces which make it a living thing." Before Gerald, before marriage and during it, I viewed sex, one root of human nature, as an efficient instrument whose goal was completing the mechanical cycle of arousal and release. But the body, like human nature, is not a well-oiled machine, after all.

In modern culture there is a great deal of reference to sexual or romantic "chemistry." What is that? You could say it's just a mutual and equal attraction, but I think it's also that each one knows how to please and gratify the other in a way that feels natural and effortless. Or at least the effort itself is a great mutual pleasure.

Of course, in my reading from adolescence to middle age, I'd come across many sexy scenes, from gorgeous sex with The Forever One in modern romance novels to equally improbable pornography, both made torrid by close descriptions of the superb body parts of luscious women, steel-bodied men, the perfection of the body. What could be better? Here's what was better: the imperfection of passionate lovemaking. By comparison, the performance of sex in print or on a screen is like watching two puppets put through their paces. Passion can't be extruded from a machine like a 3D copy. The occasional absurdity or awkwardness or misstep is part of its unpredictability, which is to say its humanity. Perfection is, paradoxically, inferior.

In *Fifty Shades of Grey*, our virginal heroine has never so much as touched herself "down there" (a direct quote) by age twenty-two, yet her first time in bed with her true love is so fantastic that she has orgasm after orgasm (as a scholar, I felt compelled to count: five orgasms before she leaves the bed). I will leave the plausibility of this to you. But then, your definition of terrific sex may not be mine; my own idea of it when I was fifteen, cobbled from forbidden books like *Peyton Place*, was not at all what it was at thirty, when, as a wife, it was a question of working to achieve (that word says it all) orgasm at the appropriate time and feeling damaged if it didn't "work." And today my idea of sexuality is just as far from that view at age thirty as age thirty was from fifteen. Transcendent sex can't be submitted to a test or a model: if you think you're having it, you are.

Of course, it must be admitted that an affair can confer a certain juiciness, especially if romantic love is the context. Oh, the places I've been, the scenes I've seen! What affair doesn't have twists of insanity, of secular divinity and blundering hilarity? If not, it might be more like exercising at the gym, or closer to a facsimile of marriage than what we think of as an affair. One of my aunts, hurried by her father when young into marrying a good match she barely knew, produced the obligatory son, then began an affair with a lover, also married, lasting many decades. Finally, when they were all nearing old age, my aunt's husband died, followed by the lover's wife. My aunt's lover then eagerly asked to marry her, or at least live with her; she politely refused to do either. Apparently she'd had enough of marriage, and preferred the facsimile to the real thing. (Of course, this story was passed down by Betty.)

And More Sex

Though I was mad for Gerald, I wasn't about to devote myself singly to a man who pursued other women besides me *and* his One-and-Only. I may have been embarrassingly naive at the start, but I learned fast. That is, I did not sit in the corner pining for him – or rather, I pined, but not in the corner – more while working the room. I'd discovered my other hobby besides love, an interesting and occasionally delightful one: casual, unromantic sex.

For the first years after Frank and I separated, even at the height of the fearsome, panic-fueled scramble to get tenure, I was very busy, though not nearly as busy as my current students seem to be in the age of Tinder and the like. As soon as I understood that I wasn't a candidate for a serious relationship with Gerald, I felt a wildness that I hadn't known even when I was young. This is not unusual for someone newly single after a long-lasting marriage, if there isn't an instant replacement. But it also came from recognizing for the first time, through Gerald, that I, classic middle-aged shlump, as my husband had called me, could actually be desired, even strongly desired.

Most of these new sexual experiences were completely unemotional, and one or two were very exciting sexually.

There was a man whose name I don't remember, if I ever knew it, on an overnight train (I think of him, with the simplicity of the inexperienced, as The Man on the Train); there was an enjoyable affair with a married colleague that took place reliably every week, same day and time, like the clockwork of much marital sex; and there was a delicious flirtation with the handsomest man I'd ever known, which culminated in the most disappointing sex I'd ever known, an instructive gap between anticipation and consummation. (So much for the lust we feel for beauties, including professional beauties.) If being in love is a potent aphrodisiac, *not* being in love with someone you are in bed with, I found, can allow for a very different sort of sexuality, enjoyable in another way than sex with someone you adore. Or it can be an affliction. I found that out too.

The Man-on-the-Train-to-Chicago (his full name) was good-looking enough that I covertly switched seats to be next to him. Some agreeable social chat as the hours went by between New York and Illinois revealed that he was a married businessman, far from his home in Indonesia. I must have been flirtatious, because as the lights were dimmed for the night somewhere in Ohio, he made his move. Sadly, those were hard financial times after the divorce and I couldn't afford a sleeper compartment. But from the quality of the superb sexual canoodling that followed all night, I was confident he would have made that compartment worthwhile. At Chicago in early morning, we said a warm goodbye and I disembarked, bleary from lack of sleep, to visit relatives, while he, I think reluctantly, continued to California, to do whatever foreign businessmen do in California.

On the other hand, my affair with the slightly

younger, long-married man I'll call Hugo, who met me weekly over the course of a year, was a reliable, carefully timed hour of pleasant, if mostly by-the-numbers sort of sex. This was not so much about the gratification of strong desire, to me at least, as a kind of comfort, a little bonbon I could count on weekly (same day and hour, like a therapy session), at a time when my life was chaotic and uncertain. In other words, the elements that made our meetings as ritualized as married life, that is, orchestrated timing and repetitive sexual movements – the very opposite of the spontaneous joy I had with Gerald – was exactly what I liked about my relations with this lover.

Hugo and I got along well, probably because we wanted from each other only what we were already giving and getting. But once when he mentioned in passing (not convincingly) that we loved each other, as though that followed from what we were doing, I found myself responding, "No, Hugo, we really don't." He didn't argue the point. Perhaps he was relieved. And I was right: he was a one-man woman with the wrong women (his wife, notably, and me), and not long after, he wound up with the right one. That is, Hugo left his wife, then the Right One also left her husband, after much agonizing, and as far as I can tell from Twitter, the new couple still seem happy today, twenty-odd years later. (So much for the truism, comforting to moralists, that a man never winds up with the woman he leaves his wife for.) I think Hugo's remark about our supposed love came from his desire to believe he wasn't just having sex for its own sake; contrary to stereotype, some men can be uncomfortable with that idea as well as women. But because this wasn't an emotional affair, we were able to part cheerfully when the time came, and with good will.

Then too, in my years-long flirtation with absurdly handsome Isaac, a colleague whom my dear gay friend Gene and I secretly called The Beauty, I discovered that I could have degrees of romantic feeling, in contrast to the conventional idea that romantic love is a toggle switch – you're either in love or you're not. I had a mild romantic attraction to Isaac, based almost entirely on his superior good looks and a certain soft charm he exuded like masculine cologne. Eventually, after finally sleeping with him, I found that I liked to tease and flirt with him much more than I enjoyed being intimate with him as either companion or lover. Two years of flirtation and hot fantasy ended after two afternoons of actual sex. Romance, it seems, has as many forms and levels of desire as sex itself.

An outstanding subject of my grand sexual experiment was John, introduced by a mutual acquaintance. John was single, age-appropriate, fiscally responsible, a decent person, extraordinarily unattractive and extremely dull. I dated him for a while because he was one of the few men I'd met who were "available," though I knew immediately he wasn't that True Love, patiently waiting all along for the golden moment when I came around to behaving in a wholesome way to reward me with lifelong passion and devotion. You're always told to give these non-starters a chance to be starters, so I did. But the truth is that I hung in there for some weeks only because it turned out, to my amazement, that John was a remarkable lover, splendidly skilled and selfless, perhaps to compensate for entirely lacking in looks. What moves that man had, like a pianist who's all technique and no soul, what fingers, supplemented by a stick with a peacock feather at the end! As long as I wasn't looking at him or talking with him much, I had a wonderful time in bed. This was entirely different from the emotion-filled passion I was experiencing at the same time (not the exact same time) with Gerald. I wasn't sorry for the difference, which was highly educational.

Soon John began pressing for me to stay overnight. He wanted a *relationship*, good lord! At first I evaded this, because it was way too intimate; like a stereotypical male, I found my date whiny and clinging. Then one day he shocked me by declaring that he couldn't go on because he and another woman he'd been dating at the same time were falling in love. John explained rationally that he felt he couldn't have that mutual love with me. I heartily agreed he could not, while privately I tried hard to imagine John as someone's object of romantic desire. It seems that love is not a meritocracy, after all: there are too many intricacies of hope and projection in romance. The one who was quite low down on my own hierarchy of love was apparently someone else's dream, or at least a man she believed would deliver what she wanted in a mate.

I didn't regret my fling with John for obvious reasons, but I do wish I hadn't gone to bed with still another man I was not attracted to. This was Keith, a younger fellow, thirteen years younger to be exact, who picked me up in a bagel shop one fine day when I was, yes, innocently eating a bagel. A graduate student at a nearby seminary, he was almost as unattractive as John, but had the advantage of my curiosity about sex with a younger man. Probably my appeal to him was based on his own fantasy about sex with an older woman. Unfortunately, he had the disadvantage of being the worst lover I ever had, without exception; he either didn't know, or didn't want to know, what to do beyond the crudest actions possible in the shortest time allowable. Since he wasn't fun to be with out of bed either (specifically, that bed was a dirty foam futon, if my memory is right), I wasn't about to show him, even if he'd been interested. This little adventure was very brief, but his contribution to my own course of study was clear: sleeping with someone because of that person's youth is not a sure-fire path to sexual happiness.

There is one man from this time that I think of with loathing and a bit of shame. I'd begun to date, online and through fix-ups, to see if I could find that legitimate romance which must be the healthy and desirable goal of every unattached woman. Larry was an online date, a professor, proper in every way a date should be: single and sincerely looking for a relationship, not unattractive, with similar interests, cultural tastes and socioeconomic profile to mine. This all signaled that we had the much-ballyhooed *so much in common*. Larry was exactly the sort of man I'd been told I should look for and cultivate openness to appreciating, as an antidote to my futile love for Gerald. Who knows, I thought, this could be the one to rescue me from lonely old age!

I dated Larry exclusively and liked him in a minor sort of way, the way you like a pleasant person you chat with on an airplane and then wave goodbye to. But I stayed in it purely because it was an appropriate relationship, not because I enjoyed his humorless company or particularly desired him in bed. He apparently was no more enamored than I was, because he ended it after some six weeks by email, explaining that he was dating someone else he preferred. This was fine with me, though I would've made a phone call, myself. But he also felt compelled to ask, while he had my attention, *why* I'd requested a certain sexual position (and not one unusual or exotic), graciously providing me with his own unflattering psychoanalytic explanation (most of these are unflattering, I find). Even if this everyday sexual act had been from the Kama Sutra or *Fifty Shades of Grey*, I would have found such a break-up note astonishing, never mind one emailed after a handful of weeks. Was it his business, post-dating, to question what I did in bed or why, since he'd seemed at the time to enjoy it too? Don't most people have a liking for sex this way or that, or better yet, this way *and* that? So much for the boyfriend chosen because he checks the appropriate boxes.

This was about it for the gallery of rogues. Laughing over these tales with Gerald, always my eager audience for any stories I had about anyone or anything, almost made the bad ones worthwhile. Whether our sexual involvement was off or on, Gerald and I were like the couple in *Les Liasons Dangereuses*, an eighteenth-century novel, openly sharing what was happening with us as part of our closeness.

The best man to come out of this adventurous period of my midlife was Matthew, an attractive colleague who'd recently broken up with the woman he'd been living with. At the time we met, he was dating around, though with a wounded heart. I found him smart, funny, endearing, and kind, and we spent ambiguous time in each other's company, unsure (or at least I was) if we were dating or not. It seemed to me he half wanted to, and I believed I wanted to. But once when he kissed me, at a romantic spot overlooking the Palisades where we'd been walking, I dissolved in giggles the moment his tongue touched mine, rather than felt the desire I thought I would. This made me late for another date I happened to have made, so Matthew kindly drove me there, and we wisely never attempted such a thing again. Dating or being lovers just didn't work for either of us, though I liked him more than I've liked most lovers. My journal reads, *I said to Matthew, 'Let's be friends forever... unless I break it off' – it's the kind of thing you can say to him.* Before too long, he worked it out with the very likable woman he'd left and married her. And we all did stay friends, possibly forever.

At some point in all this it occurred to me that I'd never been with a woman sexually, and it was about time. I'd always loved women's bodies, wanted to look at and touch one, so this was an enjoyable idea, what Gerald called a *frisson*, except that I had no idea how to start. Why not just go to a gay bar? said Gerald, ever helpful. But I was too shy, until one day I was at a conference and spent time with a woman I both liked and was attracted to. When I learned she was gay, I simply suggested we go to her room, in the absurd way I'd gone up to unsuspecting Evan as an eighteen-year-old virgin and inquired if he'd care to have sex. "Hell no," said my potential hook-up, looking annoyed, "I'm not about to be an experiment for a straight woman, thank you very much." How did she know?, I remember thinking. Sadly, I never ventured this close again. At this point, I am romantically attracted to certain women, but not interested sexually, alas.

Maybe the neglected angel of Appropriate True Love was invisible during this time precisely because I was still in love with and sleeping with Gerald (except for short stretches of guilty monogamy on his part). So this did complicate how busy I was.

A Happy End (That Is Not An End)

My two daughters each had the classic soft blanket that lost its ribbon and became, after years of clutching and caressing, more hole than blanket. My son preferred a nondescript brown stuffed dog with a plastic collar and floppy ears that somehow survived deep in my closet; it now shares his own little boy's bed, though poor button-nosed Jasper has lost all his fur and is more mangy than cute. Another grandson's beloved stuffed kitty looked so moth-eaten, even without moths, that his parents replaced it with an exact replica, new and clean, when he was two. Of course he wouldn't touch it: "I want dirty kitty!" cried the child, and from then on he and everyone else called this ragtag item Dirty Kitty ("Wait, where's Dirty Kitty?"), though it sounds like a porn movie.

We smile fondly at children's comforts and obsessions, their irrational attachment to random silly objects, the way these objects give children peace, repose, warmth and succor in the difficult separation at bedtime, or carry them through vexations. But why do we grown-ups treasure the nonsense we often do? The people we do? Why should this one, and not another, settle and survive in your heart, the way Dirty Kitty settled in little Liam's heart, or ragged Jasper survived to a second life? You recognize the right-seeming ones by the way you feel in their presence, just as my grand-dog Puggie knew the dog-lover of her canine dreams when she smelled those pheromones across the street.

But the familiar story also works the other way: what you loved for unknowable reasons can lose its power and allure just as unaccountably as it attained its aura in the first place. That's mysterious too, though as adults we love to think we have all sorts of justifiable motives for leaving someone or something, our surrogate stuffed animal. Children don't need these rationalizations: when they no longer feel the comfort of running a finger along the silky ribbon of a blanket, they don't attempt to get the feeling back. They're not compelled to work to keep it on track, trying harder to love, or love more correctly, or unselfishly, what they no longer want. Instead they move on to the next part of their lives, to novel desires we hope reflect a wider view of themselves, a better fit for the prospects opening before them. I did that too.

Falling out of love with Gerald did not happen to me suddenly, the way I lost my long-accustomed feelings for my husband; it came about organically, very slowly, as an Ice Age descends (before climate change). One day after the kind of encounter with Gerald that used to leave me thrilled and shaken, I found myself going about my business, la-di-dah. That was when I began to ask myself, Could it be that I'm less in love? It seemed impossible, actually, after all this time: I recall that when we began, Gerald assured me that I'd "get over him in six months," and he was off by more than twenty years.

For a while after this, romantic feeling would bob back up to the surface, particularly when he touched me, and I would feel the old way again. But then I began to recover that same equanimity ever more frequently, like a jagged line on a chart going up and down but trending in the same general direction. At some point I understood that the unthinkable had happened: I'd opened my tightly-closed fist and let the hopes go. It was a strange and disorienting feeling, as though I'd been dangling from a cliff for eons, and then gently released to ground that had been right below me all the time. This brought me both enormous relief and confidence, but also the sadness of loss; I had loved being in love.

An interesting result of this was that the less romantic my feelings became, the more I resented that through Gerald's two changes of romantic partners over the years, I hadn't measured up to his personal standard for a woman to partner with. It's not that I hadn't known this all along, but the idea had resided in some gulch of my mind, buried by the desire I had for him.

And the more I resented it, the more the romantic view of Gerald declined, in a downward spiral. It's what you pay attention to that counts.

I was amazed and amused in equal measure when I saw how liberating it was not to be in love with Gerald. I was like a subject of an authoritarian government who suddenly finds herself in a democracy after a bloodless revolution. In fact, it was a democracy in which my party was now in power.

I still have feelings for him, or maybe it's the memory of feelings, like muscle memory. Gerald and I came to have more of a real friendship, as his feelings for me did not change. But it took much too long to achieve that equality. If I'd felt less, if I'd been able to moderate my feelings so we were always equal in our desires, what would have happened with him and me, and with my marriage? I'll never know, because I wasn't able to be as I am now, given who I was, and who I was is precisely what I was dealing with. The counterfactual in romance is inherently absurd, like someone exclaiming, "If you had an ace, you could have won that hand!" Yes, it would have been nicer for me to have that ace in my hand, and

I could also have used a better poker face. But I also can't know if I would have been happy with him in any case. From my present point of view, I tend to doubt it.

For certain my life would have been simpler and easier if I hadn't fallen in love when I was married, or fallen for an unavailable man who didn't see me as a candidate for domestic partner. I don't just mean I could have avoided the turmoil of divorce or the pain of unrequited love. What made these events an earthquake in my life is that I'd never so much as imagined them in my own story, and so was unprepared to respond to these particular twists of plot. I only knew about the scripts passed down to me: good and bad wives and husbands, love is forever, my forever person, *happy endings*. Afterward, my deeper understanding of love and marriage, both the pain and pleasure, stretched my sense of the possible, just as the pleasure of romantic fiction is the sense of what one can have, do and be in love. But where there's more possibility and hope, there's also more complexity and difficulty, an unwelcome risk of strain and hurt not necessarily compensated by winning the beloved in the end.

Nevertheless, I'm very glad that I lived out this impulse as far as it would go. As a reader, I was used to the pleasure of romantic literature taking me *outside* myself, away from my lived reality, whereas this experience of romance in life, with all my errors and afflictions, gave me back a sense of self that was half-empty before. It's common to hear, in media and everyday conversation, the facile claim that the one you truly love "makes you a better person." I sometimes joke that Gerald made me a worse person, in the ordinary sense of the word. But our relationship marked the beginning of the rest of my life, living as the one I already deeply was, for better or worse – the outside coming closer to the inside. Jefferson's rational pursuit of truth and my romantic craving for deep feeling were joined in this way.

The idea that falling in love can transform you is a cliché. But in fact from that time, over a quarter-century ago, to this moment, I did in fact cease to care solely about the rules and ways of life that had mattered enormously beforehand. This change had little to do with the specific outcome of the affair. The writer Laura Kipnis calls this "redescription and denaturalization" – a conversion to understanding the habitually familiar as strange, and never quite seeing the world again in the same comfortable way, or wanting to. It was comfortable only because I hadn't thought much about it, or lived it any other way than as a habit.

I never did get back the assonance I'd fooled myself into thinking I'd had before, but instead gained some insight into the cognitive advantages of dissonance.

William Blake famously wrote, in *Proverbs of Hell*, "Without contraries there is no progression," while my former mentor, Jerome Bruner, who I was visiting a year before his death at age one hundred, told me: "Contradiction heightens consciousness." My pained sense of being pulled two ways gave me a more intense sense of life, not just my own life. "Only let go," wrote the novelist Henry James; "Only connect," said E. M. Forster. I did both: let go what I had, in order to connect what I knew was in me. This had a remarkable effect on me, though not all of that effect was "good" in the usual way at the time.

To be touched by someone you have passion for – a choice I made today, to be paid for, but never forgotten, never lost.

This was written in my journal that long-ago spring day I became both an "adulteress" and someone's mistress at the same time. The choices I made in love disinterred parts of me I didn't know were buried, in order to reclaim a life.

Or less grandly: when I'd thought of Gerald that first time as my long-awaited swing at the bat, my goal was to make the home run. I didn't, but I definitely rounded some bases, and I'm happier that I took the chance than sorry about the score.

For this reason, I consider my relationship with Gerald as having a happy ending, though it didn't end.

Chapter Seven
Passion

> Then love is sin, and let me sinful be.
> – Philip Sidney, "Astrophel and Stella"

> Without a doubt the greatest suffering, like the greatest happiness, comes from the Other. I understand that some people fear this and try hard to avoid it by loving with moderation, by favoring a match made of common interests, music, political engagement, a house with a garden, or with multiple sexual partners who are seen as objects of pleasure separate from the rest of life. And yet […] I still preferred it to certain calm and productive periods of my life.
> – Annie Ernaux, *The Possession*

I gave up my hobby of casual sex, though not of love, when a new man, this time one who was single, became the second love in my life a few years after my separation from Frank. As it happens, Nick was the man my friend Matthew drove me to see, after our failed kiss on the cliffs of the Palisades. In fact I was late because I'd lingered with Matthew, and ran into the coffee shop where I'd

agreed to meet Nick for the first time, flushed with the (failed) adventure of kissing Matthew. My relationship with Nick, coinciding with my continuing involvement with Gerald, disproved for me still another popular idea about romance, that it's impossible to be in love with more than one person at a time.

When I think of Nick now, I remember his blue eyes, in which I could see the innocence of the child with corn-yellow hair he must have been behind the mask of I've-seen-it-all worldliness. They weren't particularly large, lovely or striking eyes, but their expression of anxious vulnerability in a very masculine face drew me to him. Those blue eyes and even the unkempt hair that had once been pure blond had tremendous appeal for me, most likely because they reminded me of my father's hair and eyes. This is how romance is: you love someone and devote years of your life to him *because his eyes are like your father's*. It makes no sense, except viscerally, where logic feels absurd.

From my journal, April 30th, just before my first blind date with Nick: *I'm having coffee w/Nick tomorrow. But he's never even gone to college, so this seems pretty dubious.*

May 1st, immediately after our date: *He strikes me as in bad shape, but attractive, smart, funny and honest.*

June 1st: *Nick called me and we're going out tom night (unless I get a better offer).*

June 2nd: *He asked if I wanted to see this nut again.*

June 3rd: *Nick and I are now on hot kissing terms, and he's not a bad kisser. God knows where this will go.*

June 4th: *A good time w/Nick, who I sometimes like very much and other times feels strange and alien to me. But the strong mutual attraction is delightful.*

June 6th: *Nick is becoming more important. There's something*

there that clicks along by itself like a little train on a subterranean track.

June 21st: *Nick said he doesn't want a relationship or commitment, too soon after sobriety, but then asked me, What are you supposed to do if there are feelings, except let it evolve?*

And so it evolved.

My five-year relationship with Nick was like a fairy tale, or at least it began like one. That is, it appeared enchanted and omen-like when, during his first visit to my apartment, he fixed a bedroom door that had been hanging crookedly for ages, a task no other mortal seemed able to do. There wasn't extra money to call in a professional since my husband had left, and so I'd tapped the local talent: both my lover Gerald, who was a handy sort, and my friend Matthew, who'd done some carpentry in his time, had generously tried to re-attach this annoying loose door with no success at all; they made it worse, if anything.

Nick was a cabinetmaker by trade, so almost as soon as he'd made his way to my place, he was set the impossible task – and did it flawlessly and with graceful ease in record time. This recalled the many stories in which a succession of False Suitors fail at some Herculean labor, until the right Prince himself wins the Princess's hand by completing it. I watched in awe as this tall man, with his blue eyes and blondish ponytail, his rugged face and lanky frame, reached up with his expert hands, big and rough like my father's, banged here and there with a few assured and graceful movements, and repaired a door that two other tall and good-looking men I admired could not. (And ever afterward, whenever I saw Nick hammering, I wanted to go to bed with him immediately.) There he was, the man who was going to save me

from that lonely future with only cats by my side!

It went downhill from there, not surprisingly. Nick was lanky and appeared to be in what I'd called "bad shape", due to a vicious and long-standing cocaine habit. It had landed him in rehab from which he'd just emerged, but not until he'd destroyed a good part of his life, losing his job, apartment, and fiancée. This was even more dubious, to quote my journal, as a predictor of successful coupledom than his lack of education, but thankfully that addiction was behind him now. And he was fascinating to me, entirely unlike anyone I'd ever known. As the months rolled on, I learned that Nick was clever but not cultured or intellectual, not witty like Gerald but brilliantly funny, lacking Gerald's originality of thought but enormously enjoyable to be with, now that he was sober. We used to laugh that we were the world's unlikeliest couple on paper, having nothing at all in common. "What's a classy woman like you doing with me?" he wondered once. Not only do female professors rarely date men without college degrees, but to compound the oddness, he was younger than I was by eight whole years, the equivalent of twenty years in Man-land. Yet we got along famously, in those early days so delighted and infatuated with each other that we'd roll around on the bed like frolicking puppies, if puppies could giggle.

Pleasant as it was, this rolling around was not really sexual, however, the way it would instantly have been with Gerald if we'd found ourselves on a bed (or not). Though Nick was ready to sleep with me and spend nights with me as soon as we met, well before I wanted to be that close, the sexual connection was not at the very root of our relationship, as with Gerald. In the utopias of romance fiction, the relationship of happy lovers is not

very different from that of all other lovers; it's assumed that once in love, sex is always matchless. But in my life, and I suspect in every life, each love, no matter how small or great, has its unique reasons for being, some more sexual and some less.

The way Nick and I were together in bed was good enough, nice mostly because I loved him, and then after a couple of years, it trailed away. What it left instead was an intimate friendship, unusual for me, in which I came to fill the role of the sober, steady woman, and he the unstable, restless man who both leaned on me and also tried to avoid me, probably because he was leaning on me.

In the end, occupying these particular roles (I would almost say *stations in life*) certainly helped do us in as a couple. Nick's way of comprehending himself and his world was entirely new to me, and it felt strange for me to stand outside the particular craving of another, something like the way you feel when your very rational friend is crazy for a person who strikes you as obviously unworthy. I had no experience with chemical substances at all; there were none he didn't like. I'd never so much as smoked a single cigarette, or wanted one, and alcohol, or addiction of any sort, was never present in my family's life. Where I feared the loss of control, the blurry consciousness that came with chemical intoxication, he lusted for it. This was an encyclopedia of undiscovered knowledge as far as I was concerned.

My easy assumption that his long stay in rehab had cured him of these gross habits, as I thought of his problem, was quickly contradicted by reality. Soon after we became what he called "an item," while still in counseling for his addiction, he relapsed. This was such a blow that I made an appointment with his counselor, weeping as I talked to her about this shocking news. Her response floored me: she seemed to think it was not my concern, that I ought to step back. My journal says that when I repeated this wonderingly to Nick, he laughed knowingly: "Yup," he said in that cynical, slyly charming, seen-it-all way he had, "Co-dep, baby," adding breezily, "I'm a sick fuck, honey."

I probably should have shut that door he'd fixed right in his face at that point. I think if I'd cut off the romantic aspect of our relationship, we'd still be friends today, so deep did our unlikely affection go, so much pleasure did we take in each other's company. But I could not resist what he gave me, the charm of the hanging-out time, the sheer fun of wasting that time with him. Because that was a great part of our mutual attraction, more than sexuality, it seemed it could go on and on.

We did cobble something like a life together during those years, though it wasn't really the life I wanted for myself. Nevertheless, I think fondly of the many hours we watched terrible movies in bed, Nick leaning over to whisper reassuringly "He'll be fine" in my ear, as the villain was mortally wounded and bled to death, or entertained me by mimicking the many "snoot-faces" we encountered. He had a wonderful gift for mockery, and to this day when someone is pretentious or condescending or self-promoting, I still think of them as "snoot-faces," and imagine how Nick would imitate them for my viewing pleasure.

Reputedly, people fall in love with a "type." Yet when I think of Gerald and Nick, it would be hard to say what my type is, from this sample of two. I could be myself with highly educated Gerald in a way I couldn't with rough, largely uncultured, working-class Nick, but I could also be myself with Nick in a way that I couldn't be with Gerald, who is only too formal, well-mannered, and gentlemanly for my working-class heart. What does this say about that usual rationale for being in love, that one can be oneself with the beloved?

In fact, the cultural differences between Nick and me were more complex than it appeared (isn't that the case for everything anyway?). You might think Nick was my working-class hero, but he also could be spectacularly and purposely vulgar, to my middle-class irritation. So our relationship had vaguely Laurentian overtones – cultured, privileged Lady Chatterley and the gamekeeper (without the passionate sex). Yet while my parents were odd, uneducated, urban and poor, Nick was born into a solidly professional family – his amiable, proper, well-spoken parents were educators, in fact – and grew up in a green, comfortable suburb, pure Americana. He had casually dropped out of college after a semester and pursued becoming an addict, at first part-time and then intensively.

Nick seemed to have a subversive pride in being what he called "fucked up." When we stayed up very, very late talking in bed, a practice I generally found enchanting, Nick sometimes disturbed me with the intensity of his inward gaze as he reminisced about the past. His theme was frequently the craziness of addiction, the things you'll do for love of a substance. These tales made my stomach sink, but I didn't say so. This far-off looking away, eyes bright with the remembrance of dramatic, chaotic times, was reminiscent of Betty's talking-to instead of talking-with in storytelling.

Over the five years that Nick and I were "an item,"

I became well-acquainted with codependency, a term I'd barely heard before meeting him: putting up with more than you should because of the need to be needed. Though I despised Nick's enthrallment to stupid chemicals, something with no appeal for me (and therefore easy to be snooty about), I myself was enthralled beyond my will by certain humans, who are bodies made up of chemicals, when you think about it. Rather than say love is a kind of addiction, a common comparison, why not say addicts have a love affair with a substance? Wasn't Betty in love with her own sad and triumphant stories, aren't my own stories of love, and the craziness at the core of that love, the equivalent of Nick's tales of uncontrolled desire and need? We all, Betty, Nick, and me, probably share that haunted and hungry look while recounting the tales of our obsessions.

I belonged to the public world of rules and normalcy, but as the child of Betty and Al, always felt I was passing in it, and not very well. Nick, the child of presentable, middle-class, professional parents, must have felt that he should belong to their world, wanted to belong to it. Yet he also flouted it with a kind of devilish joyousness, not unlike the way Gerald desired and chose the monogamous relationships he bedeviled with joyful non-monogamy. Not that Nick's was a conscious rebellion against the stifling sameness and dullness of being normal; if it had been, he might not have been an addict at all, or else he'd have been William Burroughs. Instead this anarchic spirit was expressed as a conspiratorial wink he gave his buddies in the know, not a forthright middle finger or ringing declaration of independence. It wasn't a principled cause, it was a kind of great shrug to the rest of us who tediously pursued our conventionally legitimate satisfactions.

I saw this inner contradiction in Gerald too, with his promiscuous infidelities living inside his wish for a peaceful, warmly domestic, sentimental sort of love. These two touched me because both performed outwardly some part of me that felt flattened by the "normal" world – while I also believed that hidden part should be crushed and concealed. In the same way that I was a kind of stand-in to Nick for his desire to be respectable, I channeled Gerald's hidden, disrespectable and unacceptable passions. All of us (me, Nick, Gerald) lived with one foot in two irreconcilable worlds, at once needing and denying both. It's difficult to be both normal and abnormal at the same time, at least if you accept those two blurry and unstable concepts as descriptions neatly dividing the world. I no longer do.

What confused the issue for me was that Nick himself could not decide whether our relationship was a romance or friendship. When I brought it up, he'd say it was "half and half" for him. I had no idea what that meant, and he was not the sort to hold either abstract or intimate discussions about it. As I wrote in an exasperated letter I never gave him: *When I try to talk to you, you either put me off with your jokes-and-charm routine, or you act like I'm trying to perform tooth extraction without anesthesia.* Around this time, I wrote in my journal, *Nick said, "I should propose to you to shut you up." How romantic.*

Inexplicably to me, long after we were no longer lovers, he enjoyed sleeping in my bed with his arms around me, he still liked to kiss me in the same lover-like way, and most confusing, he was crazy-jealous of Gerald, whom he'd met once and found, unsurprisingly, the King of Snoot-Faces. Nick would ringingly declare from time to time that he and I were just friends, he wanted to be free to date others, and then become upset and angry when he found out that I'd seen Gerald and hadn't told him. "Dog in the manger," I'd mutter, secretly pleased. Since I'd learned from every movie and novel that jealousy is the sure symptom of romantic feeling, this seemed like a double message. I once asked what he'd do if I met a man I really hit it off with, since I'd determined, at that late point, to date also. "If you find somebody else, I'll have to go and get you back," he said instantly. *Dog in the manger.* Double the double messages. We continued to have each other's keys, letting ourselves in and out of each other's places at will. His stuff was all over my home as if we were a couple, which we sort of were, but also not.

Nick had multiple relapses in sobriety, one accompanied by a young drug user who kept calling to confide in me about him, much as my husband's new girlfriend had and Gerald's former girlfriend had (what is it with girlfriends who want to talk to me about a man we've shared?), but eventually he found someone his own age, better suited to him in every way. We were no longer an item. They married in about five minutes.

And so the deep rhythms of our closeness were suddenly broken off. He explained in a painful conversation afterward that he'd always seen me as "a kind of mother figure," though as his elder by all of eight years, I could've made headlines if I'd given birth to him. This did not seem to him either snooty or condescending. As for me, when I complained to my therapist at the time that Nick had suddenly left me to marry another woman, she asked if I would have married him. "God, no," I said, and she squinted meaningfully at me with her therapeutic eye. I suppose you could say I was a class snob while he was an age snob. Old to his young, educated to his not so much, sober to his unsober: we said no one would bet on us, and no one was proved right.

Nick was for the most part a disaster, and it was best for us that we didn't try to squeeze what we had into full-time domesticity or worse, wedded bliss (My journal: *What am I offering Nick, anyway? Certainly not pink sunsets and babies, or even monogamy. In fact, I never again want to be monogamous without a really mutual love at a very high level of satisfaction*). Why did Nick and I hang in there so long together when it didn't really work for either of us? Your psychoanalytic mumblings about dysfunctional attachment are probably true (yawn), but I prefer this: It was love, baby. Not your grandfather's love, not your Hallmark or Hollywood love, not the marital down-homey, let's-decorate-and-get-a-puppy kind of love – I doubt it was the love that *you* would choose, gentle and wiser reader, or for that matter, what Nick and I would have chosen either. I haven't seen him in a long while, but I can still hear the particular way he called me "honey" especially when I tried his patience (often) – his head cocked like Betty singing one of her ditties, in that sweetly exasperated, warmly mocking tone entirely his own: *Hunn-EEE*!

You know how people say "you hadda be there"? I *was* there, I showed up for it, and I'm not sorry I did. It was extremely entertaining, when it wasn't maddening. We like to think we know what love is, checking all the boxes: mutuality, commitment, endurance, happy-ever-after. Yet Nick was also one of the very few men I've been in love with, which is to say, who could snap my heart in two. Even though that heart was staggering and bleeding out a good while after Nick absconded, I can't be sorry, either that it happened or that it ended. I just regret that I didn't exit the main stage sooner.

The Romantic: An Argument About Passion

What did it say about me that I loved two men who would not make me their domestic partners, men who didn't want what I hoped to have with them? Explanations abound from friends and family, but usually come down to these: I must love misery/drama/rejection; or I unconsciously want someone unavailable because I'm afraid of intimacy (my decades-long marriage notwithstanding); in other words, I'm flat-out defective. As so often happens when assessing people's mentalities, any or all of these could be true, or not, or it could be something else less hackneyed.

For me, it came down to this: the very few men I've truly loved were the most desirable ones to me, meaning the ones who most aroused my passions. That is why I loved them. Whether I could have them, all the time and in the exact way I wanted them, was a separate matter to me – not the condition or test of loving itself, but a situation to be dealt with and worked out as best I could, just as a marriage is a condition, a context, a kind of institutional frame around the feelings within it. It took me a long time, nearly a lifetime, to detach myself from the idea that both the frame and the picture it encloses are the same.

I had a friend once who astonished me with her ability to turn off her romantic feelings, no matter how strong or seemingly deep, when a boyfriend did not love her sufficiently. "As soon as a man doesn't return my feelings equally," she remarked to me, with pride, "I don't love him any longer." This was no idle boasting; I watched it happen more than once, in awe. If I could purchase that skill, if there were a website in Canada with cheap rates, my shelves would be lined right now. I'm sure her family, friends, and therapists were thrilled with this self-protective faculty, and I applaud it too. Everyone agrees that a love not perfectly mutual, or not "going anywhere," meaning to the Arcadia of long-term commitment, is not serving your own interests, and is therefore not healthy. My friend might have been a bit more gifted in her ability to switch off emotion than many, but the principle is one our culture generally admires. How convenient, how expedient, to feel or not feel exactly the way you're supposed to in order to gain the most advantage for yourself.

Here is where I am romantic to the core. That is, I don't believe it's a sign of strength of mind or good character that you can easily shut off your feelings because they no longer serve your rational ends. For better or worse, I can't make myself desire or not desire someone, sexually or romantically, just because it will further my self-interested goals. This emotional pragmatism feels entirely alien to me, even a bit repulsive. But then I do recognize this comes from my own temperament and orientation to the world; people have very different emotional economies. Unlike people who risk their lives to climb Mount Everest or long for the next free dive from an airplane, when it comes to my physical survival, my desires follow my rational self-interest completely. Yet in romantic longing, my brain seems to be wired differently.

No one seems to notice how this pragmatic idea of love contradicts our culture's romantic ideals. If romance is defined as a passion for the beloved's particular self, not a utilitarian manipulation to get a workable relationship, wouldn't we presume that we love the best person, not what's best for you? If you truly desire the other for his or her unique personhood, you wouldn't think you could or even *should* erase your romantic feelings like an old scrawl on a whiteboard. That is, unless you believe that some mystical transaction from heaven assures that you only really feel love when it's embedded in a public relationship that is socially legitimate, entirely mutual, perfectly appropriate, and correctly timed. Does anyone believe that, besides my eighteen-year-old students?

If you take the idea of loving the most lovable person seriously, it makes no sense to say that you must love only someone whose own feelings and desires exactly equal yours, who matches you like some sort of twin. The implausible cultural message is that love is about the other person, but it's also equally about choosing the nicest possible life for yourself in couplehood. Love is both a wondrous miracle and yet your fault if not *both of these at once.* We are taught to expect this as inevitable, and it must be true for some, but obviously it doesn't necessarily work that way. And then what?

In Anglo-American culture there's a great deal of rhetoric about admiring passion, but only if it's selfless and proper. Then we cover this over by telling a story that combines, and in fact blurs, passion with pragmatics. The easy way out: if love doesn't lead to a committed couplehood – well then, it's not, *ipso facto*, "real" love. If a relationship doesn't work (again, the analogy with labor), or if it doesn't last, that wasn't "real" love either. What does "real" mean, then? We take refuge from life in the simple comforts of those rigid either/or boxes: love is either Mature or Immature, Healthy or Neurotic, Selfish or Unselfish, Real or Not Real.

In this view, love is a means to an end, like food consumed. It's necessary to eat to live, you hope to enjoy it along the way, but you should not live to eat, we say, and similarly, it's embarrassing and unseemly to love as Othello did, not wisely but too well. Some students can't comprehend the foolishness of Romeo and Juliet, who were "just stupid" (not a quote from Shakespeare); one student found the famous scene of Heathcliff's last meeting with Catherine before her death in *Wuthering Heights* "unromantic," because, she said, Catherine was too "clingy" with Heathcliff. Take a risk and fall in love! – but first make sure you thoroughly check it out so your love interest is an ideal partner, and conditions are optimal for you to achieve your personal goals. How often are those personal aspirations the hidden agenda, and love the convenient pretext for that? You don't want to be alone, or you're ready to get married, or you're already stuck with a partner or spouse, and therefore it must be… *love*.

Our prevailing mode of romantic relationships, not unlike in Jane Austen's world, revolves around the calculus of consumption in our society: How much will I get out of this purchase or situation? And unsurprisingly, this slops over onto our emotional lives as well. What confuses us is the rhetoric about romance as the great exception to the ethos of the marketplace, an idea with a very old history. Love is supposed to be a protected sphere untouched by commercial interests – it's love or money, supposedly never both at once. "Is it a love match?" gossips asked in Jane Austen's time, with an open understanding that if not, it was for those other benefits. In much of Austen's fiction, as well as romantic fiction through time, this unseemly division between the purposes of feeling and ambition is healed by granting both love and money to the heroine at the same time.

As a strong and central emotion, (real) love, unlike manufactured goods or business relations, is seen as natural and beautiful, a jewel of authenticity in a capitalist society with a market for everything. When I ask my students to identify what makes a place or a gift or an occasion romantic, they all say that a homemade gift, or a landscape of natural beauty, is romantic – romance is a candle rather than an electric bulb, it's a beach in moonlight rather than a tanning salon. Therefore, any suggestion that in fact we conflate beautiful, natural love with self-interest is sacrilegious. To be hurt – disappointed, heartbroken – by a passion that won't be properly rewarded, to value the uniqueness of the emotion for its own sake and not for the comfortable life it will hypothetically bring you: all of this is at best unwise, at worst unhealthy, or else, as my student said, "just stupid." Because in the end we're taught to believe that emotions can be bargained for, just as we pay as cheaply as possible for everything else in a consumer society. Unless you're getting your own back in a perfectly mutual love, you've struck a bad bargain and should cut your losses as soon as possible. Sell that stock before the recession hits!

In popular romances, "real" love is entirely requited in both degree and kind, meaning always completely repaid in coin of the same realm, and exchanged in a precisely drawn way (which is presented as the only way).

Its value lies solely in the mutual nature of that exchange, enabling the forming of a couple. Though the fictional heroine or hero is permitted to love for a time without knowing if there's a return, we, the audience, knows he or she is going to get that happy surprise. The beloved was in love all that time after all, you see, or at the very least, learned to love the well-deserving other, as well he or she should! Don't we all merit, shouldn't we all expect, both passion *and* the lifetime reward?

What I call the Stages Theory is everywhere in Western culture: Once the couple is formed, what begins in Stage One as "falling in love" will naturally evolve (if it's "real" love) into Stage Two, the trusting, caring, mutually supportive and deeper relationship that supposedly only a domestic partnership can have. Stage One is fun and exciting, but in Stage Two you will conveniently have the benefits of Stage One without that risky, always fleeting, excess of emotion, loving too well. Of course Stage Two requires (unpaid) work – not just the initial work of getting there, but constant vigilance and maintenance as well, especially to keep up, so to speak, the fun, sexy side of Stage One.

I'm all for domestic affection, but I believe there's a value in passion outside the realm of the domestic, just as there are domestic pleasures without passion. We demean passion by regulating it, defining it as aimed at one obligatory end, with a purpose for which it's built: to make a snug (not to say smug) life for yourself, building the right kind of family, namely the conventional kind. I object to the idea that romantic relationships are a rehearsal to learn how to do the "real" thing, the only thing that counts – a forever relationship – but when those practice runs don't produce, you lose; it's a fail, because you did it wrong, there is something wrong with you, or there was something wrong with the object of your desire.

At least traditional arranged marriages get right to the point and skip the hypocrisy: do away with Stage One, because it's useless, even destructive, to Stage Two. But since the eighteenth century, Western culture has increasingly tied marriage to love rather than openly admitting its aspects of property, personal gain, or compulsory social rectitude. Americans tend to look down at arranged marriages in other cultures, or our own traditional sub-cultures, as inferior to the self-evidently superior love match (as Jane Austen herself called it) of individual choice. Yet for all the ubiquity of love in words and images, we behave as though it's misguided or self-indulgent to give ourselves entirely to an emotional experience not compensated in the usual rational and practical ways that render lifestyle profit as we understand it.

Ironically, though we've co-opted the word "romantic" from the Romantic movement of the late eighteenth and early nineteenth century in Britain and Europe, the original Romantics would not have agreed with this idea. They insisted on the unique value of *feeling*, for its own sake, the sake of experiencing one's humanity. These emotions, pushed to the point of transcendence they called the sublime, were for them the means of apprehending great beauty. They wrote, painted and composed around the experience of sublimity, as opposed to rational thought or pragmatic action, because it could be the portal to a revolution in consciousness, both in personal life and also in the world. Passion (for almost anything) was not simply romantic in the modern sense, it was a way of being in the world and a mode of seeing the world. "We yearn to surrender all our Self, and let ourselves be filled to the brim with a single, tremendous, magnificent emotion," cries Goethe's romantic hero Werther in the eighteenth century (spoiler: love doesn't make him happy in the end, yet *The Sorrows of Young Werther* was widely read and imitated at the time).

The Victorians, on the other hand, ardent fans of governance and regulation in all its forms, were more often horrified by excessive feeling as selfish and uncontrollable, and while we still use some of the Romantics' vocabulary (our citified sentimentality about a park as Nature, or our openness to disclosing and sharing what we feel), we're in some ways closer to the Victorian than we like to admit. Byron lives on in our current obsession with bad boys like vampires, but now these vampires too tend to have love lives that wind up in permanent coupling, which neither Byron himself nor his poetic subjects achieved or even necessarily viewed as most important to living.

Count me in as a Romantic in the original sense, then, because I believe that what goes deepest should not be a cost-benefit analysis. Maybe love can be less about outcomes, success, and winning than an immersion, temporary or long-term, in the most human of emotions, for better or worse. We constantly learn from movies, psychology articles, self-help manuals, and TV ads that experiences are more precious than any possession; why then can't we value experiencing a beloved more than *having* him or her?

And there is more than one way to have someone. I've had more than one way.

One And Only: An Argument About Monogamy

Most mistresses in fiction, stage, and screen don't fare well. Yet from my own observation, as well as experience, of real-life affairs, there's no predicting at all how, when, or if an affair will end. They may be an hour long or lifelong, or anywhere in between; someone moves away, or someone moves on to greener pastures; sometimes they end with a psychic cataclysm and other times they dribble downhill. Occasionally they turn into great friendships or create bitter enemies. I'm not the bitter enemy type, and I have no animus toward anyone I've loved. Nor have I ever had the Tragic Mistress desire to throw myself under a train like Anna Karenina, or poison myself like Madame Bovary, or drown myself like Kate Chopin's Edna Pontellier in *The Awakening* (they were the married ones, but it didn't help them).

The complexity and variety of affairs are not confined to outcome. If Tolstoy's famous dictum is that "Happy families are all alike, and every unhappy family is unhappy in its own way," every adulterous affair is happy or unhappy in its own way. Needs and desires come in many forms: married men or women looking for pleasure while still firmly rooted in their families, as my husband claimed he was (until he wasn't), an unhappy wife failing to resist an overwhelming passion, my own position, or those who genuinely can't have what they need with the primary person in their life. Here, my subject is love affairs. Yet the one-offs or promiscuous run-arounds and lifelong loves are lumped together in one moralistic word, which seems ridiculous to me. They are all cheaters, a word that *au courant* book reviewers in the New York Times use as unthinkingly as twelve-year-olds. This, to me, is childish, a holdover from America's Puritan origins.

My theory is that non-monogamous sexuality as cheating is a concept that flourishes even more now that other sexual dramas of romance and marriage, such as the enormous fuss about virginity or childbearing out of wedlock, have withered away. Adultery in Western culture is the new premarital sex, which used to be the crucial distinction between good girls and the other kind, as if rigid monogamy is the last bastion of relationship rectitude. When tempted by illegitimate love, Use willpower!, we're told, as if we're on a diet, often with the same results as most diets. I control myself, so you should too!

Since as a society we no longer unquestioningly punish or ostracize those who have premarital sex, or live together, or divorce, or bear children out of wedlock, or marry members of the same sex or other races or religions, what's left to gossip about or righteously condemn? We must have rules to feel that our emotional lives are coherent (or even just to enjoy breaking them), and the Last Rule left to organize our moral thinking on marriage is: you must not cheat, no matter what the circumstances! Because if you break that contract, no matter how long you toed the line, there can be no understanding at all, either from spouse or the public – it simply means you're a monster who deserves to live alone and unloved in perpetuum. The monster is gendered: while a male lover is a Rat, the mistress is automatically assigned the part of Whore or Homewrecker. Infidelity is the obstacle to happiness everyone agrees is egregious;

therefore it's everywhere as a subject of drama in scripts and reality shows.

In reality, practitioners of monogamy tend to fall into three categories:

- first, those who are monogamous because they are genuinely fulfilled with one person only and don't want anyone else until they both go to the Great Beyond;

- second, those who desire others but are constrained by (they say) morality;

- and third, those who don't have enough energy or passion to want anything except what they already have. I have no idea what share of the coupled-up population is truly in the first, well-satisfied category, and neither do you. But I do know many who belong to the last two.

As for the first group, social scientists frequently ask couples to rate how happy and fulfilled they are with monogamy, but the results run into the usual problem that comes with self-assessments of a trait or state of mind. For example, what *you* mean by "happy" is not necessarily what I mean: "happy" can cover a rather wide range of feelings that includes "I guess what I have is good enough," or the self-deception I was carelessly practicing when I would have described my own marriage that way. Then too there's the question of expectations, in that my grandparents' presumption of what kind of marriage *should* make them happy isn't likely to be the same as my own. What we think will make us happy, what we are supposed to want, and what we believe about the other options on offer, all shape the way we assess our own level of contentment.

The second group, those aware of desires for one or more others but restrain themselves, often claim to be more virtuous, whereas some unknown number of these, one suspects, might be less motivated by morality than fear. If you're among those who would cheat if they could, yet resist temptation, I can only say bravo to you and my compliments to your partner. But would you want to be monogamous with someone who doesn't really want to be monogamous with you? This resembles trying to force someone to marry me, or even visit me, when he or she doesn't much care to. Why would I want to enforce monogamy with emotional blackmail or contractual obligation, even if I could?

As for the third group, whose virtue rests on lack of desire, stop holding your scolding fingers in the air, please! If there's no temptation, it's not admirable to do what you feel like doing anyway. Congratulations, you didn't act on an impulse you didn't have! In that case, you might get off your high horses and let others ride the ponies. My being or having a lover doesn't hurt you or your spouse one bit if it's something neither of you would do, any more than gay marriage hurts hetero couples, or childless couples hurt the ones who choose parenthood.

But doesn't infidelity harm the "cheated-on" romantic partner? Isn't he or she injured emotionally? That's a complicated question, like most others that involve human behaviors and emotions. It depends so much on your premises: victimhood, after all, rests on an understanding of a moral offense. And yes, when two people have a romantic commitment in our society, there's (usually) a rigid contract spoken or unspoken, and we presume the violation of that promise should cause anger and righteous outrage. Even the robot Rachel in the film *Blade Runner* knew "I should be enough for you!" was the correct answer to an unfaithful spouse when tested for her ability to pass as human. I, the victimized spouse, should be everything to my partner, so that if I don't command the entire field of his or her desire, I'm "not enough" of something or other. Thus the hurt: this supposed deficit is seen as a public declaration of one's humiliating inadequacy. If you have a partner, the logic goes, someone else can't be simply different, meaning neither more nor less, better or worse. There must be a winner.

Interestingly, the term "cuckold," a word that historically referred to males, defined the betrayed husband as an object of ridicule, demeaning his social status. A wife's infidelity was an assault on her husband's honor and social status, with or without jealousy or any romantic feeling, when a wife was considered a man's property. Even so late as the Victorian age, a man could easily divorce his wife for extramarital sex, whereas the wife could not obtain a divorce on those grounds only. The word cuckold has fallen out of favor now that women's sexuality is not as rigidly controlled, at least in our culture. Now a wife's affair is understood more as the threatened loss of the loved one more than the debasement of male status. Yet the general idea of extramarital sexuality as a kind of robbery of one's property lingers.

Here, however, is the rub, pun unintentional: when monogamy is automatically promised and presumed, non-monogamy will usually involve secrecy and lying, which appears tawdry, just plain wrong. So "you owe me fidelity" and "you owe me truth" are conflated. If sexual fidelity is a sort of business agreement organizing our bodies and emotions, the spouse is like a plaintiff who can sue when there's a violation of that promise, and the vow of monogamy is a mortgage that must be paid every day of one's life. "You owe me" employs a metaphor for love as debt collection, not exactly a romantic idea. But this pragmatism is powered by a grand moral claim – you have no right to do this, it's personal treason deserving of domestic execution, not just a deception or breach of promise. In religious terms, it has the force of sin, and there's no logically arguing with religious or quasi-religious beliefs.

I personally doubt this moral constraint on our sexual lives actually promotes the couple's love, happiness, or fulfillment, neither for the mate who suppresses a real desire, nor the one who uses a promise from long ago to repress the desires of the mate. This question of rights and morality tends to overpower a genuinely interesting question: What does this desire mean about what's going on with you, and with you and me together? For me, the issue of monogamy is not a moral imperative, but a negotiation of desires in a relationship, which is always driven by conflicting interests that might modify The Rules.

As for the moral responsibility of the cheater's lover, whether the male Rat or the female Homewrecker, my own idea is that an affair is chiefly the business of the one who made this promise and the one who received it. I as lover cannot force the so-called cheater to violate his promise to you, his chosen partner, no matter how much you want to believe that I tempted or lured that person away. I would say that the temptation itself is the salient fact, more significant than either the promise *or* its violation.

A spouse is not a talking object to be stolen from you, unless you believe your mate comes with all the sacred rights of ownership a capitalist holds dear, which many in fact do believe. In the real world there are two people in that marriage with separate and evolving desires, needs, and conditions. Chances seem high that these mates may not always be in the same place, metaphorically speaking, at the same time. You'd think each would be interested in those changes in the other.

From the point of view of the lover, I am both a person in my own right, first, and may also be an expression of the place where one person in your relationship is in his or her own life, as well as life with you. But I am not your enemy. Nothing can be done without the will of the one who is married or just committed, unless there is a weapon involved.

For this reason, I've never quite understood the popular song by Dolly Parton called "Jolene". "Jolene" is one of those country songs that tell a story of victimized innocence from the point of view of the cheated; the pleasure of the genre lies in wailing about or angrily condemning the unfaithful love, who has a cheatin' heart, and therefore deserves anything you can dole out to his person or his vehicle (presumably Jesus is not behind the wheel when the car is trashed). In the song, the wife pleads piteously with the alluring Jolene to "please not take her man." Now how pathetic is it for the singer to beg her husband's lover to just go away, as though that will alter the heart of the problem, so to speak? And why is this up to Jolene, anyway? I ask you, Dolly: where is the wife's own agency in this, to decide to be or not be with a man who's on the verge of leaving with someone else?

And then there's Jolene herself, where's her song? I was not the classic Homewrecker, in that my lovers, whether I wanted them to or not, weren't going to leave their supposedly happy homes for little old me. Let's say Jolene rejects "your man's" desire for her, goes away, just as you insist. Will that prevent him from leaving you for someone else, or for that matter, leaving you for his own sake? Or conversely, would he really be any happier with you because he shut down his desire, and will you really be happier with him?

Dear Dolly – I dare you to sing a song about that!

Since Jolene has no voice, I'll speak up for her myself. As a mistress, Jolene might say (or sing, accompanied by acoustic guitar), I'm the person that your husband has no obligation to. Perhaps that's part of his charm for me – it can be delightful to be chosen without obligation or duty. I've escaped the wire mesh of The Wife, flown over the domestic nest. I now have the liberty to be what I want to be when I'm with this man, without the loved children that entangle, household cares that weigh down, the practical plans for the future, the sometimes burdensome weight of the past.

But that's the serious stuff of life, you answer angrily, that's what's *real*, that's Life Itself.

Oh, I agree, Jolene returns, your life is serious, real and important, but is that only what's important and real? I say desire, especially deep desire, is just as real and serious, even essential to Life Itself. My valuing his desire and mine over your domesticity doesn't necessarily denigrate you. If your primary value is domesticity, you've chosen what society values and praises, and especially if you're heterosexual, what it will throw its weight and resources behind. How *nice* for you. The natural tendency is to take that privilege and see it as the only proper one, the one that is good and right for all.

I could hum the tune to this, if you like.

Here's advice I saw recently in a relationship column: "To women dating married men: You are an option – and you are borrowing someone else's spouse. When you value YOU, you will find your own love." This deep analysis implies that a mistress is not just an amoral abuser, but also a self-abuser who is *used*. She is an "option" – as opposed to… an obligation? Wisdom like this is dispensed all the time. The thinking goes this way: A man seems to love me but has not made me The One. He couldn't *really* love me, *ipso facto*, because he's a Rat, and Rats don't love, they just skitter up your legs with their filthy little rat feet, spreading infection to you, your family, and all your friends and acquaintances in sunny Happytown. So run away, Unmarried Woman! And you, Married Woman, go home to that husband you dislike half the time, and appreciate your life while tidying up. You'll be safe, of course, because wives, unlike mistresses, are not "optional"; obviously, no one can leave them.

In George Eliot's Victorian masterpiece *Middlemarch*, the heroine foolishly marries an unattractive, dull, much older man entirely unsuited to her, yet no matter how unhappy she is with him, no matter how much life she is missing, neither she nor the author seem to think of separation. Because of the marital promise, he must die in order for her to be with someone she loves, and conveniently for the happy ending, he does. Our current idea of divorce has altered radically from the nineteenth century, yet adultery today is still much like divorce was then, unthinkable except by terrible, selfish people. Unlike in the Victorian age, monogamy is now often upheld mainly by social and emotional pressure, replacing the way it was traditionally practiced, as a religiously and legally supported means of controlling (mostly women's) property, sexuality, and reproduction.

When I was involved with Gerald, friends would say to me, "I hope you know that if you and he became a couple, he'd do this to you too!", as if the only possible way of being with another person is to squeeze yourself into the same box you just emerged from. For many, when faced with infidelity, the solution is to quickly find a different mate who will surely toe the line of fidelity (because "You value YOU!"). Your purpose is to form a securely monogamous couple, after all, as if you learned nothing from the first go-round.

In the end, most spouses would probably prefer that the other be faithful (one synonym for "faith" is "hope"), but to make it a deal-breaker, a source of moral wrath and scorn, an indication of the quality or quantity of love for each other, and a cornerstone of modern marriage, seems to me not only unfair to each partner and an absurd weight on their relationship, but to be futile more often than we like to think. Studies show that adultery (based on legal marriage, not even counting other relationships) increased enormously as soon as other liberating social movements of the sixties and seventies, such as feminism and the sexual revolution, let loose a typhoon of desire in the Western world. Conservatives believe they can put that typhoon back in the bottle with ever more guilt and stricter enforcement. Good luck with that.

You have deduced by now that I don't believe in monogamy – but neither do I believe in open relationships or promiscuity as a solution to anything. I have nothing against any of those, but neither monogamy nor non-monogamy resolves the general problem of lifelong desire and romantic feelings that waver and are considered improper. My point is that as soon as you put sexuality and love into any preconceived, rigidly enforced form, you're expelling other possibilities before they happen. For that reason, I wouldn't advocate one way to express love over another. *Chacun à son goût*, as my father would say. And if both in a relationship genuinely *feel* monogamous, as opposed to presuming and swearing to it without thinking, if your desires happen to coincide with exactly what you're supposed to feel, hurray, you've won the marriage sweepstakes! There's nothing more to be said about this wonderful circumstance, so go on to the world's other problems, please.

Selfish: An Argument For Putting Oneself First (Sometimes)

We put such weighty meaning on what goes in whose orifice, where our bodies are and what they engage in, as though they're transparent vitrines displaying the value of our romantic relationships. What I wish I'd had in my own long marriage is not so much my husband's bodily chastity, someone's idea of purity, but more *curiosity*, an effort to know what my spouse was thinking and feeling – what his ideas were about me, about himself, about the quality of our relations, the truths that go beyond physical actions. It was our reluctance to pull off the masks that undermined our union on both sides, not the physical secrets of the genitals and their doings. The disaster is not lying to others; it's lying to oneself, which takes everyone else down with you.

I've said that in pop culture, adultery, even a temptation to adultery, is either punished or else diverted in the nick of time when the would-be cheater has an emotional epiphany that he is really, really happy with the One He Truly Loves after all, and would never, ever do that (again). But compelling sexual desire or emotional longing can be a stand-in for other desires that have been crushed, quickly or slowly, over the lifespan, having lived their secret lives somewhere in the dark cellar of your brain and gut. Anyone coupled up for a long time knows that people and circumstances are always in flux, that you can't predict what or when change will happen, that we may feel differently about spouses at different times in our lives, or even on the same day. Obviously new adjustments, entailing new forms of relationship, are made all the time (or sadly, never made) when people bind their lives to each other.

How then is a romantic couple going to proceed without security against another sexual relationship? This seems especially important if you have or expect to have children, who need the most stable structure possible while they're young. You'd think this question could be worked out by the couple, with thoughtful stops along the way when circumstances and feelings shift. If monogamy matters to both, why not "mostly monogamy," (what the writer Dan Savage calls "monogamish"), taking down the whole idea a dramatic notch? That way, if an affair is disclosed (and I don't necessarily believe it should be), it's not an apocalypse, but an event in a relationship to be understood, a truth coming to light. Knowing emotional facts is more important than regulating physical facts, especially because a sexual act can signify almost anything at different times in an infinite array of contexts.

Of course, it's not just a question of your own personal happiness and fulfillment; you must also concede that the selfish fulfillment of your own desire can certainly be hurtful. Many lovers or spouses are pained just by knowing the partner's desire for another (even a desire excited by fiction or images, as in pornography), much more by acting on that desire.

But ethics are almost always nuanced except at the extremes. (My friend Dora, annoyed that I frequently answer a question with "Well, it's complicated…" once burst out, "You always say that!" And I do, because almost everything *is* complicated when you think about it seriously, both the seemingly simple and also what seems mysterious.) Did my own husband harm me by having sexual affairs when I didn't know it, did I harm him with my love for someone else? And if so, did the harms in our relationship cancel each other out, so to speak? From my long view now, I think his affairs, which I knew nothing about, didn't hurt me, while his concealing what he thought and felt about me and our relationship for years did enormous damage.

The same goes for the denial of my own feelings, both to myself and to him. I caused my husband pain and humiliation when I confessed my own affair to him, it's true. On the other hand, that confession led to the end of a stultifying marriage. The truth did in fact set us free. If he's happier with the marriage that shortly followed ours, and I would have been unhappy continuing with him, as I'm quite sure I would, it seems less obvious that the affair itself was hurtful in any simple way, or that the better choice was to be paralyzed with guilt and fearful anxiety for a lifetime.

Another point that means even more to me personally: while it's obviously wrong to break a contract and betray trust, for me that has to be weighed against the damage and loss one might be causing oneself by inaction, the giving up of pieces of yourself just to keep the peace. It's not necessarily easy, and shouldn't be, to choose to put oneself first in intimate relations. But sometimes in life, especially where there's deep need or great desire, I would say *you are right to choose yourself.* Is there really a clear and unwavering boundary between unselfishness and neglecting what we owe to ourselves?

So much of our lives involves balancing the claims of others with our own, whether or not we consciously think of it that way. There's the Golden Rule, an inspiring ideal, and then there are the many decisions, from trivial to substantial, that we make in everyday life:

Must I do what my friend asks when I'd much rather not?

Am I wrong to enjoy an evening out if my toddler sobs when left with the sitter?

Should I please my parents by marrying the spouse of their choice?

Am I selfish not to have sex with my partner when I don't feel like it?

Must I open my house to that homeless person at the corner?

Should I give all my possessions to charity and live in the woods?

If decency requires us to put others before oneself, then many (most?) of our daily actions are not very decent. In reality we live with conflicting claims all the time: my needs versus yours, my desires versus the dictums of society or religion. In fact, don't we continually weigh our desires against our own *other* needs that conflict?

Selfishness and unselfishness are always selective.

Given that, where's the line for a "reasonable" sacrifice? It's all about proportion, a calculus of how strong the need is and how much you're giving up. The one exception is caring for children: their needs come first, because they're helpless. Yet – should I stay in a dead or painful marriage the rest of my life even for the sake of my children? Would you want your own children to do that? Where self-sacrifice becomes self-abnegation, morality bumps painfully into injustice… to oneself. The idea that unlimited self-sacrifice and unending devotion are a formula for happiness, much less a standard for living, is utopian for anyone not canonized.

In modern society, the priority of self versus other is never quite determined; we're frequently told we must follow our passion, yet we hear just as often that unselfishness in romantic relationships (often as part of the much lip-serviced "work") is somehow natural, even defining of romance itself.

If it's true that as a mistress I am choosing between the wife's happiness and my own, why must I always choose hers? Since Freud, following the Romantics, introduced the idea, it's been understood in Western culture that our feelings are of deep value, but (as Freud himself predicted) morality intersects awkwardly and uncomfortably with this value – thus the contradiction between the total unacceptability of cheating and the high rate of infidelity in everyday life. It doesn't help that this is presented as an absolute: you've cheated or you haven't.

Look, sometimes in the course of your life, you will probably break the rules. One of the ways we all contain Whitmanesque multitudes is that anyone who's not a saint or perfect conformist will be, at different times and places or in various ways, both a rule-follower and rule-breaker. Faced with choosing between stability and disruption, stability seems more attractive as a guide; that's a foundational principle of marriage. But should we always value stability over disruption, resignation over revolt? Whichever choice is right for the moment may be beyond formulas, outside even calculable self-interest. For women, putting your desires first has been inimical to the traditional female role of caring for others.

Living intensely might involve sacrificing the comforts of ordinariness. Conversely, what is reliable, comfortable, and enduring can suppress a vital sense of possibility essential to living. Why stay always in the middle lane? There's room in this capacious life, if we're lucky, for intense, selfish, and risky love, as well as sane, pre-approved, you're-my-rock, supposedly guaranteed affections. Neither has a certified happy ending.

Chapter Eight
All The Happy Endings

> He'd earned the right to happy endings/At least in fiction.
> – Wislawa Szymborska, "Consolation"

> Keep Ithaka always in your mind.
> Arriving there is what you're destined for.
> But don't hurry the journey at all.
> Better if it lasts for years,
> so you're old by the time you reach the island,
> wealthy with all you've gained on the way,
> not expecting Ithaka to make you rich.
> – C.P. Cavafy, "Ithaka"

Sometimes life seizes you unexpectedly, and bestows a splendid kiss on your lips. You've done nothing to deserve it; the moment is not likely to last. But the sense of it stays with you always nevertheless.

If this were a proper romance, I'd present you with a happy ending right now. And in a way, I will. There's an unusual love story coming, but it's not quite proper and you won't find it in a Harlequin novel or a rom-com. It's the story of Q.

I am a romantic failure. I never had another husband after the first one, or a fully committed romance – in the sense that committed is usually understood, entirely devoted to a One and Only. To some this may seem like the jigsaw puzzle missing that one important piece. As a woman, this is supposed to mean my entire *life* is incomplete. But it doesn't feel that way to me.

I have now arrived, mostly intact, at an age when everyone assumes you are past being desired, or desiring either, for that matter. Many of my older friends have been married for decades, some more contentedly than others, and almost all the rest no longer wish to have sex or expect to engage in a romantic relationship ("Relationships are a lot of work," says one). I have no desire at all for another husband.

I'm not ancient yet, by my standard, but definitely no longer middle-aged – just old enough to be annoyed when not given a seat on the train ("These young people are so rude") and equally annoyed when unexpectedly given one ("Wait, do I look that old?"). Age is like a flesh-eating plant; everything bodily is, of course, worse than it was, meaning it all slumps and droops on top, and ripples and wriggles on bottom; my neck-folds look like permanent smiles, while my knee-folds are in a permanent sulk. My hair, more or less gray now, is not to be discussed. I might be exaggerating somewhat, but it's in the correct direction: downward, where gravity takes you. What should I expect in the realm of romance?

Passionate love and aging don't go together, at least not in works of the imagination. There are very few novels or films that depict love and sex in old age, and even fewer that are truthful about it. If the odd movie romance happens to feature a middle-aged star, it's a still-attractive actress with personality, probably Meryl Streep, Diane Keaton, or Emma Thompson. In general, "old" women in popular culture are either incredibly wise about advising the young in love or else just absurd: good for laughs when they are "horny," or adorably cute when they find a boyfriend.

In the film *Away from Her,* the married Julie Christie is allowed a love affair because she has Alzheimer's (and is gorgeous), while the heroine of Elizabeth Strout's novel *Olive Kittredge*, grumpy and not-gorgeous, is given a settle-for-each-other relationship in her old age. As for Nicholas Sparks' *The Notebook* (more Alzheimer's)... oh please. Robert Waller's *Bridges of Madison County* (Meryl Streep, in the movie version) actually is about extramarital romantic and sexual passion, but Francesca, the married heroine, is only forty-five. That hardly makes her a crone, yet the novel treats her as well over the hill, too stodgy to do much beyond her excellent adventure of four (count them) romantic days.

The movie *Good Luck to You, Leo Grande*, features Emma Thompson as a stuffy, unsexy woman of sixty-two (the type called an "old biddy") who has the radical thought of trying to enjoy sex for once, after a lifetime of faking orgasms with her dull husband, and becomes an object of our fond amusement when she awkwardly and naively engages with a male escort. Then, after a few sessions of sexual attention, she becomes as sex-positive as the nearest millennial, and (predictably) has the orgasm she's always longed for. The scene is so contrived and fake it could be Hollywood's orgasm. Typical for the subject of aging women and sex, the film self-consciously has a well-intentioned "serious" message about older women's desire, but no awareness of how condescending the character portrait of that same older woman is.

My mother loved to sing a once-popular old song by Thomas Moore that begins "Believe me, if all those endearing young charms / Which I gaze on so fondly to-day." This is a reassurance to the beloved that when her "loveliness fades away" in old age, she will "still be adored," while "around the dear ruin, each wish of my heart / Would entwine itself verdantly still!"

The phrase that stands out to me is "dear ruin" – an older woman, dear or not, is inevitably a *ruin*? In the song, this is the measure of a man's love, that he will still want to stay with the ruined version of her! "Thank you, next," as the much more contemporary Ariana Grande sings. Our contemporary pretense that old women, such as the elderly, hot-to-trot ladies in the silly movie *80 for Brady*, have now been granted full humanity is nothing more than the other side of the coin of Moore's song from 1808: "ruined" but still lovable in their way.

The relationship of age to romance is not only about the energy of desire, which age is supposed to efface (except when it's the butt of jokes in comedy), it's based on the long-established issue of women's relationship to beauty, which has hardly changed in the last century. Pop culture fare such as *The Real Housewives* franchise, *The Bachelor/Bachelorette*, and *Keeping Up With The Kardashians* focus on showing us women actively examining every inch of their own and other women's physical and material assets, namely superior bodies and real estate, which are treated as pretty much the same thing. Glamor is the intersection of wealth and good looks. "You look amazing/gorgeous/stunning/fabulous!", the invariable greeting between women on these shows before another word is said, sets the standard for a woman's worth. This is of course replicated on all social media: anything less than an amazing/gorgeous/stunning appearance means you're near death.

To place the cherry on top, we know Hollywood is far more forgiving of a male star's decline in looks than a female of the same age: "Guys grow cold when girls grow old", as Marilyn Monroe sang; there's no lyric that states the reverse. That song is from 1949, but it's been much the same since then. Meanwhile, older men with younger women are still plentiful and perfectly allowable in both real life and media fantasy.

Betty And Al

Betty and Al did not mellow as they aged, or find peace and comfort in each other as they were supposed to. In fact, they quarreled to the very end of their marriage, which is to say, their lives. Neither left – where would they go? – but in fact there was a separation of a vague kind in the final years. My oldest brother Mel had bought a house in Florida, where they began to stay in the winter. After a while, Betty, who disliked the cold, decided to spend much of her time there. Al hated the heat and so stayed in the Northeast. Betty was fine with leaving it that way, neither wholly abandoning the relationship nor staying fully in it. At one point Betty showed me a poignant letter he'd written about missing her, saying he wished they could live together and start anew. He reminded her how long they'd been together, how much they'd gone through; it bordered on pleading, which made me cringe in sympathy. Her response was to dismiss this letter as "something out of *Reader's Digest*" – in other words, too sentimental. I knew this must have been a blow to him, and this stung me. But I also understood that her life with him had made her irrevocably bitter… it was no good for him to try to make it up to her now.

Life is not fiction, with its happy reconciliations and neat resolutions. Around this time, I wrote in my journal:

Maybe when they're both dead I will write about all this and remember how I felt about the tragedy and grief and absurdity and ugliness of it.

I was eight months pregnant with my third child, my son, when my father died. He'd had cancer a few years before, leading to surgery and radiation, but was given a good prognosis. Soon after, he retired and began the life he'd always wanted, out of the city, in a green area of New Jersey, where he could ride his bike, tend a tiny garden, and talk pleasantly with the neighbors. I remember him playing happily with my children when I came to see my parents, taking photos of them, enjoying every minute with me. On my last visit, when he was in the hospital after a frightening episode of heart failure the night before, I tried to distract him with my lively three-year-old moppet Amanda. "Isn't she cute, Daddy?", I prompted him, lifting her onto his hospital bed. "Very cute," he agreed, and then suddenly he wept – I'd never seen him cry. With dread in my heart, I said I'd see him soon and left to stay with my in-laws. As soon as we arrived, my mother called to say that my father had suddenly died. Later, we were told that the cancer had spread to the lining of his heart.

Al died too soon; Betty lived too long. My mother sold the house in New Jersey where my dad had wanted to be with her, and moved to Florida, free to do as she pleased. But she descended, slowly at first, then with shocking rapidity, into the deepest fog of Alzheimer's, almost as soon as she was seemingly liberated by my father's death. Perhaps his irritating presence was a kind of angry spark from which she drew purpose and structure.

At first when she began repeating herself, it seemed merely more of the same, since her stories about the troubles of others and her own triumphs over trouble had always been on repeat. Then there was the time we all went out for dinner and she went back into the restaurant after we'd gone through the door, scooped up the tip left on the table, and walked out again. But that too was not unlike her tendency to take bits of things from restaurants, sugar packets, napkins, even a steak knife or two. She was quirky that way.

The moment I became afraid was later on when I visited her in Chicago, where she'd gone to live with my brother Eric. It was mid-day and my brother was at work. Betty greeted me at the door and said she was hungry, could we take a walk and eat lunch out? Sure, I said, but we wandered here and there because she couldn't find the McDonald's where she said she usually ate. This was disturbing, but I was chattering as we walked around, holding fast to the normal, when she looked at me sideways and suddenly remarked, "I have a daughter who teaches at Columbia University, you know." I didn't teach at Columbia; that was a conflation of my graduate school and the news I'd recently sent her that I was now a professor. It was not unusual for her to exaggerate the facts, but it was clear she didn't know who I was. My heart plunged. "Mom," I cried, "*I'm* your daughter," but she only cocked one eyebrow skeptically, and remained uncharacteristically silent. I suspect the sideways look and the boast was her way of testing out whether it was me, after all. It wasn't clear that I'd passed the test.

So much else was happening when I was in my forties, as her memory and reasoning were racing downhill; I was unhappily in love, with all the emotional struggle that affair had brought, and my marriage had ended, with serious financial consequences to me and pain for my children. My mother's condition was an added agony. While I was slowly becoming myself at last, Betty's body went on sloughing off her mind and selfhood.

She began to weave a preposterous narrative: her beloved son Mel, her handsome prince who became the doctor that her father and early twentieth century society would not let her be, was the featured enemy. He and his wife, she began writing to me, were reporting her to the IRS for fraud; she hated them. My poor brother was so upset by this insane accusation that his wife had to hide his mother's letters so he would not read them.

After she somehow slipped out of his house and was found by the police, terrified, strapped to a gurney in a hospital, unable to identify herself, Eric, who could not bring himself to institutionalize her, had to admit that even an expensive health aide was not enough. Finally, he allowed me to find a place for her in a nursing home near me in New York. By then she had no idea who anyone was or where she was, so she didn't miss us; in fact, she seemed a bit better for the move at first. Betty charmed the nurse's aides who cared for her by telling each one they were "beautiful", one of the last words she could say. I'm sure this was to get on their good side so she would be treated well. It worked: the staff sincerely seemed to think she was sweet, not a word I'd have ever used for peppery Betty. But soon my extremely talkative mother lost all language, though once she amazed (and embarrassed) me by interrupting a holiday event at the nursing home, where Jewish songs were performed in Hebrew for the patients, by loudly singing a line of "I'm a Lassie from Lancashire," one of her best-loved girlhood songs.

The Lassie from Lancashire lived out another ten years there. We would sit together in the garden or near a window while I sang to her or later just quietly graded papers. We touched each other, now that there was no more talking: I would stroke her soft white hair, her cheek or hand, or rest my head on her lap as I had when I was a child. And exactly as when I was a child, she would absent-mindedly pat my head, as if from muscle memory, without any sign that she knew I was there, really.

I wrote at the time:

Who are we to each other? The muddle of parent-child expectations is over. Now she is the baby and I am the grown-up making all the decisions; I am the actor and she is the acted-upon, I am smarter, competent, worldly, responsible, the one who protects and nurtures and thinks ahead for us both. I am also the one who comes and kisses and embraces her, who strokes her hair and hands. If memory is identity, does she have more identity in me?

For a good while, Betty in dementia maintained a mild look of What the hell?, as if it were all slightly surprising.

But these were not bad years. I had always wanted so much for her to be happy, and now she smiled more than she ever had. I suspect this was because she had lost all memory of what she'd been angry about, worried about, even suspicious about. All I had left of my mother was a charming, teasing, slightly coy smile I remembered well. But it was a Cheshire Cat smile, remaining as if hanging in the air while her consciousness disappeared and her selfhood softly faded away.

And then nothing.

My mother had wanted me to do all she could not do: be educated, become a professional, marry well. She wanted her daughter to listen to her stories, a stand-in for a lifetime of longing for the world to hear and know her. And now I tell her story.

More Love

And then, when I was barely fifty, I began a new life with new children. As soon as my own children were no longer young, I realized that I didn't just love them because they were mine, I also loved them because I love children. Being with children… listening to what they say, observing what they do and how they think, looking at their changing beauty from newborn to young adulthood… is one of my chief pleasures in existing. I know the children in my life are probably not really the most beautiful, charming and funny humans in the world, but I can't help believing they are. The truth is irrelevant.

All English nicknames for a grandmother sound like

premises for a joke to me: Granny, Grandma, Gram, Gran, Nana. I felt I was too young to be a grandmother when my first grandchild was about to enter the world – my daughter married at an even younger age than I did – but seeing the birth of this perfectly beautiful infant, being there at her first breath, was a moment of the greatest happiness for me. And now the number of persons I love most has expanded from three to nine, with the glorious variety of personalities, gifts, tastes, and flaws found in large families. Individually, they range from reserved to super-social, quiet to very talkative, extremely picky eater to gourmand, intense and emotional to mild and even-tempered, "easy" to raise to "difficult." The men I've loved are also very different in these ways; I'm not looking for a type in either family or lovers.

Strangely, in my grandchildren, I see a connection between the passion I've had for lovers and the joy that children give me. In both kinds of passion, for babies and lovers, the pleasure of embracing the beloved is of prime importance, and you think of the other's body as not only connected to you, but as *yours*. Both are different in these ways from the affection you feel for siblings or friends.

Then too, in both kinds of love, romantic and maternal, time is suspended when you are wholly present with the one you fiercely love.

It's not that time disappeared when I was with the babies in my family, nor was it speeded up or slowed down; rather, time felt like a made-up concept, empty of real meaning, as arbitrary as whether a month is thirty or thirty-one days, or which day begins a new year. In passion, time is rich, it flows as if thickened with some delicious sauce, a kind of extended timelessness. I've only experienced that sense of no-time in making love with the two men I've loved most, and holding the children I love when they were new. I am most myself when I am caressing the body of a man I am deeply in love with. I am also most myself when I delight in watching a baby work on pulling off her shoes the way a workaholic takes on a project.

It's a tired cliché that grandchildren are more satisfying because you don't have primary responsibility for them (though some grandparents do) – the conventional explanation is that you can give them back at the end of the day. Yes, it was new and wonderful that my freedom and privacy were not restricted as when I was a mother, and therefore I escape the suppressed resentment of constantly choosing between my own desires and fulfilling their needs. For this reason, I can be free of the onerous expectations and judgments of my grandchildren that I had with my children, for better or worse; they don't have to "pay me back" for the effort of raising them by being exemplary human beings. This is not perfect love, of course – but I've never come closer to loving anyone for exactly who they are as I love the six children of my children, no matter what their parents or the world thinks of them. I doubt I could ever achieve this with a lover or husband, where expectations count heavily: judging how they are performing, noting how they are treating me, weighing their value.

On the other hand, any sort of love comes with a price. Loving children and grandchildren means I want to hear good news from and about them all the time. I want happy faces, funny moments, frequent celebrations. At the same time, I have a driving need to be there for them when they are sad or anxious or in trouble, which means listening to bad news, hearing sad stories, seeing what I wish weren't so, all of which contradicts that first desire. I didn't think of this when I chose to have children as the primary love in my life. It's the ones who make me happiest who also make me saddest.

When you have three children and six grandchildren, the odds are that at least one and usually more are likely to be miserable or worrisome at any moment. They are never all doing well at the same time. Here's the rub: it's not just that their pain or sorrow is my pain, though much worse, but in the case of grandchildren, I'm even more helpless to help them. Yes, I can advise (you can visualize the eye-rolls, I'm sure), but I don't have the authority to make decisions… because their parents have the responsibility that I'm not supposed to want, the very condition I'm supposed to rejoice in.

Romance is loving to be loved for yourself; devotion is loving for the sake of love. One is not superior or inferior to the other because one is more self-centered; it's human to want pleasure centered on yourself. These two kinds of love are only different ways to love.

Men, Again

After Nick left to marry someone else, just before my first grandchild was born, I began to date again. This wholesome activity – lining up single, age-appropriate men – was conducted almost all through online websites, once I'd exhausted the local talent. "I'd be glad to fix you up," my friends would say, "but every man your age I know is either married, gay, completely neurotic, or a horrible human being." Often it was all of those together.

Around this time, another event not only distracted me, it made me more emotionally needy while feeling less valuable in the marketplace of dating. I was treated for breast cancer: surgery, chemo, radiation, the whole experience. It seemed fine for over a decade. Then a recurrence in the same spot resulted in a further surgical mutilation of my breast. I wrote about it this way before the surgery:

So today I'm thinking about nipples in general and my left nipple in particular. It's an interesting experience to look at a part of your body that you've had all your life and know that it's shortly going away. I don't think that's ever happened to me before, unless you count cutting off hair and trimming nails.

When I've told people in person that this is about to happen, I think I see by their expressions that they're embarrassed or horrified, or maybe embarrassed because they're trying not to show that they're horrified. But is it really all that bad?

That nipple (and its twin, of course) had a long and rich life of its own, in a way. I remember very well when it first puffed out at age eleven, and my puzzlement about this, since I hadn't exactly been briefed on expecting it or what it meant. There was the curious recognition that boys were supposed to be very interested in the existence of those nipples, and not quite understanding the enthusiasm behind that for a long time.

It took a while to see the beauty of a breast and nipple, and to think my own were quite pretty. The nipple part of the breast is almost always painted as rosy and smooth, or photographed in glowing light, when in fact it's not lovely in itself, especially the bump at the end that goes into the baby's (or lover's) mouth.

Then came the babies, three of them, if anything more fixated than the boys had been, each infant in turn entirely obsessed with those nipples. And for a long time, even when they weren't needed, they were still always wanted, possibly the most wanted part of my entire body, since they'd done double service for sexual desire and nurturing.

And now – no babies, no lovers, no admirers any longer for those nipples. One was just gone, and I feared the poor remaining stand-alone breast looked wrong, probably freakish to anyone who should look at it. I didn't intend for it to be seen, though, maybe not even by myself. I recall that when my father had a mastectomy (he had male breast cancer) and swam shirtless in a pool, someone complained to the management that his surgical scar was disturbing and they made him put on a shirt when he swam. I remembered my dad's face when he told me that. And I'd seen pictures of mastectomies online and in magazines, and I thought then that they were disturbing to look at too.

Yet I wasn't very upset at losing my nipple, in spite of facing the problem of looking good in shirts and tank tops. What's the value of looking good? I'd been giving that up for years by that time. I felt like I'd made a swap, my nipple for my life, and I'd got the far better part of the bargain. I said goodbye to that nipple fondly and with regret, but it was a hearty farewell. You might say that after nursing babies and pleasing lovers, giving and getting pleasure, it had done its job long and well, and the last thing it could do for me was go quietly to save my life.

Eventually the doctors decided that nothing but a full mastectomy would do, and so I lost the breast as well. Yet here I was on dating sites advertising myself, if not for sale exactly, at least as available and worthy of a close look. I anticipated being inspected like a hog at market and failing the test.

Dating is an odd and rapidly changing modern invention, as opposed to traditional courting. Now the romantic idea has shifted to "finding your person," a process something like flipping through a pack of cards to find the Ace of Spades, though the pack of cards feels infinite online. But it's far from infinite. Studies show the market is skewed to an abundance of older women, with "old" defined as over forty. I once went on a date with an older man who helpfully made exactly this point: "You probably know," he said seriously, "that for every man over sixty who dates online, there are ten older women." "Oh, I *do* know," I said. "My point is," he went on, his voice rising, "that *I'm the best you can do*. I'm about your age, I'm a professional, and I live in your neighborhood. You're not going to do better than me." Even he couldn't argue that he was good-looking or fascinating, just that he was a precious commodity I'd better jump on while the price was right.

I know a number of older men, straight and gay, some not particularly attractive, who found online dates that became committed romantic partners in no time at all. Two of these fellows had lined up three likely candidates almost immediately after they decided to date, and the ladies were all as willing as Barkis. Once having made the lordly decision to prefer one of those on offer, the man and his date were a solid long-term couple within a week. Young women are also always in demand. My problem was not that I wasn't in demand, rather that I didn't much care for what was on offer. Some of my older female acquaintances have selected the best of the few they met online who would do for a relationship, and I have great resistance to that.

Oddly, in some ways the limitations of "dating" through electronic contact remind me more of traditional Victorian courtship than twentieth-century customs, pre-online dating. Fans of historical romance fiction revel in the strict limitations on behavior that were part of the traditional "making a match," at least among the middle and upper classes, before the automobile, the anonymity of urban dwelling, and the increasing independence of working women in the early twentieth century released young people from the restrictions. In a Georgette Heyer Regency romance, or in almost any novel that features an eligible hero and heroine, from Fielding's eighteenth-century *Tom Jones* to Thackeray's mid-nineteenth-century *Vanity Fair*, all the way to Anthony Trollope before World War I, the pleasure of reading is tracing the efforts of the suitor and his lady to work the highly structured system – or better, to work around it and wiggle their way to the goal of marriage without openly flouting the rules. This strategizing can be both amusing and suspenseful.

One of the most entrenched restrictions of the traditional courtship system that needed navigation was the assigned roles of the genders, as it has been throughout history and in most of the world. For one thing, women's behavior was carefully guarded by strictly limiting the private time of the couple before engagement. The first meeting might take place as an introduction in a social space, and the courtship would be at home or among others in social gatherings. A chaperone of one sort or another either at home or away from home ensured the all-important "purity" of the couple's relations. Unless you married your cousin (not unusual both in real life and in novels) or your neighbor, you may not have known all that much about your suitor beyond your impression of him in social encounters.

Another rule, also gendered, was that only the male could initiate courtship and make the marriage proposal, while the woman should never disclose her feelings first, or better yet, until a marriage proposal was made. Such forwardness would mark a woman as vulgar and unfeminine, since this was assumed to be unquestionably the male role. Therefore, the enjoyable game, on the part of the reader and the characters – and perhaps also for the real people engaged in this all-important pursuit – was to figure out what was really going on between the potential lovers, how to communicate feelings and correctly guess what the other had in mind. Flirting was a subtle expression for encouraging a suitor, but not subtle enough: the Victorians clamped down on this too. The label of "flirt" lowered a woman's reputation, when reputation was her safeguard for being chosen by a male of desirable value.

Since money and social class were important markers of the value or desirability of both suitor and his lady (the lady might have less money but more beauty), there were, in fact, certain boxes that had to be checked to get the necessary approval of the families involved. There was no stigma to openly prioritizing these material values, because they determined the future of the couple and their children, and were sometimes an investment in the extended family's welfare as well. We can see this in *Pride and Prejudice*, which quotes exact incomes and shows the family's hand-wringing over the fate of daughters who will not inherit property and therefore must urgently find good husbands ("good" meaning both character and resources, but especially the latter). We are also told the exact level of beauty in the marriageable young women, so we as readers can assess how much leverage they have in vying for the valuable male.

In the twentieth century, before World War II, when the practice we call "dating" began, everything changed: women were more able to hop into an automobile, have a private date in the dark of the movie theater, or even entertain in a space of their own, all without bringing doom on their heads. The emphasis on female virginity had not altered much, and males still were expected to be in charge of "asking a girl out" or proposing. But romantic love had established itself as (supposedly) the norm as a motivation for marriage, and so the couple were not only able but encouraged to grow more intimate in terms of knowing the other on equal grounds, so as to fall in love. Through dating, you spent quality time together alone as well as with friends and family, assessing how you two get along, what it would be like to live as a couple for life. Of course, the importance of social status and wealth hadn't disappeared... these were just not as openly accepted as a motivation and priority.

By the fifties and sixties, dating was something like a preview of marriage. You met someone in high school or college, or in your social set, or perhaps at work, and if, after a while, you hit it off, you were "going steady." This meant you two were temporarily committed and monogamous, halfway to getting engaged, but not living together. In real life, when my oldest brother, Mel, met his first serious girlfriend through his summer job, she was sixteen and he was twenty and in college. As soon as she was eighteen and had graduated high school, they were married, and six decades later, are still devoted to each other. One and done. But in Philip Roth's 1959 novella *Goodbye, Columbus,* the narrator pressures his girlfriend into sex at a time when it was still illegal for unmarried women to use birth control. Sex and class differences are the sites of struggle between them, and eventually break them up. Roth reveals the underbelly of this culture, the hidden issues in dating relationships that weren't supposed to be there.

The sexual revolution, the invention of the birth control pill, the women's movement, and the gay rights demonstrations in the late sixties and seventies were the stepping stones to the much looser form of dating we have now, in which sex is played up and social status is (purportedly) played down. Virginity was widely ignored as a requirement for women, though men still asked women out and paid for dates. Then, at the very end of the twentieth century (Match.com began in 1995), online dating disrupted the previous system entirely, slowly expanding over the next decades to apps that specialize in types – ages, ethnicities and religions, educational level, sexual preference, and much else. It makes you think of Adam Smith and the division of labor in the eighteenth century.

Has the automating of dating elevated our chances of finding The One, or made the dating experience better? I would say that by demoting the value of knowing someone in their natural setting of family, friends and work, we've gone back to the box-checking of pre-twentieth century pragmatic courtship. As with all consumer products, there's an ever-growing tendency in online dating to want more with less effort: we can now efficiently target a potential date's location, profession, tastes and preferences, while blatantly using programmed marketing techniques of selling yourself in language and carefully selected photos. This rational sorting of possible mates has a similar connection to passion as the Orgasmatron machine in Woody Allen's futuristic comedy, *Sleeper*, has to… well, an actual orgasm.

The result of all these efforts can either be fruitful or astonishingly bad, depending on your status in the market. This is determined by the cold facts of looks, age, and (admit it or not) resources, not just financial status but the social status of profession – more free than it used to be, less restrained, in other words, especially for women, but not all that different from the boxes-to-check in courting and marriage in traditional society as a substitute for passion. I certainly had many interesting experiences thanks to online dating, and met a few interesting men (not the same thing), but generally speaking, I feel I've wasted half a lifetime looking at photographs, reading what a potential date is looking for, and meeting a fleet of men I would barely want to talk to if they sat next to me at a dinner party. Yet a number of men I know have found this process fun; all the women I know find it exhausting, if not demeaning. One man's profile helpfully warned: "Serial first-date dinner-daters, please note that I keep permanent reservations at the exotic Grey's Papaya hot-dog stand, just for you. If your purpose in being here is to secure free meals, I'll take you instead to a supermarket and treat you to a cart-full of food you can prepare for yourself at home." Sweet.

At first, I met up with anyone who would have me, and engaged in a couple of weeks-long pseudo-relationships I was relieved to ditch. One of these was Owen. I didn't like his company all that much, but he seemed kind, so I gave in to his pressure to have sex. It was so bad, so empty and unsatisfying, that… well, let me put it this way: I'd far rather have sex with my former husband. Still, I thought it might be my fault for being critical when it was only the first time we were intimate, so I agreed to it again. It was worse, which I didn't think was possible. Bye-bye Owen.

This sort of dating taught me that your lifelong expectations for how people should behave in romantic encounters quickly comes up against the expectations of others. Owen, who I'd labeled a "very nice guy," was pleasant until I gently told him I was ready to call it quits after six weeks; then he angrily upbraided me in public because I hadn't given him a chance, and followed that up (in case I hadn't understood) with accusatory emails. I can understand disappointment, but Owen seemed to think I owed him more time, as if it were a given right.

Years later, I tried again, and decided to write down my adventures for my friends:

May 25th: It's not like I haven't done this before, and that's what scares me. I'm all too familiar with the rising hopes, the sadness when I confront the reality of who's out there, the humiliation of rejection before I'm even given a chance to meet, and the sheer boredom of wasting my time in trivial conversation with men who don't attract me. Too bad. It's part of the process, and it has to be done, like check-ups at the dentist. Except that's not a good analogy, because after my teeth are cleaned, I feel good, healthier than before, having gotten a concrete result with minimal time and effort (though a lot more money). I can't say that about dating: on the contrary, I often feel a little dirty after these encounters online. And I don't mean in a good way.

But hey, hope is that thing with feathers that flaps around no matter what mean and pessimistic thoughts I have. So here goes, and we'll see if my experience lives up to my cynicism.

May 30th: I was feeling quite down when I wrote the above. But… according to Emily Dickinson, hope not only has feathers but "perches in the soul" – it's somewhere in there, or I wouldn't be doing this at all. And meanwhile, I'm getting lessons on the human mind, and the social construction of gender and age, and good stuff like that. Plus they say that suffering is good for character, and my character could use some goodness.

It's a given that there are going to be lots of men I won't like and will find ridiculous. But this doesn't mean I don't like men. On the contrary, I find men naturally delicious, if I like them or love them, or even if I'm just attracted to them. I adored my father, I'm crazy about my brothers, feel that my grown son can do no wrong, worship the ground my four grandsons walk or crawl on, and I probably have more male friends than most women my age do. And let's not even start on men I've loved romantically, every single one of whom I actually still love today (there aren't very many). So I'm far from a man-hater.

On the other hand, my fear of being hurt is in direct proportion to the pleasure that men can give me, and that produces, at least in the beginning, a certain defensive cynicism along with longing – you might call it a hostile edge to hope. I know this, but it's very hard to distinguish between standing up for myself for the first time in my romantic life, as I want to do, or just being "too picky" about men, as I've been told I am.

June 3rd: An email from Columbia University advertised an alumni speed dating event, and I thought, "Well, why not? That might be interesting and fun." The link said, "Are you interested in meeting fellow alums for romance? Sign up for our speed-dating event, ages 20-40!" Sigh. Sob. I saw 40 a long time ago. Apparently I now don't exist in the speed dating world.

Fred seems downright ugly in his profile picture. But the guy has his profession going for him: he's a high-achiever in a field that interests me. So I wrote one of my come-hither letters, and responded right away. Yes, I have an appealing profile, he says, but he's "seeing someone more or less regularly. Good luck." He did not come hither.

This was food for another meditation about men and women and age and looks. Every man who has a high-status profession, no matter how repulsive or how old, seems to make out like a bandit, while high-status me, ten years younger than Fred and (excuse me for saying so) a lot better-looking, lies gasping on the shore. I'm not sure if this makes me hate men, or the women who choose these guys, or the whole sex-gender-age system. But damn, it's unsatisfying to hate a system: so abstract. Therefore – irrationally, I admit – I hate Fred instead. Don't worry, no actual men were harmed in the course of this emotion.

I had a session with a personal trainer yesterday (comes free with joining my gym for the summer) and after we talked about my "goals", he informed me that I'm "starting from a very good platform." I asked what that means, since I'm totally out of shape and have less muscle tone than a Cabbage Patch doll. It turned out he meant that I have a good body for my age, no weight issues or bumps in the wrong places. Well, a girl has to hang onto something while being battered by Match.com. At least I have a good platform.

June 6th: Phil has a pleasant face, sent a flattering email suggesting dinner at a place of my choice, and best of all, volunteered to come somewhere near my neighborhood, contrasting nicely with Quentin, who clearly thought meeting me in Manhattan was an imposition. So in spite of misgivings, I impulsively set up a meet-and-greet for today.

My misgivings about Phil were based on his work history – he's a businessman, has owned a men's suit store, and done other business-y things. I've never yet dated a businessman (or scientist, for that matter) who has the same sensibilities I do. But in the spirit of Broadening the Scope, I suspended my disbelief.

Except it turns out that Phil did not invite me to dinner. After numerous confusing communications involving a link I'd sent him to a restaurant where we could have a glass of wine and tapas, it turns out that wasn't what he meant at all. This was revealed when he asked what kind of place I had suggested, even though I'd sent him the website so he'd see the address. "It's a restaurant where we can have a glass of wine and tapas," I replied. He wrote back plaintively, "But I said I'd take you to a diner. I want to go to a diner." Had he said that? I found the email he'd sent, and sure enough, it said, "I'd like to meet you and take you to a dinner, you choose the place." Now, I did think that dinner at two pm (the time he wanted) was peculiar, but then, what isn't peculiar about this whole process? After this misunderstanding, we agreed we'd just meet halfway and look for a place he considers sufficiently diner-like. That was yesterday.

This morning, bright and early, he called to say that he'd "hurt his leg somehow" and would remake the date next week. I can't say how glad I was. Of course I didn't hear from him again, and did not consider this tragic.

I'm detailing this trivial event because it illustrates an important principle in this online dating business, if not in life. How do we come to judgments about people (not to mention situations) with little actual knowledge? Interestingly, there are two books on the New York Times bestseller list today that argue, respectively:

1) we should go with our gut in making decisions, and

2) we should not go with our gut in making decisions.

And they sell because this question is terribly confusing in real life. People want someone to tell them, once and for all: how do I know?

So with Phil, I see now that I said yes to the immediate date because his relatively pleasant looks compared well with the unattractive available men I've been seeing online; because Phil's willingness to travel from his neighborhood closer to mine contrasted nicely with the humiliating reluctance of Quentin; and last, because of his flattery, evidence of good taste in women. None of this was predictive.

June 9th: Today I had lunch with Ron, who'd been too busy to see me the last two weeks. He's the one whose wife is in a nursing home. A lovely man, unfortunately not in the physical sense.

We talked about politics, about which we mostly agree, but it was the usual: he was eager to tell me his opinions on current events, not to hear my own aperçues. That's fine when someone knows more than I do, or has fascinating things to say, but alas, not in Ron's case. I'd like to tell all single men that the secret to capturing a woman is to ask her questions and actually listen to the answers. It really isn't all that hard to do.

So then I asked about Ron's life (he was totally uninterested in mine). He's been married over forty years, and his wife was an unusual woman. Though she didn't go to college, she rose from secretary (his word) to a high-level position at a financial firm, making tons of money before she became ill. I was way more interested in her than I was in Ron himself.

Ron then revealed that when he proposed marriage to his wife, she broke down and told him the awful truth that she was seven years older than he was. He emphasized this as though she had been withholding the news that she had Ebola. Ron related that he immediately withdrew the marriage proposal in the face of this horror: "When I'm forty-three," he reported thinking, "she'll be fifty!" His tone was: Can you imagine such a thing? Of course this made me feel about a hundred years old. Fortunately for the lucky

Ron, some time after dismissing her, he realized he missed her and stooped to marry her, but apparently her advanced age bothered him for decades. I pointed out that he is eleven years older than I am, did that bother him? No? Wasn't that a double standard? He looked mightily confused, but came back with: I just go by what pleases me. If a woman doesn't like my age, she's free to withdraw.

Though I liked Ron, I can't see hanging out with him. And one reason is that he feels too old for me. Put that in your irony pipe and smoke it.

A friend points out in an email that it's "all a crapshoot anyway. Our very individual existence is a biological accident, so how can there be any method in the pursuit of love?" He recommends meeting without knowing anything about the candidate and just flopping into bed.

June 15th: Stewart had one of the longest and most detailed profiles I've ever seen. He's done a good deal of traveling, and he appears to have listed every place he's visited on the globe. Plus he has a tremendous lust for seeing the many sights of New York, all of which were also listed, and he is a marvel of athleticism in a variety of sports, which were listed too. It made me tired just to read it all, but he was dashingly handsome in his picture, sporting a bicycle helmet.

He responded right away, ready to have fun with me in exhaustive detail. It dawned on me that what he is dying for, being alone in a new city, is a companion in his hyper-energetic travels.

The next morning there was a two-sentence follow-up email from Stewart, solemn and earnest: How much time did I devote to my job? Was I off for the summer? I felt like I was being interviewed for a position, those niggling last questions before you're made the offer or declined. I answered, out of politeness, but Stewart then wrote a last regretful note: "I guess I have to accept the fact that I really want someone who has time and freedom."

That's what I get for being lazy. However, not only did Stewart talk exclusively about himself, the usual turn-off (he was curious about me just once, asking how much time I would have… for him), but it was very clear that he had a strict agenda of his own: rigorous companionship in his daily travels.

"So what do you want from this, if you're not going to give it a chance?" asked my friend Dora reasonably. Good thing I have reasonable people in my life to ask me unanswerable rational questions. In the same way that I complain about the way this online dating process makes romance into work, complete with resumes and interviews, figuring out what I want in advance feels weird and unromantic. What do I want? Love, liking, sex, company, pleasure, spontaneity… actually I'd take one or two of those. (Yes, that's correct: in advance I want… spontaneity.) And it's truly amazing how difficult any of these desires is to fulfill.

Actually, I sometimes think if I could meet someone who makes me laugh, I could forgive many sins.

Maybe I should have followed a friend's advice to reel them in: First, lie about your age ("If you don't lower your age, you'll look older than you are because everyone else is doing it"), and second, say you have a rent-controlled apartment or a country house, even if you don't.

But the real problem was not reeling in the fish; the problem was that the older I've grown, the narrower my tolerance is for the way I spend my free time with assorted fellows out there. And that violates what I call the Dating Platitudes:

Platitude One: You can't tell on first or even second date whether you will like someone, because he could be a hidden gem.

Platitude Two: If you are free of other attachments, love is bound to happen.

Platitude Three: If it doesn't happen, it must be your

own fault.

The latter particularly bothers me; I call this the "If you build it, they will come" (and date you) theory.

It seems unfair to me that wanting too much (the story of my life) is an explanation for why I haven't found someone I can love in this supermarket of relationships. Consumer choice is about the quality of the goods as well as your own resources; it's not just about your eclectic tastes. If the market narrows and the choices on the shelves grow bare, it's not necessarily a reflection of your bad character that you don't find what you want. You know the song: It's nice work if you can get it, and you can get it if you try. Actually you can't predictably get it just because you try. And you're unlikely to get it if it's not really there.

I may have become too undomesticated, a former pussycat on the hearth gone feral, to be with someone who does not give me a certain degree and kind of pleasure. It doesn't help that I've developed an allergy to the Alpha Male – this may appeal to mass-market romance heroines, but not to me. I just don't want anyone telling me what I can or should do or be any longer.

On the other hand, I made a startling discovery: there are numerous young men who particularly seem to lust after older women. Who knew?

From my journal:

Online dating this summer has surprisingly revealed that I am popular with men from 20 through 88. Maybe there's some kind of prize for Broadest Appeal? But trophies aren't boyfriends, though I've heard they can be wives.

There were a number of young men like Trevor, age

twenty-nine, as I noted at the time:

"Hello, i am Trevor. I really enjoyed reading your profile and wanted to introduce myself. I work on wall street by day but evenings i am an artist, a painter and a photographer. I am successful and educated and looking for a nice lady to enjoy life with. Would you like to talk?"

I said no, too young, but I hope he finds that wonderful woman he can enjoy life with. He came back with: "For now sex is good, I am too busy otherwise. Wanna meet up?"

I replied that it wasn't going to happen, alas, and wished him luck. His final words: "Okay, I will wait for a time when you might need good sex and amazing pillow talk for hours."

I'm mighty fond of Trevor. Talented with the pitch, for sure.

That was when I wrote in my journal, many years ago:

Having sex with someone I'm not all that attracted to, as I did in my energetic forties, is not something I feel like doing any longer. In fact, there are very few men I see that I want to touch, so dating has not been a gratifying experience, and I've pretty much given it up. That doesn't mean I don't miss sex, but what I miss specifically is the way it was when it was great, not the way it would be with the men I've met in recent years.

Why am I not sad that the sexual part of my life seems to be over? You'd think I would be, given how important it was in the middle of my life. But I can never go back to the way it was, and that long period of obsessive, unrequited love was so torturous that I wouldn't want to. Nor could I possibly want to return to the kind of ritualized, chilly sex I had with my husband, or still further back, the confused and conflicted sex I had before marriage. If sex should return to my life, it would have to be different, because my life is different. The next stage will tell its own story, and we'll see if it includes sex or not. My guess is not, but then I've learned never to say never.

Then "never" happened… it's the story of the splendid kiss. It's not a happy-ever-after, and kissing was the least of it.

The Story Of Q

The story of Q is an out-of-body experience, but with bodies, at least some of the time.

I had never told anyone, not even my brother Eric, my confidant who knew everything about me, the story of Q. This wasn't because I thought my brother would disapprove; we never criticized or judged each other. It was more that it seemed irrelevant to the rest of my life. My relationship with Q tracked alongside my real life with a kind of delightful shadow existence. It was a little talisman I kept in my pocket and turned over once in a while with pleasure.

And we had never met, so there wasn't much to tell that wouldn't seem absurd. He had messaged me on an online dating site, a very accomplished man but younger than was called for, even younger than Nick. This was enough to disqualify him from my romantic fantasies, though it infuriated me when men disqualified women on the basis of age. His online message was charming, but he was married: I'd been there, done that sort of thing, no thanks. Yet he persisted, and I couldn't resist answering his amusing letters; no harm can be done through electrons only, I thought.

From the first, he was conflicted about what he wanted, and I was conflicted about wanting him. But the pressure was off when he retreated from his original purpose about a year in, got cold feet about meeting after all, and so we… just kept writing once in a while. These weren't romantic or seductive notes: I had glimpses into his burgeoning career, nothing like my career, and Q sympathized with my worries about children and health, though he had no children and was himself in perfect health.

We wrote back and forth every few months this way for over ten years, not quite friends but not lovers, closer and closer not-friends-not-lovers in this liminal space as years spun by, without ever making plans to meet. As it happened, he lived within walking distance, but he could have lived in Tokyo for all it mattered. I had no idea what he looked like, in any case. His letters were so delightful that I kept replying, telling him at ever-increasing length and depth my woes and resolutions, complaints and observations about the world, the sort of thing you tell good friends, but somehow different with him. I loved his attentive responses to what I told him, his interesting behind-the-scenes descriptions of his work, and the sly sense of humor that unexpectedly made me laugh aloud.

I thought of him as my dear, clever, funny, always interesting confidant, a secret, *confidential* confidant. He was an indulgent but harmless enjoyment from afar, popping up with semi-regularity to give me momentary comfort and amusement. At one point in our correspondence, I lamented that I hated Valentine's Day because it felt like a fake holiday, yet always made me feel like single-woman trash. On every V-Day afterward, without fail, he sent a sweet but non-romantic note, such as a supportive description of the torture the real St. Valentine endured.

It amazes me now that I never so much as had the curiosity to search for Q's photo online, so little did I have a sense that we would meet, much less become lovers, much, *much* less that he would become one of the most important men in my life. I had imagined him as looking a certain way, and that was that; it was like not wanting to see a movie actor play a beloved character from your favorite novel, whose image is already firmly fixed in your mind. No, that actor is not my Darcy!

Then one year, to my great surprise, he hesitantly confessed that he'd begun to imagine that he'd seen me on the street, and then one day, after another two full years of hesitation and wavering on both sides, we finally agreed to meet. I waited at the place we appointed, nervously. What I feared was that our becoming embodied to each other could be an awkward disaster, ruining the lovely, delicate, secret relationship conducted entirely across the ether for years and years. If I disappointed Q, or he disappointed me, perhaps we wouldn't be able to go back to that unique and deeply gratifying relationship we had, all of it in words. Most of all, I was afraid I would fall in love, when I'd finally loosed myself from the chain of loving Gerald with not enough return. To counter my anxiety, I went the other way and refused to treat this meeting as an occasion: instead of dressing to be attractive, I wore an old pajama top that I lounged around in at home. Ha, take that!

I'd fixed on a spot outside, in a nearby park; I wasn't about to invite a man, who suddenly seemed a stranger, to my home. The moment when this figure in the far corner of my life came toward me in the flesh, smiling rather sheepishly, is both the weirdest and most wonderful of my memories. Of course he looked nothing like the Q I'd envisioned. "Is it really you?" I asked dopily. It was (as I told him) like the scene out of Woody Allen's *The Purple Rose of Cairo* where Jeff Bridges steps out of the screen, except I look nothing like Mia Farrow.

Talking with him on that park bench for an hour or so was, remarkably, exactly like reading his letters. But much, much better. Almost immediately, we had a sense of comfort with each other as though we'd been familiar friends for years – which we were, though we'd met ten minutes before. I learned more about his situation after that, why he'd reached out for a romantic relationship in the first place, and I was about to learn a great deal more about myself.

Before we met at that park bench, I had carefully reminded Q that I was old, to make sure he wouldn't be unpleasantly surprised. He'd found a long-ago blurry photo of me online and liked it, which alarmed me, so when he proposed meeting, I wrote back, "Wait, do you really know what a woman in her sixties actually looks like?" Later, when he complimented me on my adorable dimples, I pointed out that those were not dimples, they were *wrinkles*. "Oh stop it," he said, and cheerfully went on. He's like that. "Why do you keep doing that?" he finally asked me curiously. "It's because I'm trying to say, 'I'm *old*, get over it'," I said. But he was already over it when he'd first reached out to me twelve years before.

We did not disappoint each other, just the opposite, and then a time in my life began that was like no other before or since. After the park bench meeting, we agreed to take baby steps and see, but if a toddler walked as fast and far as we did with our baby steps, it would be a marathon runner by age two.

I wrote to Q about this:

I completely agree with you that we're still taking hesitant toddler-ish steps and feeling our way around (so to speak). Have you ever seen a baby learn to walk? They hold on both before and after taking their brave steps forward, clutching on to the reality they know before walking into the reality they don't know – though we sort of fell into a pool and started swimming very well, to my surprise. (Wasn't it just a short while ago I had that rational plan to have sandwiches and a nice talk in the park?)

It's difficult to express how odd it felt to be a woman barreling towards seventy and falling in love once more, and not incidentally, having the best sexual experiences of her life. Why would anyone, much less a younger man, want to spend hours making love to an often grouchy older woman with thinning hair, sagging neck and arms, and various intermittent complaints of aging, who lost a breast to cancer (and stubbornly refused to replace it)? Yet he did want to, very much, and I'm as sure as I am of anything that he loved it too. You can attribute this to the stereotypical idea that men will sleep with anyone, or simply that what most people of any gender really want in a relationship, sexually or emotionally, is mutual pleasure.

But I knew how it would be when this began in the flesh, because I'd been there with Gerald. Once more I came to know every hidden line and curve and shadow of a beloved man's body, one who does not, in the usual way of thinking, belong to me. Again, that body was stamped as owned by another.

So again, I did all I could to put the brakes on this new dubious real-life relationship. Once again, as in the first days with Gerald, I scolded, denigrated, and lectured myself, I was analytical, and I was insightful. You know you shouldn't do this; you can see how it will end. And again, none of this did the slightest good. This affair was impossible, I knew, yet its very existence proved that the impossible can sometimes become possible.

I was having what I called Qualms about it all, and wrote this to Q after his first visit:

I'll let my subconscious tell it; here's a dream I just had (my very first dream about you): You'd invited me to a big dinner with your entire family. No one seemed to know who I was, but you came over to me, put your hand on my shoulder and touched my cheek. This was surprising and nice, but then I looked up and saw that you looked very different than I remembered, morbidly overweight, badly dressed, kind of greasy… "Oh, I'm not attracted to him after all!" I thought happily – and woke up. You don't need the collected works of Freud to get this one, though Alice in Wonderland, where an infant turns into a pig, is also appropriate.

In other words, the Qualm has to do with your situation, the state of being married, which is the context for anything that happens between us. You know this is not a moral qualm – I personally think the huge fuss made over monogamy is ridiculous. And it's not that I think we should all be "swingers"; I just believe you can have deep feelings for and a good relationship with someone though you're not monogamous, and obviously the reverse is true too – monogamy is no guarantee of the quality of love. It's the nature of the feeling that I value, not some rule or contract. But it doesn't matter what I believe: marriage is a powerful institution and has an enormous limiting effect on what any relationship outside the marital couple can be – even friendship.

Think about it – here's what I can't do as your mistress, a list just off the top of my head:

1. *See you in the evening.*
2. *See you on weekends or holidays.*
3. *Be seen with you in public – even restaurants or movies or museums are problematic and have to be carefully considered.*
4. *Fall asleep next to you, or wake up and snuggle into your warmth.*
5. *Call you on the phone or text you, no matter what the occasion, even to say happy birthday or just to ask a question.*
6. *Find out how you are every day, and tell you how my day went if I like.*
7. *Plan a trip or travel with you anywhere, ever.*
8. *Meet your friends and family, or introduce you to mine.*
9. *Have breakfast with you.*
10. *See if you're sexy when you haven't shaved or showered yet.*
11. *Spend as much or little time with you as I want to, if you also want to, any particular day.*
12. *See where you live and how it reflects you.*
13. *Touch you whenever I feel like it, which would be often.*
14. *See you naked every day.*
15. *Expect you to put me first in anything important whatsoever.*

So this is the chief Qualm: I will never know you in any of these ways. These limitations have been very convenient, in fact a downright advantage, when the man in question isn't someone I want to spend much time with and have little feeling for. But where there's strong desire and/or feeling in these circumstances, there has to be repression, and I absolutely hate repression – I think because

I wasn't allowed to do or speak about what I felt or wanted until I was an adult, really, and then I held a lot inside during my long marriage as well. I'm not hoping to make you feel bad about all this, just make you aware of what you might not ever think about, because the above list is likely not a problem for you.

Are you still with me? Do you remember saying you liked my honesty and directness and would rather know what I'm thinking and feeling than have me bite my lip? Are you regretting that now?

Anyway, there's an opposite side to this, which I'll call the Anti-Qualm. The Qualms list was long; the Anti-Qualm list is short. Here it is:

1. Desire

That's it; there's no 2. And guess which wins out, the Qualm or the Anti-Qualm? Which is more powerful, the intelligent part of my brain, that has generated all these well -thought-out reasons not to see you, or the Reward Center, which doesn't really give a fuck what the frontal lobe has to say for itself? My brother the psychologist says the frontal lobe is small compared to the rest of the brain. Generate reasons all day! says the Pleasure Center, You're a laugh a minute!

Q replied:

Yes, yes, yes to your honesty and directness. I'd always prefer you to speak about whatever reservations or irritations you might be experiencing. I know that many people feel otherwise, but I can't understand why. If you sensed that someone you care for might be feeling X or Y, how could you possibly wish them to keep it to themselves?

As to the Qualm: Well, that was extremely well-argued. By the end of it you pretty much convinced me of the folly of your having anything to do with me. If I were simply a friend of yours whom you were asking for advice, I'd urge you to steer clear of this cad with whom you've been corresponding. You've read the novels, mem-

oirs and biographies; you've seen the movies. Does your character in this particular drama ever find a happy ending for herself? I think not. And I have no counter-argument to offer – none whatsoever. Except for the assurance (which you don't need) that I'll happily write to you whether you choose to sleep with me again or not.

Here's the dilemma: love has the capacity to give great joy, but it also has the power of a dictator for those who don't order their lives by rationally regulating their emotions. There is simply no escaping this paradox, except with fantasy or fiction, a magic carpet of the imagination to slide you past all but the most readily assailable of difficulties.

When I began to encounter Q as a person in real life, it was fascinating to trace backward the suggestions of the man I came to know from the letters. I could not have predicted from the writing alone who he turned out to be. Part of the intense delight he gave me was discovering both who he was, and who I was with him. The latter was quite different than the part of myself that had burst forth with Gerald, because Q is entirely different, and so we were very different together. I loved who I was when I was with Q, either in writing or in person, because it was the self that most reflected my interior life.

But I soon encountered the problems that emerge when traveling from the zone of the imaginary, or unrealized life, to the complexities of an actual relationship: I saw aspects of Q I hadn't suspected before, and he learned about disagreeable parts of me. Like an idiot, I asked him not long after I met him how he'd feel if I began to date another man. I wanted him to be jealous; he claimed his definition of love made him want me to be happy with someone else, since he couldn't give me romance, meaning a public relationship. I thought this definition of love was horseshit, most likely an excuse not to tell me how he really feels (I meant indifferent emotionally), and furthermore, my idea of romance is not limited to a relationship in public. We had to wrangle these opposite views together. "What else can I say that will offend you?" he teased when I'd pouted about his answer as he was getting ready to leave. "Let's see," I said, "How about 'The money's on the table'?"

Does Q love me? Does Gerald? The two men I've loved most have both said they do, but to this day I don't know what either one means by that, which seems appropriate, considering who I am. Is it an expression of friendship, or romantic love, or something ambiguously in-between? Is it like Nick's half- friendship, half-romantic?

There's no use asking Gerald because the answer would be evasive. Here's how it went when I tried, long ago:

Scene: a restaurant, where I'd proposed we have lunch so we could talk about our relations, not his favorite sport. Pause after the waiter leaves.

Me: So I've wanted to ask you something for a long time: how do you really feel about me?

Gerald: (shifts around, clearly uncomfortable): Well, it's complicated. You're important to me… I do love you, but…

Me:… but it's not a romantic love, is it? You love me as a friend?

Gerald: (getting angry): I don't like this. It isn't fair. You set this up as a kind of test, and I can't win, because you already know the answer.

Me: (realizing he is right, I begin to cry mutely, humiliated to be exposed in a public place, just as the food arrives)

Ugh.

However, I did pounce on poor Q when he claimed romantic love has no real definition, as it's entirely constructed by society. He might be right, but this is not the reply one wants to hear. Many pages of torturous prose from me followed. At some point it occurred to me that Q could have fobbed me off with a quick "Of course I love you passionately!" to make it easier on himself, but would not do it. Cupid's arrows were no match for him and his annoying integrity.

But even if you're in a committed relationship, let's say a marriage or partnership, as it's unattractively called these days, do you really know exactly what the other person means by "I love you", or do you just assume you know? Is it certain he or she would know either?

"It's really something, isn't it, the complications that ensue when two minds in the ether become two embodied people in the real world?", I wrote to Q – having had the habit of writing for so long, we simply continued to do it more frequently after meeting, between his visits to me. "It was all so easy for the twelve years before we met. What isn't peculiar about our relationship, from its origins onward? One thing I love about you is that I seem able to display myself to you in all my peculiarities and moods. You are unfazed. I must say I've never encountered anyone quite like you in that way before – at least at such close quarters. And we've been in close quarters, you and I."

How to describe Q? Quietly intelligent. Mild-mannered, like Clark Kent. Gentle, sweet, patient, *good* – like Jesus. Maybe if Jesus were an adulterer… who makes you laugh. And I left out all the best parts, which are too indecent to describe.

Here's one that's not indecent: *He has a certain way of putting things in words that's new to me*, I wrote in my journal the day I met him in real life. I had rarely been with a man in my life who didn't talk *at* you. All the men I'd been with romantically or professionally were conversational performers, of one sort or another; it had always seemed like the price of being with someone who has an interesting mind. When you're with a performer, you either listen passively, as I did the first half of my life, or you perform competitively, as I did for the second half. Being with Q was like listening to a soft, subtle voice reading fiction aloud, or quietly asking a question, provoking thought without demanding attention. Q in reality has no such voice, literally speaking, but he spoke with his writing voice, replying in a way that makes it delightful to talk. To my surprise, he is exactly the persona I imagined in his letters: fascinating yet entirely unpretentious. That strikes me as a rare combination.

Because showing my poor mutilated chest to anyone was something I had not done before, I announced to Q soon after we met that I was never going to bare my bosom to anyone besides a nurse or doctor. I expected suppressed cringing, or else declarations of tolerance. "So I'd have to go to medical school…?" asked Q instead. You haven't lived, in my opinion, until you've laughed so much you nearly fall off the bed in the middle of making love.

It was better every single time. Just when you thought it was the best, it was better. And we had very little time, so it had to be hoarded, like the food that could not be wasted in my childhood fantasies of survival. He appeared semi-regularly like a ghost at my door, and because our time together was so limited, we began making love when he'd hardly walked a foot inside. After he left, I would watch through my window as he walked down my street, on his way back home, stunned that he was leaving. Once, he asked why I looked sad; I said it was because I already missed him, though he'd barely just arrived.

Almost a year later, Q wrote that he could no longer go on seeing me. The guilt of it was making him ill, no matter how obviously justified his situation seemed to me. He sent an explanation in the form of a page-long, beautifully detailed metaphor in which I was the South of France, a fabulous destination he could no longer afford to visit. Since he's a writer, his letters are always filled with excellent metaphors, but in this one he outdid himself. I was ninety-percent broken-hearted, and ten percent flattered.

For a long time afterward, I grieved as if he'd suddenly died. He still lives within walking distance, yet I felt I would never see him again and still doubt I will. But we went on writing, because it was the backbone of our relationship, the through-line of our narrative. This has never altered or paused at all, except when I've declared I had to take a break because I wasn't sure I could go on without knowing if I will ever see him again. My breaks have never lasted longer than weeks, because something always happens that I want to tell him, *need* to tell him. He has never taken a break.

The shadow relationship of our writing once again became our whole relationship, as it had been before we encountered each other in real life. I still have a compulsion to narrate my life to him, to know he listens, to read his responses, which are not like anyone else's, and to learn whatever I can of what he thinks and does. In short, I love him, embodied or disembodied, and I know *exactly* what that means. It's not a mystery to me.

Last Valentine's Day, Q sent me an image of a candy heart that said "The money is on the table," the silly joke I'd made when he was on his way out the door almost ten years ago. That man has a good memory, a trait very handy for romantic love, constructed by society or not.

The end of romance in real life is not like closing a book, because unless you're Romeo or Juliet, your existence goes on. Plunging into love is to travel with no real end, an often arduous journey through a near country, a too-near home, the self.

But falling in love is also like visiting a faraway and exotic destination. Maybe you can never really know it, even if you live there a while; maybe you romanticize the vistas while ignoring the slums. Nevertheless, when each visit to the South of France gives you more pleasure than you've known before, why would you not want to go again and again, even if you have other obligations or can't afford it?

Happy, And After

Little bits of memories, the detritus of small pleasures and concerns that filled our days, swirl by in old age as if in a tornado, taking everything up again.

The freedom of playing alone in my little dark place behind the armchair. My desires before they had a name. The fear of being left alone. The intensity of my longing. An infant at my breast who needs me. The power of knowing someone wants you. The power that comes of knowing yourself.

My brother Eric was the one always there for me, the one who gave me the understanding I needed when I truly needed it. Because he eventually moved to the country where his wife was born, we didn't see each other often in the last decade before he died suddenly in his sleep, after a pleasant evening with his wife and daughter. Our confidences were in long emails, bulletins on our families and health, of course, accomplishments and worries, and secrets we told no one else. There were also thoughts about questions that absorbed both of us, some connected to our work: ideas I was teaching, his experience of human nature in his forensic psychology practice. His emailed letters were so long that I used to print them out to read them; the longest was eight pages. Eric's death took out half my heart. But Q was there to give me that rare sense of intimacy and unquestioning acceptance I had with my brother… and he still is.

Looking backward, I return to the questions that preoccupied me when I began: How did romantic love come to have enormous and peculiar power over me in particular? Where did my romantic sensibility come from, and to what has it led?

Remembering the crisis of my first love affair and the end of my marriage, I wince reading the journals of that time. I see what I should have done: put an end to the affair or (and) the marriage early on, or else enjoy my lover, shore up the memory as one of the treasures of my life, and then go back to the normal and try to make of it what I could, without bitterness. Like so much advice from friends, neither was what I really wanted. Yet when I think of simply avoiding the experience in the first place, that doesn't feel right either. I learned so much from it, changed so much because of it. I no longer want to cajole and scold my younger self, but rather weep alongside her and reassure her: Look, I happen to know that it will be okay, you'll be all right eventually.

I know I felt more powerful when I was engaged in my first affair. Some of it was egotism, that I could relate to Gerald in ways his legitimate mate couldn't. But it was also tremendously liberating for me, in terms of finding out what I really wanted, breaking rules of domestic relations and questioning all over what family values are and what it means to be a wife, or a person on her own. Someone once asked me what I'd say to my daughters about having had an affair. My answer was that I'd tell them it's a struggle to come to terms with the opposition between one's own self-interest and the necessity for a world of justice and compassion. And I hope they see it's not easy to find a way, and that understanding might come more from experience than from abstract morality. I agree with John Stuart Mill that you should have as many experiences as possible, or by proxy, great toleration for the many kinds of experiences of others.

Would my marriage have been better if there hadn't been adultery on both sides? I would say no. Frank and I would have been the same people, and even if we could have revolutionized our relations and made them more "romantic," or more in conformity with what they "should" have been, I could never have felt for him what I felt for the men I have romantically loved. In a way

I hid behind marriage so I could continue to protect myself against the world; I thought I needed that protection because I believed the version of me that my husband had, that I was smart but also in a way dumb, and certainly incapable of strength in a crisis, and incompetent to deal with, well, reality. In fact I feel so different now about this supposed weakness that I can't imagine continuing to be Frank's wife, or anyone's wife, for that matter.

Yet my heart still hangs open like a purse, exposing its valuables, when it's supposed to be snapped shut.

In the end I'm not sure why I never found anyone I could love as much as the ones I couldn't be with. Popular romance features the girl who gets the distant guy without chasing him, just because she's so adorable. Apparently I wasn't adorable enough. Or I didn't see the gems available to me, or else (my own view) I'd just had enough with compromising and settling in the first part of my life. I still can't bring myself to pay that price. Perhaps, like many older women, I don't want anyone constantly telling me what they think of my tastes and behavior.

I do know that I'm tired of hearing that if I have a bottom line and no one marriageable has risen above it, there's something wrong with me. Maybe there is, but I don't want to be another way. I choose not to alter my standards for a partner, or my expectations for what a gratifying relationship is. I think many (male and female) are satisfied by the institution itself; marriage as a social and emotional contract gives them what they want, maybe more than the specific person they're married to. By reverse engineering, they believe they are in love, or at least love. That simply doesn't apply to me: I know when

I'm in love, and I know who I love.

I suppose the question I'm asking myself is whether I'm getting too cantankerous for this world. Maybe I should just be put out to pasture alone, where I can ruminate over these questions while chewing grass and bothering no one.

Dating has been unsuccessful (except for Q, who was not a date) because I am picky, I'm told, in the same way I'm too picky about modern fiction, and hold writers to too high a standard – if they're not George Eliot or Chekhov or Faulkner or Zora Neale Hurston or Annie Ernaux, I'm not interested. I've matured and become smarter in some ways over my lifetime, but I can't help noticing that I'm mostly stuck with myself more than the optimistic world of psychoanalysis and Lifetime movies (where people are always having life-altering epiphanies) would suggest. Who I am is exactly the peculiar person who wants what I want, whether I can have it or not.

I do see, looking back, that I've had the same fear of being alone all my life. It dominated my childhood, in fact, along with a terrible fear of abandonment, which is of course a related anxiety. The solution I would like, to find someone I could deeply love who would be always with me and devoted to me alone, has not worked, but I've been able to work on the fear instead. The problem with the former is that it depends on another person, and that's not controllable or predictable. Managing your own feelings is far better, though it requires devoted effort, because I'm a high-intensity feeler, and therefore my feelings are not much subject to rational efforts to change.

Yet to my great surprise, my childhood loneliness has evolved into a frequent need to be alone in order to be entirely myself. When you spend your life trying to please a man and care for children, it's a luxury to please yourself first.

This brings me pride and dignity. I cherish not being "on" all the time in the effort to be lovable and desirable enough to keep the love object near me. To hell with that, I say. So if I feel dismay that I won't have company on New Year's Eve, for example, I also feel good that I can do anything I want to do. I've had so many New Year's Eves when I went where I was invited in order not to be home by myself, and then was bored or irritated.

Being part of a couple will not save you; it will make life easier in some ways, more annoying in others. It will make you less lonely sometimes; it will also limit, suppress, and flatten you out, how could it not? There are people who stick with the same mate no matter how unsatisfying, or go straight from one to another, never really growing up because they don't know how to just be in the world. I was one of those. I had no idea how to be on my own. Now I do; I've gone from a lonely person who had to have someone with me, to a much less lonely person who vitally needs to be alone at times. I'm self-contained like a snail moving slowly through the world, most comfortable when curled up in my own protective shell, not dependent on someone else's shelter.

We are all wired, as well as molded, differently, in our emotional systems. This is who I am: someone who has and wants passion, not sentiment; who values moments of beauty, not prettiness; who lives for joy, not contentment. Marriage is a structure, a home or a prison, a container of intense or wild or anti-social emotions. I am a vessel of desire, a container for pleasure – an unquestionably leaky container.

Most important of all, I have had the pleasure of love in various ways: love of children, yes, an essential to me in the pursuit of love and beauty, necessary but not sufficient. As for passion, I believe this: When you find someone you can wholly love with both your body and heart, for however much time, in whatever way… that is extraordinarily fortunate, whether or not it works. I suspect it happens far less often than people expect it to.

Many are temperamentally fit for (and fitted to) marriage, in the form it's now understood to take: commitment for life, but only if it succeeds. I'm not particularly a fan of marriage myself, except as a system for rearing children, mostly because I see too many who sit back and relax into its comforts, regularity, and familiarity. This relaxation is precisely what the married like about it, and precisely what repels me. This is because it can easily slip into a kind of smugness, the closed-circle "we-ness" of "*We* think that's a good idea… *we* enjoy that show… *we're* off to the Cape for the summer." As a person committed to singularity as well as love, this feels to me as if there's a pretense of two as one brain and body, a science fiction movie I don't want to see or act out.

The predictability, the reliability, the daily solace of the commitment for a lifetime, all of these strong pillars of the legitimate and respectable domestic relationship, can also be its great weakness: the tendency to become wearisome. Here's a benefit of being a lover: the erratic becomes erotic. On the other hand, affairs are easily weakened by tempests of desire and feeling, the guilt of lying, the fear of exposure, the frustrations of restricted time. Committed relationships may be short or long, affairs may also be short or long, and romance of any kind may be either deep or shallow, brief or enduring, casual or transformative. They are all simply different forms of being with someone else, with varied levels of feeling, different goals and ways to get there.

Old age and sickness make us see the body as a different kind of being. With advanced age, if you're fortunate enough to attain it, comes the understanding that both you and the world could be erased in an instant, or slowly fade to black until you disappear. Time is leaving people and events behind me now, while I'm carried forward in a riptide I can't swim away from. When I was younger, I used to feel I was racing, or at least crawling, toward something, an idea, a plan, a position in the world, or a relationship that would "make me happy." But now, when I think over my life, I see that the best and worst that happened to me was entirely unexpected, and that includes the best and worst in my romantic life.

The Ends Of Romance

In many stories, we learn about characters as they react to a provocative situation outside their ordinary lives – conflicts, challenges, crises, temptations. Their responses are not always predictable by who they seemed at first to be. In the best literature, these responses are holders of interesting and provocative truths, markers for the ways we singularly approach life when something new and unexpected arrives, tragic, fearful or alluring. Here I am a character in my own narrative, neither heroine nor villain, only feeling, acting, choosing what I could at the time. The story I've found myself in, have put myself in, is sometimes fiercely romantic, sometimes critical, a combination I call semi-romantic. Romance is something like Christmas for me; I celebrate the holiday without believing in the religion.

This is because I've discovered that what I live for is love itself, not only in the banal sense of being loved, or giving love as a kind of gift, but in loving the sensation of loving, the richness and intensity of it, love experienced for its own sake. This is the opposite of how society scripts it for us in every way: the forms and structures of romance, a specific chronology of events, its hierarchies of value (good and bad romances), the proper labels and acceptable objects for love, the way it should feel and be and go – with any deviation noted, if not shamed.

Paradoxically, the Romantic is often a call to freedom, but the rigid conventions that surround its wild impulse can be a sort of penitentiary. I think there should be an opening for a different definition of romance that is fluid rather than closed and limited, a space filled with a force field of emotion, a way of reframing the meaning and value of the romantic, especially for women.

Popular romance is often criticized for raising unrealistic expectations, especially in women, the way pornography might raise boys' sexual expectations to an impossible bar. I believe there's a real risk to women in heterosexual couples of diminishing their own pragmatic power because they believe too much in their romanticized emotional power, just as there is a consequence for women leaning on feminine beauty to get them through. If women invest in romance more than men do, if they need it more and deny their dissatisfaction with relationships because they need it more, the advantage goes disproportionately to men. Real-life consequences never quite escape us in certain conditions, and one of those conditions is gender.

Romance is broadly historical and (as Q said) socially constructed, yes. Love is also a belief system with contradictory beliefs. Like mythology and religion, it imagines another world of beings, but with actual humans.

Yet at the same time, it feels deeply personal and individual. I would like to dismantle romance as experience that has to be hooked up to an institution like marriage and coupling, the rules that function to make it legitimate and approved, and return it to the realm of deep feeling.

At the interesting conference on romance fiction I attended some years ago at the Library of Congress, an unusual mixed audience of readers, romance writers, and scholars discussed the readers' insistence on what popular romance lovers call the HEA, the Happily Ever After. Both readers and writers were very protective of the particular niche they enjoy and its definition, carved out of a certain type of love story over the ages. As one of the scholar-speakers, I proposed that the definition of romance as a genre must be broader than the Happily Ever After. This is not an original idea: some writers do want to modify the formula so the conclusion of romance doesn't always have to be marriage, only a pledge of love, a commitment, the Happy For Now.

The fervent fans of romance at this conference vehemently disagreed: the tale of Lancelot and Guinevere, *Romeo and Juliet*, or any text that doesn't end in a couple skipping in meadows or celebrating golden anniversaries is out of bounds as a "romance" because it's no longer pleasurable. A colleague claimed that in the classic film *Casablanca,* Ilsa rejects Rick because her true love is Lazlo. Telling Rick she loved him was just a trick to get her husband out! I was fascinated by the difference in our understanding: to the contrary, I think the movie illustrates two kinds of love, romantic and domestic, and Rick sacrifices romance to save Ilsa from a concentration camp. Romantic love isn't seen as inferior, but as a kind of luxury that can't always be afforded.

The Happily Ever After, or the Happy For Now, I believe, is just a way to organize and socialize the unruliness of passion. I have more than one friend, advanced in years, who began their loving relationship in adultery, the husband vowing to stay with his very ill wife until the end, the mistress enjoying what they had for years, until it happened that they were able to be together. I wonder, would that qualify as an HEA, would this be a story that romance lovers would be glad to read? My friends' love stories are actual life, with all its complexity, exactly what we don't want in romances.

I'm not judging a reader's desire for the HEA – enjoy whatever you enjoy, I say. For many, romance is about hope.

Romantic love has been for me too the hope of deep pleasure, which itself has been bittersweet – in a way, the hope itself is the greatest pleasure. I genuinely want couples I like to be happy, and when I like fictional characters, I hope to see them together forever, past the time I can read about them. This is true whether it's a TV show, a movie, a Noel Coward play, or a classic novel. I want Cupid and Psyche to be an item for always, and I want Petruchio to learn to love Kate, even though – or because – I loathe his misogyny. I root for the couples on the reality show *Married at First Sight* to succeed. Needless to say, my desire in reading *Wuthering Heights* is for Cathy to leave her tediously pleasant and virtuous husband for Heathcliff. I remember reading a scholarly article in grad school claiming those two could never have a good marriage: *Well*, I thought, while I was married and still in my twenties, *to hell with that*. You mean a marriage like yours, right? But why does their marriage or anyone's have to be like yours?

What bothers me about the HEA are the implications for defining real love, the exclusionary nature of that idea. A psychologist I once met at a party was holding forth about romantic love as an inferior form of love because it's about the objectification of the beloved, whereas the good thing about committed relationships is that you really know and accept the other person, which is… yes, here we go again, real love. This is related to the therapeutic bias against any kind of love that comes with a risk of pain. The truth is that *any* desire comes with a risk, ranging from rejection to death, while the dogma of "real love" names only desires weighed against the likelihood they'll be satisfied.

Reducing romantic love, including extramarital love, to a simple either-or can short-circuit the infinite varieties of human feeling and experience. The entire publishing phenomenon of popular romance and romantic comedy would shift in unknown directions, if we allowed fictional romance to follow the complex and layered rhythms that love has in the lives of actual men and women, including an ambivalence that sometimes never goes away.

The frequent criticism that romantic love in real life without a happy ending is not real love ignores that romance is allied with imagination and art. In art, the streams of fantasy and experience meet, merging into levels and corridors of ourselves. And all the corridors are blind. Maybe falling in love evolved as a result of the human ability to imagine – that is, to imagine what someone else is like, what you are like with them, with little information in some cases.

Fantasy and play are a way of trying out what Jerome Bruner called "possible worlds" and selves without real-life consequences. In this way, it's the most uniquely human impulse. Now it's true there's a blurry line between the ability to suspend disbelief and not seeing what's in front of you. You idealize the one you love romantically, exclaim a thousand psychology articles. No doubt. But why should we not? Why must everything in life be pragmatic in motive, with a clear path before we step forward?

I realized something at the conference after all the talk about the mandatory Happily Ever After. My relationship with Q has been frustratingly limited, but I'd rather have less than I want than have a real and secure relationship with someone to whom I can't express all of myself. Such as the many men I've dated. Committing as a couple to any of them would not be an HEA, just an EA – an *ever after* that I don't care to undertake or be stuck with. After all, no relationship is really sure, never mind for a lifetime, and who's to say which ones are real?

***

Why do we need to know the definition of love if we know what we're feeling (or not)? Because if you don't think about your expectations and your experience, you won't know what can and can't be questioned and changed.

The democratic province of Love has an ideology similar to the American Dream: any commoner can garner great wealth, and all the deserving will rise to success. In reality, in Loveland, the successful couples in romance constitute a kind of superior caste: they reach the top of life's offerings as inherently worthy, the winners who are meant to be. Everyone else is relegated to the bottom rank.

Anglo-American culture gives us a great deal of lip service about passion, but our real agenda is what's called happiness rather than joy. What enables happiness is contentment, reliability, trust, safety, comfortability, the long durée. Anything that's risky threatens to capsize the well-balanced ship, resulting in a plunge into the deep, and passion is too irrational and uncontrolled to feel safe. Comfort, that need of children, is not only preferred to the extremes of emotion, even positive emotion, but is a kind of moral value: if a relationship lacks those conditions, it's just bad, threatening to the very existence of the conventional. A connection founded on uncontrolled passion is not simply different, another way to go; it's got to be ridiculed or scorned and if possible expunged from the normal.

I am not arguing that passion is somehow inherently better than a comforting long-term domestic love, but that they are distinct and equally worthy forms of life. It's true that I have a bias against couples, especially those who present as happy, meaning a comfortable combination of roommate and semi-parent to each other, but the reason for that bias is that I was one of those.

The Romantics believed their views about transcendent feelings should remake the world, but it's not arguable one way or other. Someone might bring you profound moments of joy but you prefer the low hum of long contentedness, or strong feeling itself is not in your repertoire of responses, or may be overwhelming. As for me, I will take short-lived deep pleasure over years of low-grade or questionable happiness. Would you rather have a little of what you love, or a lot of what you just like? I vastly prefer to have a bit of the finest chocolate than a lot of the cheap, mass-produced version.

I happen to be a rock climber of the heart – ever upward, whether or not I get to the peak.

My view is that understanding love within a framework of a happy ending is the ultimate use of feeling and story as consumerism, in the mode of shopping or a makeover. Buying, or buying into, a popular romance is to acquire (and require) a form of guaranteed happiness.

Americans in particular are obsessed with success. The popular idea of romance implies that you simply win at love, though in some mysterious, mystical way; but the idea of love as an achievement (working on your marriage, what sociologists call "emotional labor") is deadening to me. In the end, what was most important for me has not been what's called success in love or even pleasure, but how wrestling with love's meaning pushed me to weigh what my life means to me. Not just, in other words, what the beloved means, but what I want to live for. It's not about winning.

Love is a transformative force, for better or worse, and sometimes both at once. We can't control it, but we can be acutely aware of it. Molly Bloom of James Joyce's *Ulysses* famously ended the novel with "Yes Yes." Molly said an ecstatic Yes to sex and life, which she pretty much seems to equate, and Yes to marrying Leopold Bloom (though No to being proper in marriage). I'm a variation you can call Molly Bloomberg: I say romantic love is a kind of Yes, not Yes to the Dress, but to what is on offer in life.

At this very moment, I may have found a new companion I like, a relationship without a name. The *no-label relationship* I envision (to go with the new no-label genders and sexuality!) has no hard and fast rules or commitment, legal or otherwise, no expectation of being joined in time or space beyond what we both wish at any one time, and perhaps no vow of monogamy. I raised three children; I no longer want to take care of anyone or use up my mental energy on continually trying to please someone now. It's of great value to be taken care of, to have a companion (though statistically, women have a higher chance of being the caretaker eventually), but my independence is more valuable to me than those. It may be impossible to remove myself from the romantic system entirely, but at least I can resist being subsumed by the system.

How ironic: I've had the eager suitors, the non-committers, the rejectors and the rejected, the only too available and the only too unavailable. I've also had love of varied sorts that lasted for decades, though not as a formal couple. And now, just when I've come to value my privacy and autonomy… this comes along. The gods are laughing.

Where is Q in this? He has taken up permanent lodging in my heart in a room of his own, the room with a splendid view of my life. This is not a small or dark corner, but one whose light is in words rather than touch. I will never be happy that I had to substitute words for body, but I can live with it, and he says he wants to go on until one of us goes to that Green Pasture in the sky. Long before I knew of Q's existence, I wrote this in my journal:

This is the way life so often goes – it's not just choice A or B, but something different than you thought. In my case, it's not just Door A or B, or C, for that matter, it's an entirely different one: D.

For me, passionate love is a way of being in the world and a way of seeing the world. The mind of a romantic is always ready to infuse the commonplace with the extraordinary and the excessive, to believe a surprise will happen, *you never know*, if you open to the strongest feelings you can have. That's why it's a state that artists have always written and sung about.

I don't have a formula for romantic love, or expert advice on how to get it, keep it, or ditch it; my point is that I'm done with formulas. At this time in my life, I'm against the rules for what love is, or must be, or should be, the endless tiresome worrying about whether this is the One who is meant for you. The rigid binaries do not serve us well, as if a phenomenon as fragile, changing and complex as love can be thrown carelessly into two bins of reality; healthy love versus unhealthy love, real love or false love, true love and infatuation. Instead I see a continuum from mild, agreeable romance to wayward intense passion, a full spectrum of depth and intensities as in colors, an endurance timeline from a brief encounter that might mean nothing or else shake you, a long-term, permanent and unwavering commitment that might be quietly miserable or the source of peace and comfort. There are some who never feel romantic, or feel it differently, or define themselves by love, or define love according to who they are. All of these can intersect in a multitude of ways. None of these should invoke self-satisfied, moralistic judgments.

You often hear people say "I don't regret a thing!"

because it "made them who they are." I will admit that I wouldn't mind being someone else on occasion: less anxious, less selfish, more… you know, *heroic*. But when it comes to romance, I would do it *all* again, actually. I've carried my childhood love of adventure in books all the way to old age as an adventure of the mind. You can have your travel, you can keep your book groups and your hobbies: I still love everyone I ever loved romantically, even when that feeling no longer carries the same charge. *Je ne regrette rien* – well, maybe *un* or *deux*.

I neither reject romantic love nor feel it's best to convert it into good old reliable affection. For me, love has a way of finding its own meaning, transforming itself, whether we like it or not, and romance in story is part of our general struggle to find and shape the value of our experience. Passionate love forces us to recognize that we don't control our deepest desires and strong feelings, no matter what narrative tells us or does for us, and that is at once the pleasure, price and risk of being human.

As Rilke said: "Let everything happen to you: beauty and terror." Everything happened, and still is happening.

Is this a happy or unhappy ending to my own tale of love? Both, which means neither. It's just life. All we can do is live the story.

Acknowledgments

I have had the good fortune of working with two skilled editors who understood and supported this project: Vivien Williams and Elizabeth Ford. I thank them for their unlimited patience. Eilidh Muldoon was collaborative in her work as illustrator, and a delight to work with.

I am deeply grateful for Igor Webb, my wise publishing whisperer. I'm also thankful for Deborah Williams' invaluable advice on the manuscript, as well as for the amazing generosity of Sarah Lyons, and the kindness and understanding of my dearest friend, Anne Cliadakis. Many thanks to the following for reading all or parts of the manuscript and offering suggestions, or just being helpful when needed: Ulrich Baer, Mary Bahr, Nan Bauer-Maglin, Mary Bly, Olivia Castetter, Jayashree Kamble, Sonia Jaffe Robbins, Amy Rogers, and Sokthan Yeng.

Most of all, a warm and hearty thank you to Q, for being with me through every stage of this excellent adventure. I can't imagine having done this without your unwavering enthusiasm and faith in me.

Permissions

I would like to acknowledge the permission to reproduce excerpts from all the following:

- W. W. Norton & Company: The lines from "Translations", from *Diving into the Wreck: Poems 1971-1972* by Adrienne Rich, copyright © 1973 by W. W. Norton & Company, Inc. Used by permission of W. W. Norton & Company, Inc.
- John Benjamins Publishing, M. Freeman and J. Brockmeier, "Narrative integrity: Autobiographical identity and the meaning of the 'good life'", in *Narrative and Identity: Studies in Autobiography, Self, and Culture*, ed. Jens Brockmeier and Donal Carbaugh.
- "I Go Back to May 1937" from *Strike Sparks: Selected Poems, 1980-2002* by Sharon Olds, copyright © 2004 by Sharon Olds. Used by permission of Alfred A. Knopf, an imprint of the Knopf Doubleday Publishing Group, a division of Penguin Random House LLC.
- *Seneca Review*, Fall 2005, vol. 35: Mahmoud Darwish, "In My Mother's House."
- Annie Ernaux, excerpt from *The Possession*, translated by Anna Moschovakis, copyright © 2002 by

Éditions Gallimard. English translation, copyright © 2008 by Seven Stories Press. Reprinted with the permission of The Permissions Company, LLC on behalf of Seven Stories Press, sevenstories.com.

- HarperCollins Publishers and the Wisława Szymborska Foundation: Wislawa Szymborska, "Consolation."
- Excerpted from "Ithaka" in C. P. Cavafy: *Collected Poems*, Revised Edition translated by Edmund Keeley and Philip Sherrard. Translation, copyright © 1975, 1992 by Edmund Keeley and Philip Sherrard. Published by Princeton University Press and reprinted herein by permission.
- Excerpt from *A Lover's Discourse* by Roland Barthes, copyright © 1977 by Editions du Seuil. English Translation, copyright © 1978 by Farrar, Straus & Giroux, Inc. Reprinted by permission of Hill and Wang, a division of Farrar, Straus and Giroux.
- A short version of Chapter One appeared in *Memoir Magazine*, December, 2020.